The Process of Investigation: Concepts and Strategies for the Security Professional

CHARLES A. SENNEWALD

Butterworth–Heinemann

Boston   London   Singapore   Sydney   Toronto   Wellington

Library of Congress Cataloging in Publication Data

Sennewald, Charles A   1931–
    The process of investigation.

    Includes index.
    1. Criminal investigation. 2. Detectives. I. Title.
HV8073.S39   363.2'5   80–22802
ISBN 0–7506–9222–7 (previously ISBN 0–409–95018–1)

Butterworth–Heinemann
313 Washington Street
Newton, MA 02158–1626

10 9

Printed in the United States of America

To
TOTTIE,
CONNIE
and
THERESE OF LEISEUX

CONTENTS

Preface

For too long, the art and science of professional investigation has been deemed the exclusive realm of the public sector. Text books on investigation have traditionally been written by and for those in public law enforcement and, invariably, these books include such topics as homicide and rape. Although interesting, these subjects have little, if any, practical application for investigators in the private sector.

The close of the '70's and the beginning of the '80's mark a new era in the security industry, an era of professionalism. The private sector has come of age, and has its own rightful place in the sun!

This book was written to serve the needs of this new professional class of investigative practitioners. I have tried to cover in detail those investigative skills which are so essential in private security investigation: surveillance techniques, interviewing and interrogation, evidence, confessions and written statements, among others. An effective book on investigation must go beyond mere detail, however; the investigator works in the real world and the book must deal with the day-in and day-out challenges which confront him. Throughout the book, I have included cases and examples based on my own experiences. In dealing with these various situations, I discuss the approaches and strategies which have helped me in the hope that they can be of some assistance to others.

I. FUNDAMENTALS OF SECURITY INVESTIGATION

Chapter 1

The Investigative Process

An investigation is the examination, study, searching, tracking and gathering of factual information that answers questions or solves problems. It is more of an art than a science. Although the person engaged in investigation is a gatherer of facts, he or she must develop hypotheses and draw conclusions based on available information. The investigative process, that is to say, is a comprehensive activity involving information collection, the application of logic, and the exercise of sound reasoning.

The end result of an investigation is the factual explanation of what transpired, if the incident or issue is history, or what is occurring, if the issue is of the present.

The investigative process is not limited to the criminal justice and security fields. It is an activity found, to one extent or another, in virtually all areas of human endeavor. Academicians are investigators, supervisors faced with disciplinary problems are investigators, medical doctors are investigators — just to name a few. Sherlock Holmes with deerstalker hat and magnifying glass may be the art's most familiar image, but investigation does not belong exclusively to the realm of cops and robbers.

Just as the art of investigation belongs to no one province, so no one has all the answers as to precisely how any investigation can lead to the desired solution. Too many facets are involved in the process of information collection, application of logic and sound reasoning. Some such facets include intuition, luck, mistakes and the often touted "gut feeling." No single textbook of formulas is possible; no one book (or author) can stand alone as the ultimate authority. Our purpose, then, is an overview of investigative concepts, strategies, suggestions, guidelines, hints and examples that can be useful to any investigator.

Two Categories of Investigation

There are two categories of investigation: *constructive* and *reconstructive.* Constructive investigations are covert in nature, performed in secrecy. This type of inquiry occurs while the suspected activity is taking place or anticipated. An example might be an investigation into a complaint that a member of middle management solicits sexual favors from female subordinates and reaps favors accordingly. The purpose of the constructive investigation is to determine if objectionable activity is taking place.

Reconstructive investigations are necessary when an event has taken place and the investigator must recreate what happened after the fact. This type of investigation is usually overt in nature, carried out in the open.

THE INVESTIGATIVE PROCESS

As it pertains to the security industry, the investigative process is organizationally oriented as opposed to being community oriented. Its objective in this setting is to seek answers to the basic questions — the what, who, where, when, how and why — regarding a condition, incident or action deemed organizationally unacceptable, or to meet organizational objectives. Internal dishonesty, for example, is an organizationally unacceptable activity. The background investigation of a prospective new employee would meet one organizational objective.

Most of the investigative process takes place in the colletion of information. This gathering or collection is based on *communication* and *observation.* The answers to the six basic investigative questions will be developed through communication — that is, the written or spoken word — or by observation — that is, physical evidence that can be observed (whether by human eye or microscope), touched, or in any way quantitatively measured.

Communication

Communication includes information received from informants, information developed through the interview process, and information obtained in interrogations.

Consider a simple example. A homeowner, hearing the glass of his front window breaking, runs to the room and commences an immediate inspection to determine the cause. He observes a baseball lying among the pieces of broken glass. Sticking his head out of the broken window, ball in hand, he shouts to a silent group of youngsters in the street. "Okay, you guys, which one of you did it?'' As he asks the question, simultaneously he observes that a boy named Harry is holding a baseball bat. Based on the facts thus far gathered, he forms a hypothesis that Harry struck the ball with the bat, causing the ball to enter the homeowner's living room through the window.

Up to this point the homeowner, in a natural investigative role as a victim, has had only the benefit of his own powers of observation in forming his hypothesis. But now a couple of the boys in unison say, ''Harry did it.'' The investigative process has advanced through communication from informants. ''Did you do it, Harry?'' asks the homeowner. ''Yes, sir,'' answers Harry, dropping his head. The question and its answer are two other basic elements of communication — interrogation and admission.

Ideally, as in this example, the investigator's work is simplified if given some direction by an informant, if witnesses are available and willing to cooperate, or if a suspect is known and can be interrogated. Such simplification is not to suggest that all is easy in the communications aspects of investigation. Quite the contrary! Developing informants, or developing a climate in which employees or non-employees will voluntarily confide in you, is not easy. It takes talent. The ability to extract painlessly all the information a witness may have requires training and experience. Only a skillful interviewer can get the specialist to explain the workflow of the finance unit so it is comprehensible and understandable. Finally, the ability to interrogate, and in that interrogation to obtain voluntary admissions and confessions, requires a high level of skill.

The point to be drawn is that communication, although not necessarily easy to manage well, is often extremely helpful to the investigative process. Unfortunately, it is not always available. In such circumstances the investigator must rely totally on observation, at least during the initial phases of his inquiry, as he seeks to know the What, Who, Where, When, How and Why of a situation.

Observation

Scientific technology, in such areas as fingerprinting, infrared photography, motion picture photography, videotape and document analysis, to name but a few, plays a vital role in the observatory aspects of modern investigation. In this writer's judgement, perhaps too much emphasis has come to be placed on technology and too little on man's powers of observation.

This is not to suggest that, because new cars are too sophisticated, we should return to the horse and buggy. It is to emphasize that the common denominator of both the buggy and the car is to take one from point A to point B. Total reliance on the car could lead to immobility if it breaks down or gas supplies run short. In an investigation we want to get from point A to point B, and we should be able to walk, ride a horse, drive a buggy, ride a bicycle or use any other means of progress available to us.

A far wider range of important information is available to us through out own powers of observation than through the use of a laboratory. To see, to touch, to smell and to hear are all forms of observation. Did you ever touch the hood of an automobile to determine if it had recently been driven as evidence by its warmth? Did you ever mark the label on a bottle of liquor to determine later if someone was taking unauthorized sips? Such uses of the power or observation are as natural and commonplace as eating and breathing. Consider the example of a woman shopper who returns to her new car, parked in the shopping center's lot, only to find a scratch, dent or ding in her car door. It is predictable (natural and commonplace) that this unskilled woman will promptly inspect the adjacent automobile to determine if any part of that car reveals, at a height corresponding to the damage to her car, any evidence of paint fragments that would prove culpability — coloration of victimized vehicle on suspect vehicle, or vice versa.

If, in fact, the power of observation is natural and commonplace in seeking investigative answers and solving problems, why is it that those who are professionally charged with conducting investigations fail to understand, fully appreciate and maximize such powers? The answer, perhaps, can be found in modern technology, which mitigates against our need to fine-tune our own faculties.

Just a few decades ago people had to rely on their own resources. We do not. We hardly tap our capabilities because we do not have to. In our advanced and sophisticated society, there is relatively little need to be observant. Take the weather as an example. Today we have televised reports on tomorrow's weather based on the sophisticated use of satellite photography. Whatever the weather service predicts, we accept. Yet, even now, there are men and woman who can predict the weather with remarkable accuracy by observing nature in the raw — by observing cloud formation, density, coloration, direction, temperature fluctuations, etc. Divers and fishermen will tell you that on a calm day when all the seagulls sit in the water, bad weather is coming fast — and their predictions are at least as accurate as official forecasts. In terms of his observatory skills, man is only as resourceful as his needs.

Consider life and death. "Natural births" are currently in vogue. To observe, if not assist, in delivery is quite a revelation to most people today. In the not too distant past, most births were "natural." As for death, what can the urban man or woman know of the natural phenomenon when we live in a society where one's loved one usually dies in a medical facility and is wheeled away while the grieving survivors are ushered out, and the "remains" are not seen again until presented for viewing? In the recent past, the body, with all of the changes that naturally occur, was observed by the survivors. They saw, felt and, if there was undue delay, smelled the effects of death. They may not have used the words now employed, but they knew *post mortim lividity* and *rigor mortis*, and a great deal more.

An Historical Example

To illustrate the point that the power of observation is indeed powerful and natural to man, as well as to engage in a preliminary investigative exercise, let us look back at an incident occurring a century ago during the settlement of the American West. The careful inspection of a scene of devastation left by marauding Indians would reveal evidence as to the tribe or nation of the attackers, the approximate time of attack, the escape route and much other valuable information. Through observation, and observation alone, plausible answers might be obtained to the six basic questions that make up the ageless formula or strategy of an investigator's quest: to recreate or reconstruct the incident in question.

The accompanying map tells part of the story (Figure 1-1). Examine it carefully. The incident is reconstructed through the answers to the six basic questions.

What happened? Two straggling wagons with a party of three men, two women and five children were attacked by Indians. All were killed with the exception of a female child about ten years old. She was taken by the attackers. Death for the others was caused by gunshot, arrow and lance wounds. Two horses, all firearms, and an unknown quantity of foodstuffs were taken. Only one scalp was taken.

Who did it? An Indian party of not more than twenty braves, as evidence by the hoof tracks of their ponies. Arrows found at the scene were distinctively Sioux in terms of shaft and fin construction.

Where did it happen? On the Oregon trail, two days by horseback east of Fort Laramie.

When did it happen? Around daybreak on August 28, 1857. Discovery of the massacre was made just before noon by six riders from the main wagon train returning to check on the stragglers. In one fire pit a few small, hot coals were found at the center and bottom of the pit. A full kettle of water sat near the fire pit, as though about to be placed over the fire. All nine bodies evidenced *post mortim lividity*. (Blood in the dead body all flows, by the force of gravity, to the lowest part of the body, causing permanent dark discolora-

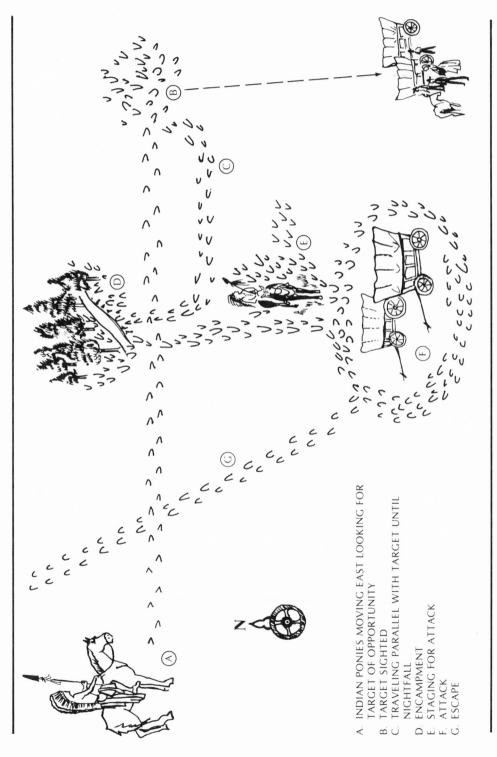

A. INDIAN PONIES MOVING EAST LOOKING FOR
   TARGET OF OPPORTUNITY
B. TARGET SIGHTED
C. TRAVELING PARALLEL WITH TARGET UNTIL
   NIGHTFALL
D. ENCAMPMENT
E. STAGING FOR ATTACK
F. ATTACK
G. ESCAPE

Figure 1-1.   The scene of the hypothetical Indian attack.

tion there.) *Rigor mortis* had set in, detectible in the jaws and neck of one woman and one child. (*Rigor mortis* commences on the average of three-to-six hours after death in the uppermost part of the body and continuing down to the feet. The upper half of the body is usually rigid within twelve hours and the whole body within about eighteen hours. The rigidity leaves in the same way it commences — in the neck and jaws — and completely disappears some thirty-six hours after the onset.)

The adults were all dressed. The four boys were half-clothed. Fresh coffee grounds were strewn about the ground between one wagon and the fire pit. The oxen had not been hitched. The quantity, location and age of horse chips found, along with the presence of two saddles, indicated that two horses belonging to the emigrants had either run off or, more likely, been taken. The discovery of a doll and a small girl's soiled clothing, and the absence of a female child's body, indicated that the girl was carried away by the Sioux. An examination of articles left behind verified that everyone else in the emigrant party was accounted for — nine dead and one missing.

Spent cartridges confirmed that some defensive shots were fired, but there was no evidence that an attacker was hit, at least seriously enough to bleed in any quantity. The disarray of food containers, and the absence of any defensive weapons, suggested to the observers that the attackers quickly searched for food, weapons and munitions, seized the two horses and the girl, and left at a gallop, as though frightened away. Failure to slaughter the oxen or torch the wagons remained a mystery.

All this occurred at around 6:00 a.m.

How did it happen?   The marauding party, moving in an easterly direction parallel to the Oregon trail, happened upon the stragglers sometime around midday the previous day. In all probability the Indians had watched the main wagon train and opted not to attack because of its apparent strength. They rode east, parallel to the trail, apparently looking for more vulnerable potential victims. Upon sighting the stragglers, they reversed direction and rode parallel to the two wagons, unseen, some 800 yards north of the main trail.

At nightfall the Indians slept in a ravine. No fire was made. Before dawn the Sioux, at first in a troop, walked their ponies to within 200 yards of the wagons. The attackers then spread out, mounted and formed a single line. The early morning fire silhouetting the unwary travelers must have encouraged the Indians to attack. They rode hard down on their hapless victims, veering into a clockwise encirclement, and killed the obviously unskilled emigrants, with the exception of the girl who was carried away.

The actions of the Indians prior to and during the attack could be determined by following their own sign. The tracks left by the galloping ponies leading away from the scene bisected the tracks of a corresponding party running parallel to the main trail but going eastward. Horse chips found in that eastbound trail were crusted on the surface with some moisture inside, suggesting they were about twenty-four hours old. Following the eastbound tracks led observors to the ravine where the Indians had camped during the night, as evidenced by ground disturbances showing the bunching of the ponies, where men had urinated, and where they had lain upon the ground. The absence of what should normally have been observable is also informative. At this campsite there was no fire, nor food scraps. The latter detail suggests one possible explanation for the attack.

Why did it happen?   Certainly a contributing factor to the attack was the apparent need for food. What happened to the party's normal source of food could not be determined. Other factors such as the treatment of the Indians by some settlers and the military, the issue of territorial intrusion, and the question of ethnic antipathy — all this was orchestrated together to bring out this small party of Sioux on a mission that was to end in the death of nine settlers and captivity for one.

The Creative Process in Investigation

The forgoing experience may appear to involve a considerable amount of creative imagination. That does not make it inappropriate — just the opposite. Be it reconstructive or constructive, the development of information by communication or by observation, the entire investigative process is as creative in nature as it is scientific.

Investigation is an imaginative process. Despite all of the modern technological assistance available to the investigator, and regardless of what marvelous things machines and computers can do, for the successful investigator there is no substitute for the God-given gift of imagination and creativity.

Chapter 2

Differences Between Private and Public Sectors

The fundamental difference between the investigative process in the public and in the private sectors is the *objective*. The primary objective of investigations in the public sector is to serve the interests of society. If those interests are best served by removing or otherwise punishing those who commit offenses against the public good, then the reconstructive method of investigation is used. When the purpose of the investigation is to inhibit and suppress criminal activity — prostitution and gambling are two examples — then constructive, covert techniques are employed.

The primary objective of the investigative process in the private sector is to serve the interests of the organization, not society as a whole. If those interests are best served by removing or otherwise punishing those who criminally attack the organization, or whose performance in any way defeats or impedes organizational goals, the reconstructive strategy is used where the conduct is a matter of history. Where that conduct or activity is ongoing, constructive, covert techniques must be applied.

It is interesting to note that what serves the best interests of society may not necessarily serve the best interests of the organization, and vice versa. For example, the society's interests are protected when an embezzler is prosecuted and sentenced to prison. There are occasions, however, when the embezzler, having banked all his thefts, would be happy to return the stolen funds in order to avoid prosecution. Such an agreement would be unacceptable in the public sector. A seasoned private sector investigator, on the other hand, is not primarily concerned with prosecution and sentencing. Recovery of the loss might be a more important achievement, better serving the interests of the private organization.

More often than not, investigations in the private sector that deal with criminal behavior result in serving the public sector's objective as well as the organization's, despite the fact that there is a fundamental difference in the perception of the crime. Wherein lies that perceptual difference? It comes from differing views of the victim. The public investigator sees society as the victim, whereas the corporate investigator views his organization as the victim.

More specifically, forgery detectives in a metropolitan police force consider forgers to be a general menace to the community. Investigators of a banking institution or credit-granting company regard the forger whose target is their organization as a very real, immediate threat to the financial stability of the organization. From the viewpoint of the private investigator, the forger must be stopped not because he is breaking the law, but because he is damaging or victimizing the organization.

Different perceptions and different objectives have a direct impact upon the strategies and the character of the investigative process in the two sectors, leading to other differences. Public investigators are usually armed, for example, private investigators unarmed. Other interesting differences that invite comparison require more examination.

Source of Authority and Funding

The public investigator represents the sovereignty of government, whose authority is vested in constitutional and statutory law. Its efforts are financed by public funds, replenished through taxation.

The private investigator represents management, with some authority derived from statutory and case laws. The same authority is afforded to any citizen, such as the power to make arrests under certain conditions, although that power and authority are unknown to most private citizens. In addition, the private security investigator has delegated authority from senior company management.

Sources of Information

In the public sector, there are relatively few limitations to such information as criminal records, government records and files at municipal, county, state and federal levels. On the other hand, there are accelerating limitations to private access to public records.

Job Security

Most investigators in the public sector are in a civil service system with clearly defined job security, and a growing number are joining the ranks of organized labor as well. The private investigator has reasonable job security (as opposed to the unreasonableness of some civil service and labor contracts), provided by the organization's personnel policies. Normally, corporate or company investigators are not part of a labor bargaining entity.

Scope of Work

Public investigators tend to specialize in specific areas of concentration, depending on the agency, department or assignment. They are burglary detectives, forgery detectives, homicide detectives, state or federal narcotics investigators, immigration investigators, etc.

Private security investigators tend to be "generalists," although some specialize in such areas as forgery or fraud when employed by finance and credit companies. They are generalists not only in the sense of working across the broad spectrum of business and commercial interests, but also in the attendant need for wide-ranging information and intelligence.

Image

Public investigators can command immediate respect and attention based on the color of authority, generally supported by impressive credentials, such as badges. Although inherited, such authority must continue to be earned to maintain that favorable image.

Although many in private security have attempted to copy their public cousins' credentials, an ever-growing number recognize that respect and attention are rightfully based on demonstrated intelligence, effective interpersonal skills, and a genuine concern and respect for others.

Civil Liability

Public investigators are relatively free from civil actions that result from day-in and day-out activities. Civil action filings, if they occur at all, usually follow only extremely aggravated incidents. In this respect governmental agencies are not as tempting a target as, for example, a utility company.

In the private sector, investigators are relatively vulnerable to civil actions as a result of exposure in their daily work, irrespective of culpability. An investigator who interrogates an employee on documented evidence of dishonesty can easily expose the company to an unfair labor practice suit, slander or libel suit, or to charges of false imprisonment or malicious prosecution. Large companies are inviting targets — the bigger, the better.

Training and Education

Once on the job, the public investigator attends publicly funded schools, classes or academies, usually of high quality, from basic in-service training to advanced and specialized courses, depending on the area of specialization. At the end of the 1950's, only thirteen institutions of higher learning offered a bachelor's degree in Police Science and Administration, or a similarly designated program. Today, approximately 800 universities and colleges offer at least one course in Criminal Justice, and many offer full degree programs.

Just a few short years ago, investigators in the private sector invariably came from the governmental agencies. The public sector was the training ground. College curriculums rarely included courses in security. This situation has been changing rapidly. More investigators are coming up within the organization, and proportionately fewer retired or former public sector investigators are entering private industry. This change is primarily attributable to the growing numbers of young college graduates with Associate, Bachelor and even graduate degrees in Criminal Justice, men and women who see definite career opportunities in large, successful firms.

In addition, there are simply more security jobs available than in the past. Loss prevention has become a recognized part of organizational existence, with more emphasis on proprietary protection and less reliance on the public sector for protective support. Thus there are more Security Administration classes in the schools, more very professional training programs such as the American Society for Industrial Security's Assets Protection course, and a host of other progressional programs, from tele-communication security to computer fraud. Most of these programs and seminars are privately funded and conducted by competent practitioners.

Technical Resources

In carrying out an investigation, officials in the public sector are able to call upon an extensive arsenal of such technical resources as questioned document examiners, crime laboratory facilities and fingerprint classification specialists, to name just a few. Within the private sector, the investigator has limited access, if any at all, to such publicly supported resources. He must seek out and assume the cost for any such services. The practical effect of this difference is that the private investigator simply cannot call upon the same resources as freely.

Professionalism

Such agencies as the Federal Bureau of Investigation have attained a high level of respected professionalism, both in fact and in profile, by virtue of their reputation, known standards and visibility through the media (both in fictional entertainment and factual news reporting). To a lesser extent, this is true of other law enforcement agencies at the state and local level. Perhaps the epitome of investigative professionalism is the homicide detective in a modern metropolitan police force. In general, the premise that criminal investigators in the public sector are indeed professional, in every sense of the word, goes relatively unchallenged — and rightfully so.

The same is not as universally true in the private sector. Investigators in this area are too often thought of in terms of "private eyes" and commercially available detectives who handle skip-tracing cases or develop evidence for divorce hearings. The general public — and, for that matter, many investigators in the public sector — have little awareness of or appreciation for the corporate investigator. When one thinks of the FBI, investigations leap instantly to mind. When one thinks of United Airlines, traveling is the first thought association, not investigations. Some people are even surprised to learn that commercial firms have investigators on the payroll. Very professional and highly skilled investigators thus go virtually unnoticed outside the upper echelons of the organization.

Regrettably, the range or spectrum of talent, from superior to marginal or poor, is broader in the private sector. There are still a large number of unprofessional, unsophisticated and unskilled "investigators" in the security industry. And where the general public may never hear of the genuine achievements of the professionally trained and qualified private investigator, they will certainly be made aware of the illegal, immoral or sloppy work of the unprofessional practitioner.

On balance, then, the mantle of professionalism is much more generally worn in the public sector, without question. But time and trends are shifting that balance. It would be interesting to reconsider this question in the year 2000.

Career Paths

In the public sector investigative agency — the FBI, for example — the entry-level position would certainly include pure investigatory responsibilities.

In a generalized agency, such as a police department, the position of investigator is a promotional and relatively low in the organizational structure, at the rank of or equivalent to sergeant. From detective or investigator, one can move up to supervisorial investigator (lieutenant), then to a management-level position (captain or chief of detectives). This means that one can advance vertically while remaining in an investigative career.

In the private sector, there is a more pronounced trend toward moving talent up into the investigative position *as a part of the individual's development and growth.* The goal is usually administrative as opposed to investigative, although some individuals may choose to make a career of investigative work. Consequently, high-ranking positions in the security industry are normally filled by men and women with investigative experience. By contrast, high-ranking positions in a police department, as an example, are often filled by men and women who have never worked exclusively as an investigator.

Assistance

Few investigations, public or private, develop in a vacuum. The very nature of the investigative process involved calling on others for information or assistance.

In the public sector, irrespective of departmental and jurisdictional rivalries (which do exist), the exchange and flow of information is rarely, if ever, denied the investigator. It is an unwritten rule that one investigator will share information and assist another if such assistance is sought.

With regard to the assistance provided by informants, it has often been said that the success of any detective in large measure rests upon his or her sources of information. Tips are provided by those seeking favor or "tolerance" — prostitutes and drug addicts, for example — by spurned or jealous lovers seeking revenge, and by a whole host of other sources, anonymous and otherwise, acting from an endless variety of motives, all desirous of seeing a culprit caught. To a lesser extent, monetary rewards also generate information.

There is little in the way of rivalries or jealousy in the private sector to hinder cooperation. An investigator for one utility company can call on a similar firm and, as a rule, count on and receive prompt assistance. This form of cooperation knows no political boundaries. Using such publications as the ASIS membership directory, which alphabetizes members by personal as well as organizational name, one investigator can call another across the country. If he is unknown at the receiving end, that party can verify the identity and affiliation of the caller by use of the same directory. Once identity is established, information is exchanged.

The use of informants in the private sector is another matter. It is unusual for employees to inform on their fellow workers; few people wish to "become involved." More often than not, a customer shopping in a store who witnesses a theft will not report that theft; the typical reaction is to look the other way. Nor does the private investigator have the same "leverage" that a police officer can use to encourage informants to talk. A powerful tool for the public sector, tips are not a significant factor in most successfully concluded private investigations.

Exceptions are noteworthy and in some area are increasing, usually within the format of a structured and well-publicized "Silent Witness" incentive award program. If such programs guarantee anonymity for the informant, they stand a good chance of surviving. And if they survive, information of remarkable value will come in.

Personal Achievement

Without question, all investigators experience a real sense of achievement when a criminal is taken into custody at the successful resolution of a case, especially if the investigation has been lengthy and difficult. Bearing in mind, however, that the real objective of criminal investigations in the public sector is the *successful prosecution* of the offender, it must be recognized that there is a high (and rising) level of frustration for investigators in this area. The work of the investigator can bring little lasting satisfaction when, as happens all too frequently in the present climate, trial court decisions are reversed in the appellate courts. And if appellate reversals based on liberal interpretations of the law do not bring frustration, wrist-slapping sentences handed down by the court will do it. The reward of satisfaction for the professional investigator must be found in the investigative process itself — the means, not the end. To bring a case to a conclusion, identifying the suspect and causing his incarceration — even if only temporarily — brings a sense of personal achievement (and helps to preserve sanity), even if the final result fails to accomplish the ultimate objective.

Because the stated objective of the investigator in the private sector lies in the protection and general welfare of the organization, such down-the-line possibilities as unsuccessful prosecution, light sentencing, appellate reversals, or even failure to indict, although certainly disappointing to some degree, do not bring anything like the level of frustration commonly experienced in the public sector. Why? The mere exposure and eradication of a gang counterfeiting corporate negotiable instruments, for example, and the destruction or seizure of their means of continuing production, genuinely satisfies organizational goals. The investigators can take satisfaction from the knowledge that they have put an end to a source of loss or threat. Similarly, to identify and subsequently to cause the termination of an employee who ingeniously falsified his time records or travel expenses — organizational activities considered more a violation of trust and of the employer-employee relationship than criminal acts — can and does bring real job satisfaction. For these reasons there is probably a healthier climate of self-worth and job satisfaction today in the private than the public sector of investigation.

Conclusion

In dwelling at some length in this chapter on the differences that can be observed between public and private investigators, it is not our purpose to widen the gap between them, but rather to identify those differences for better understanding of common interests and goals. With increased understanding, how much easier it is to communicate and to work together!

Chapter 3

Qualities of the Investigator

To the uninitiated, the aspirant and the distant observer, there is an aura of romanticism surrounding the investigator and his work. That illusion is quickly dispelled in the light of reality. The real world of investigative work is hard, demanding and rarely glamorous. Occasionally a case may come along that is exciting, or one in which the answers come easily, but as a rule investigation is a tedious, exhausting, frustrating, time-consuming and sometimes dirty (in the literal sense) process. Invariably the novice investigator is somewhat dismayed by the difference between his or her preconceptions of the nature of the work and the reality.

Crimes are not solved by ingenious and clever supersleuths but by hard working men and women who universally share one common denominator: perseverance. In the words of Samuel Johnson, "Great works are performed, not by strength, but perseverance." This investigative virtue is defined as "holding to a course of action, belief, or purpose without giving way; steadfastness . . . continuing strength or patience in dealing with something arduous. It particularly implies withstanding difficulty or resistance" in striving for a goal.[1]

Perseverance is the one overriding human trait or characteristic among the many deemed necessary, or at least highly desirable, for investigative work. What are the others? One authority, Donald Schultz, lists fifteen "desirable attributes of an investigator."[2] Charles O'Hara boils it down to three: character, judgment, and the ability to deal with people.[3] And the familiar "green book," *Municipal Police Administration,* has its own list, including "the ability to be deceptive."[4] Collating, modifying, deleting and adding to the suggestions in these sources, we have identified twenty-one qualities or characteristics that are necessary in the effective investigator. He is

1. Observant
2. Resourceful
3. Patient
4. People-oriented
5. Understanding of human behavior
6. Knowledgeable about legal implications of the work
7. A skilled communicator
8. Receptive
9. Possessed of a sense of well-being
10. Dedicated to the work
11. A self-starter
12. Skeptical
13. Intuitive
14. Energetic
15. A good actor
16. Capable of sound judgment
17. Logical
18. Intelligent
19. Creatively imaginative
20. Of good character
21. Professional

Invariably a successful investigator, man or woman, will possess, in varying degrees, each of these traits, either as innate or learned qualities. (Following the discussion and amplification of each trait, a self-scoring survey is provided for personal insight at the end of this chapter.)

Powers of Observation

Skill in observation does not come naturally. It must be learned, and it must be practiced. It requires *seeing* as opposed to merely looking; and, after seeing, the ability to draw intelligent conclusions.

An underlying characteristic of a good observer is curiosity. If you are curious about a person, the power of observation can reveal a great deal. In personal appearance and grooming, for instance, are fingernails manicured or dirty? Are the nails chewed? Is the hair of conventional cut, long and shaggy, or carefully styled? Has the hair been colored? Is clothing color coordinated? In current fashion? Are the shoes shined? Heels run down? Is the person dapper or sloppy in appearance? If in casual dress, are there any stains such as paint or grease that could indicate what the person does around the home or at work? Are there any personal items of jewelry or accessories that might tell you something? If a man, is he wearing a college ring? Fraternal or service ring? A Timex or Rolex watch? Religious medals? If he is wearing a metal belt buckle with the Coors logo, is he a martini drinker?

Apply the same close observations to an automobile. Fingerprints on the interior of windows suggest children. The same is true if there is popcorn on the rear seat or floor. What kind of decals or stickers are visible? Would a bumper sticker reading "I'd rather be skiing" tell you anything? What kind of debris is present on the front floor mats? Are there cigarette butts in the ashtray? If so, what brand? Is there lipstick on the butts? Are there a great many butts?

Obviously, there is much to see, and much can be learned by observing. This is not to say that intelligent, concise or totally accurate conclusions can always be drawn from any given observation. But valid conclusions can often be made. Think of the wife who waits up for her husband and observes lipstick on his collar. He can speak eloquently of the power of observation!

Resourcefulness

The resourceful person is one who, when one path or strategy is blocked or comes to a dead end, finds another. He thinks in terms of alternatives: If this does not work, something else will. If the information is not available at one source, he will turn to another. The person who lacks resourcefulness has a tendency to give up when the initial plan or strategy fails.

In one investigation concerning activities that were occurring in a cocktail lounge, it was vital that I get into that bar during the evening hours, unnoticed. But on the preceding evening the bartender had become suspicious of my presence and purpose and begun pointing me out to the patrons as an investigator. He would surely do the same if I went in again on this critical evening. If he could be lured away from the location just for thirty minutes, I could go in and secure the last needed evidence. The questions was how to get him out?

Across the street from the bar was a pay phone. I entered the booth. I knew the bartender's name and also his home address. Dialing the bar, I asked for the bartender by name. He came to the phone, the noise of the bar audible in the background. I identified myself as a fire captain and asked if he lived in the apartment building at 7373 Hightower Parkway. "Yes," he answered. "Why do you ask?"

I told him the apartment building had caught fire and many items of furniture and personal property had been carried out by tenants and firemen. "Can you come right down and identify your effects?"

"Who's calling?" he asked in disbelief.

"Captain Glotz, Engine Company 461," I replied.

"You say my apartment building caught fire?" he asked incredulously, obviously alarmed.

"In this confusion I can't say specifically whose apartments are damaged. I'm telling you the building has been fire and water damaged, and there are a lot of personal effects that need to be identified and secured. Are you coming or not?"

"I'll be right there, Captain. Give me fifteen minutes."

From the phone booth I watched him leave the bar, get into his car and drive off. I entered the bar and accomplished my mission before he returned.

I saw him in court later. We looked at each other. Nothing was said because nothing needed to be said. He knew.

Patience

The quality of patience is not only a virtue in investigative work, it is essential, particularly in surveillance assignments. It is not uncommon in surveillance assignments for investigators to have to sit in a parked automobile day after day, week after week. The average man would give up, but patience pays off for the investigator. We did hear of one impatient investigator — but he did not last long.

Interaction with People

The investigator must be people-oriented. He must be comfortable around and with people. Our two key sources of information are observation and people. People communicate, and there is a direct relationship between the amount of rapport between two people and the amount of communication.

The individual who likes and enjoys others acts like a human magnet; he attracts people. Those who are uncomfortable around others subconsciously avoid or shun them — and that is perceived. The investigator who enjoys people is usually very adaptable in adjusting to a wide spectrum of different types of people. He is comfortable with the dock worker as well as an executive, with a person on welfare or resident of a main street flophouse as well as a political or government official.

There is also something to be said for kindness and respect for others: It pays off when the investigator is seeking assistance and information. This applies not only in developing informants but also in the day-in and day-out gathering of what appears to be inconsequential information.

Understanding Human Behavior

In addition to the human understanding involved in being people-oriented by nature, there is another aspect of understanding human behavior that is important for the investigator. It belongs in the area of practical psychology. The investigator has to have a fine sense for what makes most people "tick."

There are times when it is appropriate to cry, even for men; there are also times when it is not appropriate. That is true of laughter, sarcasm, anger, resentment and the whole range of emotions and responses. Sensitivity to the reactions and emotions of others can throw light on the investigator's task. Dealing effectively with human responses can make the difference between success and failure. With the person who is experiencing shame, the empathetic investigator can keep communication alive. The investigator who fails to appreciate or understand that person's feelings may act or react in a way that closes communication.

Understanding the Legal Implications

The investigator in the public sector today is very sensitive to the legal implications of his actions. This is not always equally true in the private sector. This may be due, in part, to the very clear distinction between public and private law enforcement that has existed in the past, particularly in the private security man's immunity from such restrictions as the Miranda requirements.

That situation is rapidly changing. The private security investigator may or may not be caught up in the same legal problems as the public law enforcement officer, but the lines of difference are no longer so clearly drawn. And many other legal ramifications affect the work of the private investigator, particularly as it pertains to making arrests and the discharge of employees. The trend is to focus on how and what the investigator did, rather than what the accused did. The investigator must therefore be sensitive to the gray areas of the law, as well as clearly defined legal limitations on his actions.

Effective Communication Skills

Because report writing is such an integral part of the investigative process, the investigator must have writing skills. In addition, he must have the ability to articulate his case effectively, be it an oral presentation of the status or findings of a case to management or testifying in an administrative or judicial hearing. Cases are lost and won by the manner in which witnesses project, especially verbally. Good delivery, in terms of enunciation, clarity, conviction and choice of words, adds credibility to the facts of the case. Conversely, mumbled, hesitant or hard–to–understand oral presentations, and presentations filled with slang or other poor choices of words, tend to discredit an otherwise good case.

Receptivity

The quality of receptiveness means being open-minded. That includes an interest and willingness to listen to other opinions, and even to ask for them. Further, it includes the willingness not only to listen but to *consider,* weighing the merits of other ideas, suggestions and opinions and, when appropriate, accepting them. The unreceptive person who rejects external sources, who has strong tendencies to pursue an investigation in his or her own way, tends to work in a trench, becoming blind to alternatives. The effective investigator must remain open for fresh input.

By way of illustration, in 1978 we were approached by someone who asked if we would be interested in meeting with a graphologist to discuss the possibility of utilizing graphology in background investigations. Graphology, the study of handwriting for the purpose of analyzing the writer's character, struck me as something akin to fortune telling. The caller asked me to keep an open mind and at least give the graphologist — a young woman — the opportunity to prove her ability to identify indicators of dishonesty in the handwriting of our employees. With some skepticism we agreed.

We gathered sample handwriting of four of our most trusted employees and the handwriting of four former employees who had been discharged for dishonesty. There was absolutely no way the graphologist could know anything about the eight individuals. The "test" analysis was overseen by my very able assistant, an attorney by education and a former FBI agent. To his dismay, the young woman not only identified the former employees as having "traits of dishonesty," but she was also able to identify other interesting personality characteristics of several employees in the sample with startling accuracy.

We called on the graphologist again to assess the promotability of three key security executives in the organization, and her analysis of the three was so accurate it was uncanny. We asked another security executive to identify the three subjects by reading her analysis only; he was able to identify each of them correctly.

By being receptive to a new idea, graphology, we broadened our own horizon.

Sense of Well-Being

An investigator must feel good about himself, his skill, his ability to perform the task at hand, no matter how complex or difficult. This feeling is more than self-confidence, because it includes experiencing the rewards of a job well done.

The sense of well-being also includes personal and professional security. The investigator is not always looking over his shoulder, wondering how long he will remain in the investigation unit; he is comfortable in the knowledge that his performance level is high. Another expression of this quality is self-esteem.

One who lacks this sense of well-being will spend more time and energy on himself than his assignment, and his work will suffer in consequence.

Dedication to the Work

How many wives and how many husbands have said, "You're more dedicated to your job than to me!" Outstanding investigators are unequivocally dedicated to their work. Invariably, families suffer, personal affairs are neglected, yard work goes undone, personal business goes unattended — all because the demands of the job take priority.

A dedicated investigator does not wear a watch to know when to go home. He wears a watch to record in his notebook the time of an event, interview, receipt of information or action. This dedication is not unique to investigators, of course. It can be found in doctors, educators, scientists and military officers, to name but a few — invariably in successful ones. There is something awesome and wonderful about so loving one's work, as long as the dedication is not an escape from some problem. Of the many who may have suffered because of that single-mindedness, most have survived and are richer and stronger for their trial. And for those dedicated individuals who caused the suffering, the time comes when they make it up, many times over, for they too are richer and stronger because they have fought the best battle.

Self-Initiative

The demands of the investigative process require an individual with initiative, a "self-starter." Working within the guidelines established by the organization, he or she accepts assignments and pursues them in a uniquely unstructured fashion. Rarely is there only one way or one specific time to resolve the issue at hand. The investigator must be able to act on his own. The work should never require official or managerial prodding or supervision.

Most supervision is advisory in nature. The man or woman who counts on a superior to say "start" and "stop" should not be in the investigative business.

Healthy Skepticism

A healthy skepticism in investigation means taking everything in with "a grain of salt," not fully accepting anything with blind faith, yet not necessarily rejecting anything because of the source. Everything is listened to, everything is look at, nothing is sacred, nothing is a fact until it is proven or measures up to known and acceptable standards. Healthy skepticism keeps investigators sharp and accurate. If someone says it was raining on a given night, and that information is vital to the case, the healthy skeptic will confirm that information with official records of the weather service.

This quality has to be private, not open. Only a fool would openly display the attitude, "I'm from Missouri, you'll have to show me." Such a posture can be self-defeating, because many people resent skepticism, particularly when it is directed toward what they say or believe.

Intuition

The notion of "a woman's intuition" would seem to preclude men having the same instincts, which is far from the case. To be intuitive is no more or less than the familiar "gut feeling." It is the sense of knowing something without the use of a rational process or evidence provided by the five physical senses.

Intuition is commonly manifested in the area of attempted deception. An experienced investigator may have no concrete proof that someone is lying, but nonetheless experiences a strong intuition that the person lied. It is a hunch, a feeling that cannot be explained but is an indicator for action or direction. Many cases have been resolved because an investigator paid attention to this intuition or followed a hunch.

Energy and Stamina

Investigators are not desk-bound executives. They are workers, always on the move — looking, probing, digging, asking, comparing. Their work requires a person with a high energy level. Its demands impact on the mental as well as the physical reservoirs of strength and stamina. Despite the fatigue and frustrations, despite the setbacks and reversals, despite the failures that inevitably occur, the investigator must have the reserves of energy that enable him to keep going.

Acting Skills

In Shakespeare's *Hamlet,* Hamlet instructs the troupe of players, "Let the words fit the action and the action fit the words." The advice suits investigators as well as actors.

The investigator must be able to assume a wide variety of roles, and he must be able to change roles quickly and fittingly. Whatever the role — fire captain, credit verifier, old wartime buddy, the "bad guy" in the interrogation strategy, or friend — each calls for versatility. Call it deception if you will. The ability to act or be deceptive is a prime requisite in the effective investigator.

In one case, evidence suggested that the firm's computerized list of customers had somehow fallen into the hands of an insurance agent. The agent appeared to be soliciting business through mailings to our customers. It was determined that the insurance agent had contracted with an independent mailing service for a quantity of mailings. Further investigation revealed that the principal of the mailing service — call him Mr. Brown — was a part-time operator, his regular employment being that of supervisor with a major mailing service — the very service subscribed to by my employer. The circumstances appeared to indicate that Mr. Brown was building his own mailing lists by making extra runs of the lists of his employer's clients. It was necessary, however, to confirm this suspicion.

Brown ran his part-time business out of his garage. I contacted him at his residence by phone and said that a friend had referred me to him. I told him I was in town for a very short time, that I was from another part of the state, that I was the director of a Christian fund-raising foundation, and that we were interested in expanding our appeal to a select part of the Los Angeles market on a test basis only. If the test reflected a favorable response, I told him, we would then be interested in discussing a contract. In the meantime, all I wanted was to purchase a list of 1,000 residents in a specific geographical area with a given income range. The geographical and income requirements matched those of my company's customers.

In response to Mr. Brown's questions, I gave him a fictitious name for myself and the foundation. When he asked for my telephone number I told him that I was almost impossible to reach because I traveled a great deal. We agreed on a price for the mailing list, with payment in cash, and set a meeting time in the lobby of a large downtown hotel the following week.

At the appointed time and place, after a brief discussion of my foundation, I examined the multi-page list of names and addresses Mr. Brown provided and paid him for the list in currency. We parted on my promise to get back to him within thirty days.

Careful comparison of the purchased list against our customer list proved negative. During additional phone conversations I asked for more lists, but Brown was unable to deliver new names. Another appointment was set up in the hotel lobby. This time I was accompanied by an investigative associate.

Our intention was to disclose our identity and determine how Brown had obtained a few of our customers' names and addresses — the few we knew about.

Mr. Brown was astonished upon learning my true identity. During our quiet interrogation in the corner of the hotel's coffee shop, he admitted taking home overruns and set-up runs of the address labels which were considered waste or trash. This was subsequently confirmed. The handling of "waste" at the primary mailing service's facility was also corrected. Our investigation established beyond doubt that our computerized customer list had not been stolen or sold.

The particular strategy of deception or "cover story" used in this case was considered the best way to insure that we arrived at the truth. And it worked.

Good Judgment

Good judgment simply means the ability to make the right decision most of the time. When someone claims to exercise good judgment, he is really saying that his batting average is over .500 — that he makes more good decisions than bad ones.

There are two elements involved in sound judgment. The first is the *willingness to make decisions.* Many people — including those in management roles — find decision-making difficult as well as unpleasant. The effective investigator is not reluctant to make decisions. The second factor is that most decisions, based on experience, intuition and accumulated wisdom, must prove to be right. Note the qualification: *most* decisions, not all.

Bad judgment is somewhat easier both to identify and to define. Bad judgment occurs when the decision runs counter to the available data. Overloading an airplane and attempting to take off on a short runway is poor judgment. So is the attempt single-handedly to arrest a felon known to be armed and dangerous in a dark alley.

Another indication of poor judgment is making the same wrong decision more than once. The investigator does not live who has never made a mistake. The good ones do not repeat it.

The Exercise of Logic

A logical person is one capable of consistency in reasoning. In investigative work, logic is necessary in drawing reasonable conclusions based upon earlier events. A logical mind is able to see relationships between events past, present and future.

For example, it is discovered that over the past six months quantities of titanium have been smuggled from the plant. Considering the availability of the material and existing controls, it is logical that the titanium was removed by an employee. Because titanium has little value or appeal for personal use, it is logical that the thief has a buyer, someone with a commercial need or a commercial source for titanium. The next logical investigative step might be to identify and contact the major legitimate suppliers of titanium in the area to (1) identify industries and firms that regularly purchase titanium; (2) determine if any regular customers have reduced their purchases of the metal while at the same time maintaining or even increasing their level of production; and (3) depending on the professionalism of the titanium supplier, advising them that stolen metal is in circulation and requesting that they pass along any information that comes to their attention. These are logical steps, in a sequential pattern that is reasonable.

Intelligence

Without question, an effective investigator must have higher-than-average intelligence. Most of the qualities already discussed — resourcefulness, understanding of people, communication skills, receptivity, initiative, skepticism, sound judgment and a logical turn of mind — imply an agility of mind beyond the normal. Simply stated, a good investigator cannot be average; he must be smart.

One aspect of intelligence essential to the investigator is mental recall, or memory. The ability to remember small details, even those seemingly unrelated to the present case, can help make logical connections that aid in resolving the case at hand. Such details might include names, events, faces, an automobile, a phrase, a criminal's M.O. *(modus operandi)*. The investigator must have strong powers of memory.

Creative Imagination

The creative imagination is capable of transcending the reality of the present or apparent. Puzzles offer a useful demonstration. In Figure 3-1 there is a picture of a cake. How can you cut the cake with a knife, using only three straight strokes, so that you end up with eight pieces of cake, each of equal size?

As another example, how can you change the number 9 (in Roman numerals) into the number 6 with the addition of only one line?

Solution: IX + S = SIX

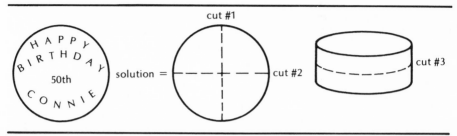

Figure 3-1.   Creative puzzle.

Such exercises are illustrations of the ability to see things in a different way, demonstrating a creative imagination.

In a practical way, *Municipal Police Administration* puts its finger on the essence of this ability: "Uncovering the facts of a crime by means other than direct interview and examination of physical evidence in the strict sense requires an active and practical imagination and the ability to substitute the mental processes of the culprit for one's own."[5] In other words, you must be able to think like a thief. What would you do next if you were the criminal? How would you dispose of the evidence if you were faced with his problem? Where would you go if you were in his shoes?

For this writer, it is difficult to conceive of conducting an investigation without that creative imagination as part of the overall strategy.

Good Character

For many years I worked for and with a "grand lady," a woman of strong principles, Koral Vaughn, Senior Vice President of the Broadway Department Stores, now retired. She used to say that personnel employees and security employees must be, "like Caesar's wife, above reproach." It is hard to add to that.

Sense of Professionalism

An investigator, in particular a criminal investigator (and the bulk of investigative work in the private sector is criminal), is always "on stage." On or off the job, what we do, how we do it, what we say and how we say it reflect on the image of our profession. Like other professionals the investigator must maintain high standards of conduct.

One good rule to follow will be familiar to most investigators: What you do on the job, hear on the job, see on the job and say on the job, should *stay* on the job. But discretion is only one aspect of investigative professionalism. Because of the investigator's high visibility, such qualities as courtesy, a sense of fair play, gentleness, good grooming, pleasantness and humility will evoke respect and admiration for the investigator individually and, collectively, for the investigative professional.

A Self-Quiz

Figure 3-2 provides a self-quiz for the present or potential investigator. Bearing in mind such qualities as good character and a sense of professionalism, grade yourself as fairly and objectively as possible. Whatever your score, there will always be room for improvement. Make it a goal to move those X's one box to the left.

MARK APPROPRIATE BOX WITH AN "X"	STRONG	ABOVE AVERAGE	AVERAGE	BELOW AVERAGE	WEAK
	5	4	3	2	1
1. Are you really observant, seeing instead of looking?					
2. Are you resourceful, able to find other ways to go?					
3. How patient are you?					
4. Are you comfortable with and do you really like people?					
5. Do you have a feeling for how people tick?					
6. Do you know the legal "down-side risks" of the job?					
7. Do you write and speak well?					
8. Do you invite and accept other people's input?					
9. Are you comfortable and confident as an investigator?					
10. Do you consider yourself dedicated to your work?					
11. Are you a person of initiative?					
12. Are you a healthy skeptic?					
13. Do you get "gut feelings" and act upon them?					
14. Are you considered energetic on the job?					
15. How good an actor are you?					
16. Do you have a reputation for using good judgement?					
17. Are you strong in logical reasoning?					
18. Rate your own I.Q. range with 110 as the average.					
19. Are you a creative person?					
20. How would you rate yourself as a person of principles?					
21. How do you rate your sense of professionalism?					

Each box has a numeric value as shown in the top line.
Add up the columns and enter the total score here.
Maximum score attainable is 105. The average score is 63.
An investigator should score above 75.

Figure 3-2. Investigator's personal quiz.

Chapter 4

Managing the Investigative Function

There is a school of thought which supports the concept that a good manager need not possess the technical skills of those being managed. Where that approach may be valid in some or even many areas of management, the concept proves invalid when it comes to managing or, more precisely, supervising investigators. The reason is that the very nature of the work demands far more freedom of movement, more alternatives and more creativity on the part of the investigator than other security functions. To manage the highly motivated and creative individuals who perform in this more "free-wheeling" kind of work requires that the supervisor be someone who has already been down that road, one who understands, through experience, what is going on.

The manager of an investigation unit performs five different roles, each of which requires investigative experience. Such a manager functions as

1. An investigative counselor
2. An investigative trainer
3. An investigative controller
4. An investigative motivator
5. An investigative evaluator.

THE MANAGER AS INVESTIGATIVE COUNSELOR

Because the investigative process is not a precise science, the investigator on assisgnment — including the experienced investigator — needs the active counsel of a knowledgeable person about where he (or she) has been in the case, where he is now and where he should go next.

This counseling activity is an informal and open exchange of ideas. It is exploratory, creative and thought-provoking. It involves bouncing ideas off one another and "off the wall." It means bringing together the sum total of yesterday's experiences that should throw light on the direction of today's investigation.

This counseling role should not be misconstrued as one in which the manager sits as the oracle of wisdom. He functions, rather, as a participant in the discussion, one who can make significant contributions by virtue of his investigative skills and experience.

The key to effective counseling is the process itself. It should be a process that creates a climate in which one person stimulates another with ideas or strategies that could materially contribute to the successful conclusion of a given case. The following exchange exemplifies this kind of dialogue.

Investigator: "The guy has simply dropped out of sight. He's not been seen or heard of for over a year."

Supervisor: "What about the last known residence? No request for forwarding mail, or information about a moving or storage van?"

"No, he was in a cheap hotel, lived out of a suitcase."

"Check for address changes at the Department of Motor Vehicles?"

"Yep. Nothing."

"Is he an ex-GI?"

"Yes."

"Did you check with the Veterans Administration to see if he carried National Service Life Insurance and if the premium payments could give a lead?"

"I checked that. He does have an old $5,000 life policy with them but no payments have been received since last year."

"Could he be locked up somewhere?"

"Checked that too. I know for a fact he's not incarcerated in a federal institution or in any of the neighboring states."

"How about a monastery, like that Trappist place in Utah?"

"I didn't check that but I really doubt it. He was too much of a party guy and boozer. Say, that gives me an idea. He drank big. He could be in a state mental institution. Never thought of that before . . . ."

In this exchange the manager is not giving advice in the strict sense of the term. He is stimulating the investigator with questions that, in this example, led the investigator to discover a logical step he had not taken.

In some circumstances the counseling process may be advisory in nature. This is simply another dimension of the process. The investigator who has doubts about the wisdom of interviewing a given witness, for example, can have the benefit of his manager's feelings. The essence of the process is dialogue, involving the exchange of ideas and agreement on strategy.

THE MANAGER AS TRAINER

You cannot teach a student the art of calligraphy, how to fly an airplane or how to wrestle until you, the teacher, have first mastered those skills. The same is true in teaching investigative skills. Teaching and developing such skills is a vital responsibility of the manager. This is particularly true in the training of newly assigned investigators, or novices.

In his role as trainer the manager has a number of options and combinations of options. Ideally, a combination of all available options would be used, including the manager's direct involvement, on-the-job training with an experienced investigator, classroom instruction, and participation in college progams and seminars.

Direct Involvement

The manager may personally conduct an investigation from beginning to end, with the trainee working alongside. As the case unfolds, step by step, the manager explains the why's and wherefore's and answers questions. The student thus learns the logic or rationale of the investigative process, and, with the manager as teacher, he or she learns the business the right way from the start — the manager's way. For all practical purposes the manager's way is the right way, when one considers the fact that the manager is the evaluator of the investigator's performance.

On-the-Job Training With Others

A second training option is to assign the novice to work with an experienced investigator for so-called "on-the-job training." Although this is the most popular method of training, it does have its drawbacks. The most conspicuous problem is that the trainee tends to pick up the more experienced partner's bad as well as good habits. An otherwise excellent investigator who tends to be sloppy with his note-taking because of an unusual capability of mental recall will pass along to the novice the notion that note-taking is not important. If the novice does not have the same recall ability, this flaw in the learning process can have serious consequences later.

Although the manager may choose to delegate the training to a seasoned subordinate, the manager must still assume the final responsibility for training and follow-up to insure that bad habits or gaps in the learning process are corrected.

Classroom Experience

Another form of training is the formalized or structured classroom experience. Here there is a wide variation of possibilities, from instruction given by the manager to instruction by a number of seasoned investigators, each teaching in areas where they have particular expertise, to utilizing an outside training counsultant. This form of training has genuine value as part of the learning process.

The quality and creativity of classroom training are limited only by the manager's imagination. Take, for example, a program we designed for instruction in the art of interrogation. We held a one-day interrogation workshop for all investigators of my organization. In preparation for the seminar, all participants were required to submit an actual interrogation situation in which they had experienced difficulty. On the day of the training session, selected situations were read aloud to two randomly selected investigators, one of whom was charged with playing the role of the interrogator while the other acted the interrogatee. The "interrogation" was acted out before the assembled group of investigators. At the same time the interrogation was filmed on video-tape with sound. Following the dramatized enactment of the interrogation situation, the confrontation was subjected to a critique by the entire group. This proved to be a meaningful learning experience for all involved.

As an extension of this classroom experience, we later developed a self-study interrogation workbook which covered the basics of interrogation, the do's and don't's, and then exposed the student to one of the previously videotaped situations. The video-workbook program contained three situations. After reading the first situation, the student was instructed to close the book and turn on the television set. The situation he had just read about was dramatized on the screen. At the conclusion of the first filmed sequence a message on the screen directed the student to turn the set off and return to the workbook, where a series of questions about the interrogation just witnessed had to be answered. After the student had viewed all three situations and answered the questions about each, he or she could then compare the answers with those printed in the back of the book.

This variation on the classroom approach to learning had three clear advantages: (1) The novice investigator engaged in a learning experience alone, without tying up the time of the manager or another investigator. (2) The learning experience was non-threatening. The student's answers were unknown to anyone else, and thus his own private and confidential assessment of doubtful or incorrect answers (as measured against those in the back of the workbook) could serve as a useful guideline. And (3) the learning process was experiential. The student could privately live the role of the interrogator on the television screen.

Outside Classes

Another way the manager can discharge his responsibility as trainer is to arrange or require attendance at local college classes in relevant subjects or seminar sessions on investigative skills. While the availability of such programs will vary in different areas, this type of formal training is rapidly increasing and is of unquestioned value.

THE MANAGER AS CONTROLLER

In the manager's role as controller there are four areas of concern: organization and span of control, records, expenses and equipment.

Organization and Span of Control

Span of control as a management concept refers to the number of subordinates reporting directly to a superior. In an earlier book we took the position that a good span of control in a security organization is six persons.[6] But in the case of investigators, this effective span of control can be extended because of the nature of the worker and the nature of the work. As Schultz observes, "Highly qualified and motivated investigation personnel obviously require less supervision, thus making it possible to extend the normal limits of a span of control."[7] In the organization diagrammed in Figure 4-1, for example, only one manager or supervisor is needed for the investigation unit.

However, as Schultz concludes correctly, "Under no circumstances should a supervisor in investigation be required to have more than 10 subordinates reporting to him."[8] Thus, if a security organization has more than ten investigators, organizational design as it pertains to investigations comes into play. Here another principle of organization is applicable, the logical division of work, according to which investigators are divided by either their purpose, process or method, clientele, time or geography.[9] In the organization shown in Figure 4-2, three supervisors working under the manager should be capable of exercising effective control over as many as thirty investigators.

Records

The primary or master record in the investigative unit is the Investigative Assignment Ledger. Every investigation conducted by the organization is posted in this control ledger by date received or date the case was opened, case file number, name of suspect or arrestee, if any, the name of the investigator

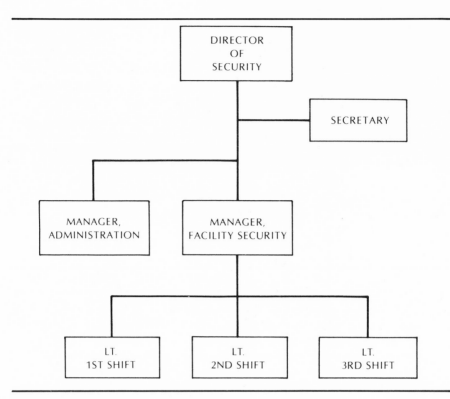

DIRECTOR
OF
SECURITY

SECRETARY

MANAGER,
ADMINISTRATION

MANAGER,
FACILITY SECURITY

LT.
1ST SHIFT

LT.
2ND SHIFT

LT.
3RD SHIFT

Figure 4-1.   Organization with less than 10 investigators.

to whom the case is assigned, status report dates, remarks and final disposition.

The simplified illustration of ledger entries shown in Figure 4-3 tells the manager who examines it on March 7th the following information:

Investigator Childs: On January 4 he was assigned a company burglary investigation (file designation B), the second of the year (file #2 = B-2-80). He filed his first report the following day, a supplemental report six days later, and another report on March 7. The matter is pending.

On January 9 Childs was assigned the first background investigation of the year (BI-1-80), which he completed and filed on February 2. On January 13 he was assigned the first malicious mischief case for the year (M-1-80). Four days later he filed his first report on this case, with a second report following almost a month later. The problem of someone cutting the exterior fenceline is still pending.

Investigator Moss: On January 6 she was assigned a special investigation, the first of that classification for the year (SP-1-80). The same day she identified juvenile Learant as the suspect and referred that juvenile to the police, who took over the case. There was nothing more for her to do and the matter

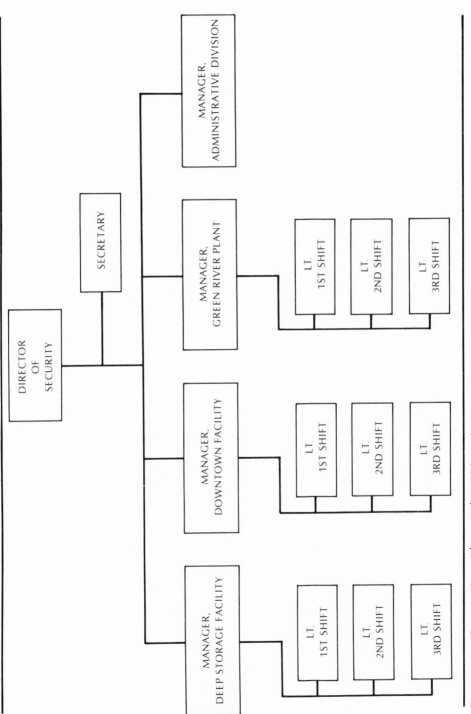

Figure 4–2. Organization with more than 10 investigators.

DATE	FILE #	SUSPECT/ARRESTEE	INVESTIGATOR	1st REPORT	REPORT	REPORT	REMARKS
4 JAN 80	B-2-80		Childs	5 JAN 80	11 JAN 80	7 MAR 80	
6 JAN 80	SP-1-80	Learant, Oscar	Moss	6 JAN 80			Arrested juvenile. Turned over to P.D.
9 JAN 80	BI-1-80	Turner, Helen	Childs	2 FEB 80			Update OK
9 JAN 80	S-1-80		Hernandez	11 JAN 80	9 FEB 80		Lewd calls to Accounting Div.
10 JAN 80	E-2-80	Farmer, Charles	Moss	11 JAN 80			Employee terminated.
11 JAN 80	B-3-80	Jackson, Wiles & White, Samuel	Hernandez	12 JAN 80	13 JAN 80	1 MAR 80	Detective Hogan reports arrests. Recovery being held as evidence.
13 JAN 80	M-1-80		Childs	17 JAN 80	11 FEB 80		Fence cutting
16 JAN 80	E-3-80	Reed, Malissa	Hernandez	19 JAN 80			
16 JAN 80	E-4-80	Borowiler, Harry	Moss	18 JAN 80	21 FEB 80	6 MAR 80	Employee resigned
17 JAN 80				21 JAN 80			

Figure 4–3. Investigative assignment ledger.

was closed (cleared). On January 10 she was assigned the second employee investigation of the year (E-2-80); the next day the case was resolved by the termination of the employee. On January 16 Moss was assigned another employee case, the fourth of the year (E-4-80). This case was cleared from the books some weeks later, on March 6, when the suspect resigned.

Investigator Hernandez: On January 9 he was assigned the first sex crime of the year (S-1-80), a lewd phone call problem that is continuing but has not been resolved. Hernandez has kept abreast of the case, filing monthly supplemental reports. On January 11 he was assigned the third burglary case (B-3-80). He filed his initial investigative report the next day. On the following day the ledger reflects a report from a local police detective advising that the patrol division had picked up two suspects. The case is awaiting trial. On January 16 Hernandez was assigned the third employee investigation of the year (E-3-80). He submitted his first report three days later, but since then no activity in connection with that case has been recorded.

It should be borne in mind that this sample reflects only the assignments over a two-week period, and the three investigators would naturally have other cases assigned prior to the initial date of the sample.

Obviously, then, the Investigation Assignment Ledger provides the manager with a wealth of information.

- It is a single source that reflects the total case load of the organization.
- It is a single source that reflects the quantitative status of a given classification of case. By the 16th of January, for example, four employee cases had been formalized. By August the then current page of the ledger might tell the manager at a glance that the 64th employee investigation for the year was just assigned.
- It serves as a reminder to follow up on cases still pending.
- It serves as a guide as to which investigator might or might not be assigned to the next case.
- It is the source for the compilation of monthly activity or production statistics, by unit as well as by individual investigator.

The ledger (which should be bound as opposed to a looseleaf format to insure against the removal of pages and modification of entries) is a strong supervisory tool. Consider, for example, Hernandez' case #E-3-80. Examining the ledger on March 7, the manager notes that Hernandez submitted one report on this case on January 19. There are no remarks to indicate an activity or status, and the case is still open. Thus the sheet signals a possible problem. It should alert the manager to go to the investigation files and pull #E-3-80.

Let us say, for the sake of illustration, that the one report dated 1/19/80, as indicated in the ledger, concludes with this statement: "Investigation will continue when the subject employee returns from his medical leave of absence." More than six weeks have passed. Is the suspected employee still on medical leave? Or has the employee returned but Hernandez has failed to keep up with the case? Whether the employee has returned to work or not, the investigator should have checked within a thirty-day period and, if the employee was still on leave, a brief supplemental report to that effect should have been written. The manager can point out this lapse to Hernandez.

The other key record is the monthly activity report for each investigator. Such a report is simply a summation of each investigator's work, covering the number of cases assigned, the number closed, number pending, number of arrests or apprehensions, value of recoveries, and any other data deemed significant to the organization. Such data are computed in terms of the month in question (for example, February, 1980), this month last year (February, 1979), this year to date (January-February, 1980) and last year to date (January-February, 1979).

Expenses

Ideally, the investigative unit of the security department should have its own salary and sundry expense budgets, originally prepared and subsequently monitored by the manager.

In *Effective Security Management*, summarizing the chapter on planning and budgeting, this area of the manager's responsibility is expressed in a nutshell: "Planning and budgeting go hand-in-hand; a budget is a plan stated in financial terms. Budgeting requires a realistic estimate of programs and their costs, and an allocation of resources to achieve planned objectives.

"Because budgets are prepared well in advance, effective budget management requires thinking ahead, anticipating needs based on relatively predictable conditions. The budget then becomes a tool . . ."[10]

Each month the manager should analyze the expenditures of his section. Let us say that he originally planned for 40 hours of overtime for his staff but during the last month actually incurred 80 hours of overtime, a 100% increase over the plan. The manager must review the work record to determine who worked the excess overtime and why. The extra overtime may or may not have been necessary. Periodic review and evaluation of these and other expenses are simply another important way of controlling the operation of the investigative unit.

Equipment

Equipment used by investigators, such as two-way radios, binoculars, recorders, weapons, surveillance trucks, cameras, etc., requires strict controls. All forms of such equipment should be secured in a locked equipment room with the key controlled by the manager.

When an investigator has need of equipment — say, a camera — it should be assigned to the investigator on an equipment control sheet that reflects the following: Date checked out, description of equipment (by equipment number or serial number), case file number, investigator's name, person checking the equipment out, condition of equipment going out, signature of investigator taking possession, date equipment is returned, condition of equipment returned, and signature of person receiving the returned equipment. Unless such controls are in place and faithfully administered, equipment will invariably end up missing or mysteriously damaged.

With respect to the condition of equipment and record of damage, this control is not designed to make investigators pay for damages. It is designed, rather, to prevent a situation in which equipment is urgently needed but is discovered to be broken or otherwise inoperable. With proper control, if any piece of equipment is damaged on one case, that damage will be caught and promptly repaired, so the equipment will be ready for use the next time.

THE MANAGER AS MOTIVATOR

Because most individuals in investigative work are or should be highly motivated, managerial expertise in this area will best be demonstrated by what he should *not* be: a de-motivator.

What can cause a motivated employee to lose dedication and enthusiasm? In large part such de-motivation is the result of managerial styles or practices that restrict the investigator's decision-making opportunities, emphasize criticism rather than praise, take credit when that credit rightfully belongs to the investigator, restrict the investigator's freedom of movement, or in a host of other ways express the negative characteristics so frequently found in the work environment.

Really effective and motivated investigators may indeed be prima donnas, but of all employees they require a light touch on the reins. The best managerial approach to them is expressed in an article entitled "Give Your People the Opportunity to Fail," in *Security World* magazine. It reads, in part, ". . . we find the decision-making process is the result and reflection of one's judgement and/or creativity. Management either respects and values the judgement and/or creativity of each employee, or they don't. How can an employee's true capabilities be known if the individual is over-supervised, over-ruled, unduly limited, reversed and corrected?"[11]

Even those who might take issue with this thinking in general would be hard pressed to refute its logic as applied to the work climate of those engaged in investigative work. The manager responsible for investigators must have outstanding people-management skills as well as a strong background in investigative field work. Unskilled managers can and do drive valuable investigative talent to to look for work with other companies or in the public sector.

THE MANAGER AS EVALUATOR

There are two common managerial errors found in performance evaluations as applied to the investigative function. The first is the attitude or belief that evaluations should be an annual event, usually preparatory to salary reviews. The second is the error of rating the person rather than that person's performance.

The effective manager recognizes that the evaluation of each investigator's performance is an ongoing process, based on case after case, and one that should be reviewed at least monthly. That review will begin with the monthly individual statistical summary. If the investigator's work is rated marginal, questionable or below accepted standards for the month of March, the matter should be discussed at that time, not months later. To put this in another way, the investigator should never be surprised by his or her standing in the eyes of the manager. Everyone needs and wants to know how he is doing, and it is encouraging and stimulating to know that your work is under constant review as you progress through the year. Even the knowledge of failing to meet acceptable standards, when this evaluation is handled in an objective way, provides encouragement to the employee in terms of knowing exactly what is expected of him and what he must do to reach accepted standards of performance. On the other side of the coin, rare is the employee who is not motivated to even better performance when praised for his or her work.

Objectivity in evaluation is essential. The manager cannot afford to rate investigators as personalities. Each must be rated on the basis of what he does or fails to do — on performance. It is all too easy to fall into the trap of rewarding likable and popular personalities with high marks, or to rate less attractive people with lower marks. Even the wisest manager can sometimes be blinded by the halo effect of an outstanding but isolated incident or swayed in his judgement by the fact that an individual is highly popular. Avoid these traps. Evaluate everyone, like it or not, based on the record.

II. METHODS OF SECURITY INVESTIGATION

Chapter 5

Undercover Investigations

Undercover investigations are essentially intelligence or "spy" operations within any given area or unit of a corporation. As such, the investigation is definitely covert in its nature and operation. Effectively, no one should know an investigation is in progress other than those directly responsible.

The obvious advantage of an undercover operation is that it gives management an accurate picture of what is occurring in detail, on a day-to-day basis, in a designated area of the organization. As a rule, management does not really know what is going on in line units. It relies on supervision to keep superior officers apprised. Obviously, poor or dishonest supervisors will not report on themselves or their subordinates.

Another invaluable aspect of this covert activity is that the undercover investigator is in position not only to observe dishonesty but also to participate in it, along with all the other employees who have chosen to become involved. This provides security and management with intimate details of employee theft and other illegal activities. As an example, the shipping and receiving supervisor might be compromised by a female subordinate as a result of an overnight love affair. The female employee and two other receiving clerks are stealing from the firm by signing off receipts which reflect more goods than actually received. The differences are being divided among the three and various truck drivers delivering the goods. The compromised supervisor knows what is happening but conveniently disappears from the dock when trucks come in. An undercover agent assigned to work in that area as a forklift operator would (assuming he is an effective agent) soon become involved in the thefts. He would also readily discover why the supervisor never seems to be in the area when the illegal activity occurs.

Undercover investigations may be conducted on a random basis or they may be undertaken with specific targets — for example, when there is information or suspicion of dishonesty in a given area, such as the shipping and receiving department in the illustration above. Random assignments are simply tests of work areas. If dishonesty or any other form of unacceptable conduct exists in that area, it will be discovered. Unacceptable behavior might include the use of alcohol or drugs on the job, cheating on the time clock, gross carelessness that causes damage to materials, equipment or goods, or any number of other actions that commonly constitute problems in the work environment.

The objectives of constructive or undercover investigations in the private sector are:

1. To discover internal dishonesty.
2. To identify all parties involved in the dishonest activity.
3. To identify the organizational, operational or physical failure that contributed to or permitted the dishonesty to occur.
4. To purge the organization of all guilty employees (or outsiders who contract for or otherwise service the organization).
5. To correct those deficiencies identified in #3 above.

Additional benefits from this particular protection strategy include discovery and subsequent correction of conditions which are counterproductive to the best interests of the organization, such as poor supervisory practices, unsafe conditions, wasteful practices, sanitation problems, legal compliance failures, industrial espionage and internal sabotage.

It should be clear that undercover investigations in the private sector focus on internal operations involving employee conduct and performance. It follows that the strategy used to detect and apprehend shoplifters (customers, not employees) who commit theft in a retail organization is not the same as an undercover investigation. Rather, it is a plainclothes, constructive, *observatory* program (as opposed to participatory) that has little, if anything, to do with employee dishonesty.

TECHNIQUES AND METHODS
Penetrating for Job Placement

A very important aspect of the undercover operation is the need for the investigator, agent or operative to assume a false identity in the work force. To all intents and purposes, the agent is an impostor, posing as a janitor, assembler, stockman, clerk, accountant, waitress, EDP operator, warehouseman or anything else — not excluding a possible role as a security employee within the security department. The fact that the false or assumed identity would not stand up to any searching scrutiny (as in a security background investigation) presents no problem, since the agent is security's operative. To fake a work history to meet a job's requirements is not difficult, and co-workers usually accept others at face value.

There are two effective ways to penetrate the work force clandestinely. One is to have the assigned agent simply present himself to the unsuspecting personnel department representative as an applicant. In this approach the agent should be armed with a pre-designed and memorized background and work history appropriate to the position sought. The other way is to work in close harmony with the personnel executive of the target unit or facility. This latter method requires written policy that specifically defines the relationship and responsibility of the personnel executive, including—*and this is most important*—the admonishment that the executive is bound to absolute confidentiality regarding the presence or placement of an undercover agent, even if queried by the unit manager under whom the agent will be working.

This written policy should preferably be included in the personnel manual. It should state, in essence, that the placement of undercover agents in the work force as necessary is an acceptable protection strategy that has the full support of senior management. This is important because invariably you will find personnel people who believe that undercover operations are "dirty" or unethical — that undercover agents go about trying to entrap perfectly good employees, and report unfairly on management and personnel. Often there will even be those in personnel who, despite written policy, remain steadfastly opposed to the strategy of undercover investigation and will do whatever they can to undermine the program. One solution to that kind of problem is to place an undercover agent in the personnel department itself, without the knowledge of the staff or the personnel manager.

Important elements of the written policy would include the following:

- Personnel management should endeavor to place applicants sent by security unless, in their judgment, the applicant is totally unsuited for the position or placement would be a conspicuous deviation from normal standards that would arouse suspicion.
- Only the personnel manager should know that an undercover agent is on assignment; absolutely no one else should be privy to that knowledge.
- Personnel records should not be coded or in any way otherwise reflect the fact that an employee is an undercover agent.
- Once the undercover agent is in the work force, he or she should not be laid off or otherwise terminated without consultation with the security department.
- The true identity of the undercover agent should not be revealed, even if such a request should come from the personnel manager's own supervisor.

Reporting

An undercover agent must submit a handwritten report for each shift worked. Typewritten reports are not satisfactory; and handwriting provides some protection against forged, altered or fictitiously prepared reports. Each report should be signed and dated. Although the practice has questionable judicial or administrative value, the affixing of the agent's signature should follow some form of personal statement to the effect that he affirms or swears that the contents of the report are true and factual. While it can never be known for sure, such a statement may have some influence on the agent's concern for the truth. (The veracity of undercover agents is discussed later in this chapter.)

The thrust of the report should be the equivalent of a "shotgun" rather than a "rifle" attack — that is, the agency should comment on a wide variety of incidents, observations and conversations during the last shift worked, instead of zeroing in on a specific highlight of the day or a particularly interesting facet of the job. The agency is not the one to determine what is or is not important, because he is not in a position to weigh the value of everything he hears or sees. A full overview, uncensored, of what occurred in that agent's life on the job can be carefully evaluated by the investigator or security administrator. That is good raw intelligence.

The written report goes to the undercover agent's primary employer, the outside agency supplying the service. That report is transcribed into a typed report, in which the identity of the agent goes over to a coded numerical designation. For example, in 718-4423

718   = location, e.g., St. Louis
4423   = agent Conrad Bastilla, the 4423rd agent hired by the agency

The handwritten reports are maintained by the agency. The typed reports are forwarded to the security management of the company using the service. Obviously, if such reports ever fell into the wrong hands in the company, the identity of the undercover agent would be protected by the coded designation.

If possible and practical, it is desirable to have each agent also make a telephonic report on a phone answering/recording device maintained in the supervising investigator's office. That recorded call is a summary of the written report, which may take as much as five days to move through the typing and mailing process. The phone message will not only be fresh and current, but it could also provide the signal for closer supervision, including daily personal contact with the agent. When a case starts developing and the end is in sight, undercover agents must have specific instructions and directions. Sometimes they need encouragement. One's heartbeat tends to increase, or another's courage tends to sag, as the drama approaches its climax.

Concluding the Case

The duration of a typical undercover investigation is usually measured in terms of weeks, and the undercover agent's effectiveness at a given location normally ends with the successful conclusion of the case. The reason is that the agent's involvement with dishonest employees necessitates his or her "termination" along with everyone else implicated in dishonesty. This strategy protects the agent's real identity and mission, since he is treated or processed no differently than the others involved.

This procedure suggests administrative rather than judicial action for detection of employee dishonesty. Why not follow the normal criminal justice system, beginning with the police arriving at the scene and taking into custody all participants? The answer is not simple. Following are some of its component parts:

- Once the police are aware of the investigation, the corporate investigator becomes "an agent of the police" and loses, in large measure, control over the investigation.
- The loss of control would handicap efforts to surface other incidental information that could be just as valuable to the organization as the original criminal theft investigation.
- The identity of the undercover agent would, in every case, be disclosed in court.
- The disclosure of an undercover agent in court automatically invites charges of entrapment.
- With the growing liberalism in the courts, convictions are increasingly harder to obtain. Even when won, they remain uncertain because of the possibility of appellate reversals, some of which are based on questionable logic.

All this means that the degree of civil liability exposure is growing almost by the calendar month. The investigative efforts of the security department should be to protect the company, not to increase its exposure to civil liability.

Administrative resolution of internal misconduct cases, including theft, normally by means of termination of employment, is an acceptable and safe alternative to criminal prosecution. As a matter of fact, many people are far more concerned about losing their jobs than they are over facing a confrontation with the police and court systems. The police and courts do not scare people as much as they used to. During the last decade, many people brushed their teeth in the morning knowing full well that they would be in jail by nightfall. Demonstrators for civil rights, Viet Nam war protesters, and current anti-nuclear groups are good examples. But threaten a protesting assistant professor with discharge from the faculty and you will have numerous experiences with arrestees who beg to call their employers so they will not lose their jobs. There is a great deal more trauma and pain to employment discharges than is generally credited.

The undercover agent, therefore, is "terminated" along with those he or she identified as being undesirable employees, and no one is the wiser. That agent then awaits the next assignment, at another location.

Security department investigators would normally never go undercover in their own company. Undercover agents should be provided by an outside service agency that hires, trains, assigns and supervises such agents as an ongoing part of that agency's professional services. The rationale for not using career security people in undercover criminal investigations is that, at some point into the investigation or at least at its conclusion, the undercover agent will be viewed by any number of employees as a partner or co-conspirator in the criminal activity. Why? Because the undercover investigation is constructive, covert and *participatory*. The agent's task is to be accepted by the employees who are engaged in dishonesty. That acceptance often includes such intimate relationships as wining, dining and, yes, even romance (although the latter rarely occurs as part of the investigative plan). The resulting close association, which is a key to the success of the investigation, is treated as such at the moment of truth, the day the case is resolved. That resolution frequently includes "capture" of the undercover agent along with all the others involved in criminal conduct. A regular company investigator could hardly resume his normal role of investigator after playing the part of a bad employee. Besides compromising his effectiveness, that revelation would immediately invite a charge of entrapment.

PROBLEM AREAS

The Issue of Entrapment

Undercover investigations and entrapment are two processes closely intertwined in the minds of most people, so linked that separation is quite difficult, if not impossible, for some to perceive. But entrapment is easy to understand when one reflects on the process of planting seeds in a garden. Entrapment is the process where one person plants the seed of an idea to do wrong in another person's mind.

Following are two vignettes of employees in situations where theft occurs. In one case there is entrapment; in the other, there is none. Which one entails entrapment?

Vignette #1: The Warehouse Dock.   Two warehouse dock employees, Charlie and Roy, are working on a Saturday with their supervisor, Mr. Morgan. Charlie is an undercover agent. The facility is normally closed on Saturdays. This is an overtime assignment for the three; all the other employees are off duty.

At lunch time Morgan decides that he would like fried chicken and French fries. He asks the others if they would like the same and volunteers to go get their lunches from a nearby fast-food franchise. Charlie and Roy agree. Rather than walk through the building and leave by the authorized door, Morgan decides to take a shortcut to the parking lot. He jumps off the dock, unlocks the gate that is part of the security enclosure around the receiving area, and leaves that gate open for his return.

Charlie watches Morgan's car disappear down the street. He then approaches Roy and says, "Morgan won't be back for another twenty minutes. Why don't you pull your van over here and we'll both get ourselves a color TV set. No one will ever know the difference." Roy thinks the idea is a good one, and the theft of two TV sets occurs.

Vignette #2: Kitchen Cleanup Time.   Two kitchen helpers in a large hospital, Bill (the undercover agent) and Harris, are the last employees to leave late each night. Final chores include the garbage run (final trash and garbage trip down the service elevator to the dumpsters in the basement) and the mop-down. As he is dry-mopping the tile floor, Bill notices that the "walk-in box," or refrigerated room, was inadvertently left unlocked. He comments on that discovery to Harris. Dropping his mop, Harris hurries over to the door in question and tests it. The door opens. Harris then tells Bill, "Quick! Go get me a couple of plastic trash bags from the supply closet." Bill asks why, but Harris doesn't answer. He gestures with his hand toward the supply closet. Bill complies with the request.

Harris then motions Bill to follow him inside the box. He tells Bill to hold the large green plastic bag open. Harris then proceeds to place in the bag a carton of steaks, a ham and several pounds of butter. Now humming mischievously, Harris waves Bill out of the room and locks the door to the box. He takes the sack from Bill and pulls it across the floor to the cart already loaded with four garbage cans. Harris seals the bag containing the stolen food items, places that bag in a second one, and seals it. He then makes room in the nearly full garbage can for his bundle and covers it with garbage.

The bundle is deposited, along with the refuse, in a dumpster in the basement. Harris drives his car down to the trash area after work and picks up the stolen goods. Bill claims half the loot as his, but Harris only gives him the ham, promising more later. The ham is turned over to the hospital's security management as evidence.

Note the clear distinction between these two situations. In the first case, Roy was the victim of entrapment. Charlie, the undercover agent, planted the seed of the crime in Roy's mind by suggesting the idea. Roy's "garden," or mind, was devoid of the idea of stealing. In the second example, however, there was no entrapment — even if the door was intentionally left unlocked. Leaving the door unlocked, and the agent's discovery of that condition, simply created an opportunity. Harris could ignore it, correct it or take advantage of it. No seed of theft was planted. Had Bill, upon discovery of the open door, said, "Look! Some fool went off and left this thing unlocked. We could take off with half the stuff inside and no one would be the wiser" — *that* would constitute entrapment.

In either case, the key question in determining entrapment is this: Whose idea was it to commit theft? Who planted the seed?

Deception or "Double-Cross"

Another hazardous aspect of undercover investigations which must be understood and dealt with accordingly is the ever-present possibility of the undercover agent fabricating information. In some instances such fabrication may be the result of an agent's anxiety to please an overzealous investigator or supervisor who is pressing hard for derogatory information. In one actual case an undercover agent reported the daily thefts of a co-worker, actually going so far as to plant stolen goods under the front seat of the accused worker's auto and reporting the observed theft to security. When the truth was eventually, and painfully brought out, the reason for this maliciousness on the part of the agent proved to be a personal one. The agent passionately disliked the co-worker. He envied the other man's popularity, good looks and "All-American boy" image, and he used this undercover position to "bring him down a notch or two."

How does one deal with this possibility of deception? First, recognize the possibility itself. Second, verify, directly or indirectly, all information submitted. If the agent reports that a group of employees attended a party at one's home on the weekend, it should be possible to verify that information. Even if it would be difficult or impossible to verify what happened and what was said at that party, at least a part of the agent's report would be confirmed. Third, look for inconsistences which might occur between the written and verbal reports. A good time to reconcile information is just before interrogations commence. The agent's verbal summary, with some details, should not conflict with earlier reports if the agent is reliable. And lastly, be sensitive to the natural and normal reactions of the suspected employee during the interrogation. On occasion, detecting natural reactions of disbelief and innocence during an interrogation, this writer has suspended the questioning of the accused and commenced an interrogation of the accuser, securing admissions of deceptive and fabricated reports, some designed specifically to hide the agent's own acts of theft.

The Absence of Professionalism

There are some undercover agents who are truly professional. They have devoted years to this unique and fascinating kind of work, and their effectiveness is something to behold. But these are outnumbered by men and women who lack professional bearing or stature, let alone formal training and experience.

Many individuals take such assignments either out of curiosity or to supplement their income while going to school. Using agents of this type in undercover work may be acceptable, but they need to be closely supervised, from the security side of their activity. Perhaps the application of the term "undercover investigator" to such agents is a misnomer. They are really intelligence agents used in an investigation supervised by investigators. To consider them as investigators in the strictest sense of the term might confer on them a degree of responsibility and decision-making that could prove counterproductive, if not simply unproductive. This use of undercover agents, in fact, comes down to security deploying non-security people to assist in a security operation.

The people engaged in this very specialized work are normally provided by a contract service organization that deals specifically in providing undercover agents for any given need. Those agencies recruit through blind ads (using a post office box only as an address) and actively recruit college students. The service companies are the primary employer of the agent. Once that agent has been accepted by the security department of the hiring company and has been placed on an assignment, he is paid the same as any other employee doing comparable work, but at the same time he is being compensated by his real employer, the service agency. If, at any time during the course of the agent's assignment, his services are no longer wanted or needed, he can be terminated and instructed to report back to the primary employer. There is no employment commitment or guarantees between the company using the undercover agent and the agent, because the agent actually works for someone else.

This distinction is important with reference to the company's need to be consistent in its termination practices. To better understand this, consider, as an example, an undercover agent who decided that he liked the position he was filling as an undercover agent, and disliked the service company that was paying him to function as an agent. Suppose that he stopped sending in his daily reports and even went so far as to tell everyone he worked with that he was an agent. When called up and terminated, he could not claim discrimination or inconsistent termination practices, because his assignment was secondary to his primary employment.

Conclusion

Regardless of the absence of widespread professionalism among undercover agents, and the potential risk of fraud or charges of entrapment, undercover investigations are a viable and, indeed, often essential part of the overall strategy of protecting the company's assets. Failure to employ undercover investigations is like a man denying himself eyeglasses when his vision is impaired or needs correction. It can leave the company blind to what is occurring within the organization, with particular reference to employee misconduct. There is no adequate substitute for this effective, internalized self-inspection and feedback process.

Chapter 6

Surveillance

Surveillance, an integral part of the investigative process, is the visual monitoring of a location or individual to determine what activities or conduct are occurring. This visual monitoring is accompanied by a "log," a diary-type record of what is occurring within the surveillance picture. The log provides a documented chronology of what was observed.

The surveillance may be stationary, moving or a combination of both. It may also be covert or overt, with an objective of detecting the commission of a crime or serious policy violation, gathering intelligence, preventing a crime, or all three. And surveillances may be conducted by the human eye or by means of electronic and mechanical hardware.

Covert vs. Overt Surveillance

There is a useful rule of thumb in determining the difference between covert and overt surveillance. Covert surveillances are normally detection oriented, whereas overt surveillances are usually prevention oriented.

As with all such rules, there are exceptions. For example, a covert surveillance of a fashion jewelry department operation with a primary objective of prevention could be an intelligence-gathering mission, developing every available detail surrounding that operation with an eye toward taking appropriate corrective action to reduce losses. Such intelligence could include (1) traffic patterns (customer counts by the hour, or fractions thereof); (2) number of customer theft incidents (customer-to-thief ratio); (3) type of merchandise stolen; (4) exact locations of thefts; (5) time of thefts; (6) what employees were doing when thefts occurred; (7) how thefts were effected; (8) employee staffing (break schedules, number on duty, etc.); and (9) employee dishonesty (discounting to friends, failure to record sales, putting jewelry on during store hours and then wearing it home).

By the same token, an overt surveillance of a precious jewelry department by means of the conspicuous placement of a television camera could fail its primary objective of discouraging a robbery but at the same time provide a tape of the robbery that could lead to the identification and subsequent apprehension of the robbers.

The distinction, then, between the objectives of covert and overt surveillances is not hard-and-fast. It does, however, offer a functional differentiation in most situations.

Surveillance by Human Eye

Whenever practical and possible, surveillances should be conducted by the human eye, without the use of any device or hardware, save binoculars. There is no substitute for the total comprehension afforded the observer — in terms of clarity, detail, color and dimension (depth of field) — when he or she personally views the scene of an unfolding event.

This is not to suggest that the same scene should not also be recorded on film or videotape if possible, but the human eye provides the most reliable view. It may be sophisticated and less uncomfortable to monitor employees handling cash at a cash register with a history of shortages by means of CCTV with a pinhole lens, but any investigator experienced in such surveillances will testify that the human eye is more discerning, with less room for doubt and error. The flat surface of the television monitor fails to give the viewer the depth of field our minds are accustomed to and expect.

In addition, there is the interpretative value of the human mind where the observer directly witnesses an act or event. Most surveillance films cannot stand on their own. They require some interpretation.

Visual Surveillance Devices

Despite their limitations, surveillance cameras, in particular video cameras with time-lapse recorders, are invaluable in a number of situations, not least those kinds of cases where it is impossible to conceal an investigator to conduct the surveillance. Another advantage of cameras is that they allow a multi-location coverage with one operator monitoring all locations, either simultaneously or in any sequencing pattern of switching from one location to another.

In the security context, the camera has materially contributed to the investigative process. Many a dishonest employee has been caught on a time-lapse video recorder while exiting the facility with stolen goods through covertly monitored doors, rummaging through office desks and files, or carrying out a whole host of other security-related violations, such as kicking vending machines to force out candy, drinks or extra change. Such cameras have also captured on film outside culprits who victimize the company, such as bad check passers and holdup artists.

The camera's eye is effective in providing general information — who is entering a given door, who is receiving goods through a dock door, who is within a security-controlled work area, etc. For very specific or detailed information, the camera has shortcomings. In one investigation of thefts from a payment processing unit in which employees opened customer's envelopes containing statement heads and payments (not always in the form of bank checks), the camera was unable to detect the actual theft. It did, however, indicate to the investigator which employee was stealing by showing her suspicious behavior and furtive movements, which eventually led to her capture. The camera's deficiency in revealing specific details, in this particular case, included such puzzles as this: Did the subject put a customer's white envelope into the pocket of her work smock, or was that a white handkerchief or a note?

Although VTR's (video tape recorders) with time-lapse and time-generator capabilities are in wide use today, there is still a need for the relatively old-fashioned but reliable 35mm camera. Be it a motor-driven, time-phased, sequential shooting camera that exposes one picture every 10, 30 or 60 seconds (and whose film is never developed unless there is a need), or a camera hidden in or disguised as a clock that will only activate when a desk drawer is opened, these surveillance cameras are a viable part of the security investigator's arsenal of weapons.

The Surveillance Log

The recording of what a surveillant observes can be by voice on a tape recorder or handwritten. If it is taped, the notes must be transcribed at a latter date. An advantage of the handwritten notes is that they are immediately available. There is nothing fancy or special about the log. Its purpose is no more than to record, briefly, what is observed and when, as exemplified in Figure 6-1.

There should be a separate log for each calendar day, even though one day's report could have several pages. Each day, or each shift, should have a heading similar to that in the example, showing the date, case under investigation (name and file number), and the identity of the investigator or investigators. If two or more surveillants are watching the same scene, only one should maintain the log. If two or more are surveying separate areas while on the same case, separate logs should be maintained. These logs will then become a permanent part of the official case file.

June 16, 1980   Miller Case 51 73-80   Dick Smith

7:00 AM   start surveillance. Yard empty.

7:32 AM   Miller and Hedgeman enter yard
from Bldg 201

7:37 AM   Miller opens truck gate

9:11 AM   green 4 dr chev XLM 441 78? 2 male
occupants ① M CAUC 25 6'0" 170 GLASSES
BLOND HAIR ② M CAUC 45 5-7 150 bald stop
by gate and dismount. Miller talks to
them. Miller keeps looking around.

9:19 AM   chev & 2 occupants drive away north
bound. Nothing happened other than talk.

11:27   same chev is back with same occup.
Miller waves at Hedgeman and leaves
in chev. Miller empty handed.

Figure 6-1.   Sample surveillance log.

THE STATIONARY SURVEILLANCE

Stationary surveillance positions may be *fixed* or permanent, *short term*, or *very temporary*.

Fixed Surveillance

Fixed or permanent surveillance positions are designed or contructed into a building or any other structure, allowing for the visual monitoring of a given location within that building according to need. Examples would include fixed positions over the back office of a cash counting room, where large sums of currency are counted and prepared for deposit; permanent installations over gaming tables such as in gambling casinos; and positions affording surveillance opportunities into sensitive work areas, such as receiving or delivery docks, or where the general public has immediate access to valuable company assets, such as a precious jewelry display in a retail store.

The fixed positions themselves may be disguised or so unobtrusive that only the very alert or trained eye would detect them, or they may be conspicuously obvious. Examples of unobtrusive surveillance positions would include full mirror where one would normally expect to see one, such as a single full-length mirror in a men's clothing store, or louvered vents that look like heating and cooling register openings in the upper portion of walls. An example of a conspicuous position of surveillance would be a ceiling-mounted, closed circuit TV camera that pans back and forth in full view of employees or customers, with or without a light suggesting that it is functional. Another conspicuous surveillance position is the protruding two-way mirror configurations commnly seen elevated on market and drug store walls with a view down aisles that have the greatest history of shoplifting losses.

Short Term Surveillance

Short term surveillance is for specific problem-solving situations. Positions selected might include rented houses, apartments or rooms affording a view of a targeted portion of company property, such as stockpiled assets, box cars on company railroad spurs, loading docks, a door or window through which there might be illicit traffic of people and/or goods, or a section of perimeter fencing where unauthorized penetration is suspected.

One case involving this type of surveillance developed after the discovery that a set of double doors on the front of a department store were being found unlocked several days a week. There was no question that the doors were locked each night at closing time. A test of the swing of the doors with the burglary alarm on revealed that they would open one foot before the alarm actuated. This created the possibility that someone could remain in hiding while the store was being closed and, later, could unlock the door, open it less than twelve inches, and pass out through the narrow opening large quantities of merchandise without setting off the alarm. The same culprit could then return to his hiding place and emerge only after the store was again open to the public. This possibility had to be resolved.

Two investigators rented a hotel room that directly overlooked the front doors in question. For several nights they took turns observing the closing procedure through binoculars, insuring that the doors were indeed locked, and monitoring the doors until they were opened again in the morning. After close to one hundred consecutive hours of work, it was discovered that the door had a faulty tumbler in the lock mechanism. The vibration of passing buses during the early morning hours would infrequently cause the bolt to fall. The problem was solved, though not with the solution anticipated.

It is not uncommon to place under surveillance locations other than the immediate company property. Examples might include the residence of an employee suspected of dishonesty to observe him or her unload company equipment or property from his auto after work; the gathering place of suspects, such as a local bar; or any other location where stolen company property might be stored, divided up, or otherwise disposed of.

When property other than a hotel or motel is rented for surveillance purposes, it should be done surreptitiously, using some pretext, and ideally under an assumed name. Investigators, like criminals, can obtain good false identification; and as far as references are concerned, other members of the investigative staff or even personal friends can vouch for the "roomer." As a rule, however, establishments in the areas where surveillance is needed are not especially discriminating about who is moving in.

The point is that the owner or landlord should be given no reason to be interested in or curious about the rental. To take a landlord or apartment manager into your confidence borders on pure folly. Being privy to a secret operation creates an overwhelming irresistible itch that must be satisfied — a satisfaction that comes from telling someone else. In this way the contagion spreads. The rented facilities must obviously remain covert in nature, and if handled as such usually prove very productive. Certainly there is some risk of a leak, but the short duration of the surveillance, and the professional status of the management concerned, will tend to minimize the risk.

For short term surveillances, vehicles, particularly campers or vans modified to accomodate surveillance personnel, can be very effective. The van innocently parked on the street or in a parking lot rarely arouses suspicion.

If the vehicle must be parked dangerously close to the surveillance objective, ruses can be employed. For example, the vehicle can be boldly driven to the desired spot, where two investigators dismount, each on his own side, slam the doors shut and, in animated conversation, leave the scene. Secreted in the rear of the closed van is the surveillance team. If there is no legal or reasonable way to park where it is necessary, or if overnight parking would be either illegal (hence no reasonable person would do it) or suspicious, an effective ruse is for the vehicle to "break down" at the desired location. As long as the van is not needed for moving surveillance, visual proof of the breakdown can be offered by having the driver (and passenger, if manpower is available) jack up one corner of the vehicle, remove the wheel, place blocks under the axle to prevent the vehicle from slipping off the jack, and then depart — with the surveillance team hidden inside. It is amazing how acceptable a disabled vehicle is, even to those who should be wary.

A Dodge van was used as a modified surveillance vehicle in one case where warehouse employees were peddling stolen television sets, radios and stereo component parts to a "fence" in a neighboring community. The fence was, in fact, a storefront rented by a combined public and corporate investigative team. The store was wired for sound recordings. The van parked in the rear alley next to the store's back door, where all the nefarious activity took place, was painted and disguised as a fresh fish delivery truck. On each side of the van was mounted a ship's steering wheel, a decorative addition to the seafood theme. The hub of each wheel accommodated the lense of a 16mm motion picture camera, manned by a team of two investigators secreted inside the van.

Very Temporary Surveillances

Very temporary surveillances can last anywhere from one half-hour to two weeks (at the outside), depending on the circumstances. They may be conducted, for example, from adjacent building rooftops or office windows, with the owner's knowledge and permission, often on the basis of reciprocity should the need arise.

In one case an undercover agent phoned from a pay phone and reported that an employee was going to stash a stereo set in the trash area outside a certain door at lunch time. Later in the afternoon he would leave work early, drive his car to the trash area, put the stereo in the trunk, and drive off. The only place from which we could survey the trash area was a neighboring company's rooftop. Within a half-hour we had identified the management person responsible for that building, presented our case, and obtained permission to place an investigator on the roof. The roof was flat with an 18-inch parapet. A head showing over that parapet would have been disastrous as far as our case was concerned. However, because the roof was flat, there were 4″- × -8″ water drains through the barrier, creating little windows through which a man in a prone position could observe the area under surveillance. Equipped with binoculars and a walkie-talkie, the investigator observed the secretion and later recovery of the stolen merchandise. Following his directions over the radio system, investigators were able to block the culprit's car with their vehicles, and he was captured.

Hardware Used in Stationary Surveillances

Hardware that can assist in stationary surveillance work includes telephones specifically installed for the case, two-way radios, 35mm cameras with telephoto lenses, 8mm or 16mm motion picture cameras, video cameras with recorder (regular speed or time-lapse), binoculars, tripod-mounted telescopes, and "jeri rigs," or improvised devices limited only by the imagination.

Improvisation can be an important part of the investigator's art, as two examples may suggest. One is a trigger device activated by a string attached to the sliding door of a boxcar. When the boxcar is entered at night, the string is pulled, turning on a small, unobtrusive light. The thieves are unable to see that light, which signals that a crime is in progress. Another device was improvised by students of a college who were experiencing frequent forcible entries into the soft drink dispensing machine sitting outside their dormitory. They wired the coin box so that, if it were removed, all the dorm lights would go on along with a loud bell. They all slept peacefully during the "surveillance." When the machine was again attacked, the surprised thief found himself surrounded by a large number of very incensed young men.

THE MOVING SURVEILLANCE

Moving surveillances are by far the most difficult to achieve and the most vulnerable to discovery. The objective of a moving surveillance is usually that of determining an unknown location — where the subject lives, works, plays, conducts affairs, disposes of stolen goods, meets others, etc. Once the location is known — the Where of the investigative quest — then other strategies, including stationary surveillance, can surface details connected with that location.

Moving surveillances can be accomplished on foot (especially in crowded urban areas), or by means of bicycle, motor bike, motorcycle, automobile, public transportation, or — though it sounds like the implausibility of television drama — by plane or helicopter. Any means that is available and practical can be used, as long as it enables the investigators to follow the subject to a location the knowledge of which is germane to the investigation.

The risk in the moving surveillance, as in any covert surveillance, is discovery by the person or persons being followed. Such discovery — called "burning" — can have disastrous consequences for the investigation. It may cause the subject to destroy or otherwise dispose of evidence, to discontinue criminal activities before the case can be fully developed, or to suspend those activities temporarily only to resume them with a whole new set of strategies. It will induce a heightened awareness in the subject resulting in appropriate defensive maneuvers. And it may result in public or organizational exposure of the security department's surveillance activity, which would have embarrassing consequences. (The notorious Watergate affair was neither more nor less than the discovery of a surveillance, although that case involved illegal means to effect the surveillance, a strategy not propounded here.)

The trick, then, is to avoid discovery. Following are some suggestions to minimize that risk.

Foot Surveillance

- Keep several people between yourself and the subject being watched.
- Never watch the back of your subject's head. Many individuals can sense being watched or stared at.

- Watch the subject from the waist down, especially the legs and feet.
- If the subject stops to window gaze, visit with someone or buy a paper, and if your stopping would be obvious, keep walking past him. If possible, enter a building or store ahead of the subject and, from its recesses, watch for him to resume his movements and to pass by.

Public Conveyance Surveillance

- Never sit directly behind the subject.
- Sit several seats ahead of the subject, on the same side of the vehicle, as long as there is no way for him to exit behind you unobserved.
- Watch the subject from the waist down, especially the legs and feet.
- Absolutely avoid eye contact with the subject.
- If in a bus that stops, or will stop within the short distance of one block, remain in the bus to the next stop after the subject alights if he appears nervous, or if you can see through a rear or side window the direction the subject takes after leaving the bus.

Auto Surveillance

- Whenever possible, have two or more vehicles involved in the surveillance, with voice (radio) contact capability.
- Use female investigators as drivers as well as riders.
- Female investigators riding in the car should sit close to a male driver.
- Follow as far back as distance, traffic, road design and conditions will allow — the farther back, the better.
- Do not follow in the same lane in which a subject is driving. That lane tends to be more "blind." Other lanes permit turns and expressway exiting in a less *reactive* manner.
- With multiple vehicle surveillances, a decoy vehicle can follow the target relatively closely. When the subject makes a change in direction, turning left or right, the decoy should continue straight ahead. The intent of this maneuver is to cause the subject, if he is at all suspicious of a tail, to enjoy a false sense of confidence that he is not being followed.
- In multiple vehicle surveillances, have the autos "leap-frog" each other at appropriate time intervals, the trailing vehicle moving up to the forward position and the lead vehicle dropping back to the end of the line.

- Be aware of the importance of "body language" while in a moving surveillance. Tense concentration is discernible. An arm draped over the seat backrest, or resting in the door's window frame, gives the appearance of a relaxed and unconcerned driver or occupant.

Hardware Used in Moving Surveillances

All of the hardware listed for stationary surveillances is used also in moving surveillances, with the exception of time-lapse VTR (video tape recording in slow motion) and telescopes, which are impractical where there is too much motion. Even telephones are used, installed in the surveillance vehicles.

One additional piece of equipment used almost exclusively in moving surveillance is a sophisticated electronic tracking system, one example of which is called Vehicle Follower Model 1012. These systems — and there are a number of them — use both a transmitter (beeper) and receiver. The transmitter, a small metal box with a self-contained power source, is surreptitiously attached to the undercarriage of the suspect's vehicle by magnets. It emits a continuous signal in the 100- to 200-milliwatt range. The receiver is in the surveillant vehicle, usually equipped with two matching antennas or a loop antenna tuned to the same frequency as the transmitter. The receiver converts the transmitted signals into an audio beep. The closer the surveillant vehicle is to the transmitter, the louder the beep; the farther away, the fainter the signal. Under ideal conditions the signal can carry for as much as three miles. More practically, especially in urban surroundings, the range is about one-half mile. This type of equipment is used more commonly in the public than the private sector.

MOVING AND STATIONARY SURVEILLANCE

When the decision is made to place an individual or group under combined moving and stationary surveillance, such a determination obviously indicates the need for a very intensive and comprehensive investigation during which every move of the subjects must be recorded. This in turn suggests 24-hours-a-day surveillance, the jargon for which is "Put 'em to bed and get 'em up."

Those recommendations made for moving and stationary surveillance separately apply as well when the two methods are used concurrently. Different personnel, however, should be assigned to each type of surveillance. The demands upon the same individuals to carry out each assignment are unreasonable, particularly in view of the pressure and tension involved in moving surveillance. Moveover, the higher risk of losing a subject during moving surveillance must be taken into account. If a separate team is handling the fixed location — say, at the subject's residence — they will be in place to observe the subject's arrival home. Comparison of notes between the moving and fixed surveillance teams, with attention to the time interval, would indicate if the subject proceeded directly home from the point where he was lost or if he stopped somewhere in between.

The importance of such an unaccounted for stop is illustrated by a case in which a bartender had been observed by security consuming, on an ongoing basis, large quantities of vodka while on duty. He was subsequently discharged for consuming alcoholic beverages while on duty and for the theft of such beverages. The subject denied the allegation, claiming that he was only drinking water. He claimed that, as a staunch supporter of Alcoholics Anonymous and a former alcoholic, he would be the last person to drink again. He convinced some civic-minded leaders in the community to bring pressure on the company that terminated him.

In the absence of any physical or other tangible evidence to support the company's position, it was incumbent upon the company to prove the subject to be other than what he claimed — in other words, to prove that he was not an abstainer from alcohol. He was placed under moving surveillance in the hope that he could be observed spending time in a bar.

During the first day of surveillance, the subject went to a private residence where he spent the entire day. When he left that location, his direction appeared to be toward home. He was lost at a large, multi-signal, controlled intersection. The moving surveillance team arrived at his residence some ten minutes ahead of the subject, who pulled directly into his garage (which had an automatically controlled door) and entered the house.

The next day was a carbon copy of the first. The primary difficulty in surveillance was the controlled intersection, about two miles from the subject's residence. The interval between the time the subject was lost at that intersection and the time of his arrival home indicated that he was stopping en route, but not long enough to have a drink. Inspection of the logical route from the key intersection to his home revealed the presence of a package liquor store. On the following day an investigator was in that store's parking lot on stationary surveillance when the subject pulled in. On that occasion, and for several consecutive days, the subject was observed purchasing a quart of vodka. The company's administrative action, discharge, was upheld, as a result of evidence obtained through combined moving and stationary surveillance.

Checkpointing

A practical strategy in following a subject to his or her final destination when the subject is "tail-wise" or otherwise difficult to follow the entire distance is *checkpointing*.

Checkpointing involves piecing together sections of the subject's route, one day at a time, until the entire route is identified. Most people tend to be creatures of habit, and that is reflected in the routes they will take to familiar places. The route each of us takes from home to work each day, for example, is relatively predictable.

Checkpointing can be a strategy of choice, because it is less dangerous than trying to stay with a subject along his entire route, or it may be a necessity — if, for example, the subject makes an abrupt turn that is not negotiable by the surveillance vehicle. The accompanying map (Figure 6-2) shows the southerly route of a subject and the three checkpoints required to develop the entire route. On the first day of the surveillance, the subject's unexpected left turn onto Cimarron Avenue (west of the traffic circle) led to the designation of Checkpoint A the following morning. The surveillance vehicle was in place, facing south on Cimarron, when the subject drove by, and he was picked up at that point. Similar procedures at Checkpoints B and C enabled investigators to chart his entire route. Each checkpoint is simply a calculated anticipation or prediction, based on prior observations, of the route the subject will take.

Conclusion

All the the hardware useful in moving or stationary surveillance is, naturally, applicable to combined surveillances. A successful surveillance may also depend on additional practical considerations including allowance for biological needs. There are occasions when investiators cannot abandon a moving or stationary surveillance assignment to satisfy natural urges. Experienced investigators will carry food, water, napkins, and an empty container which can accommodate any need. Other useful items might include a small portable radio (with ear plug), a cushion for comfort, and even a blanket. These few necessities, packed in a briefcase or small tote bag, can take some of the pain and weariness out of a long surveillance. In brief, plan ahead!

The fruits of such planning and attention to detail can be substantial. Surveillance is clearly a vital investigative strategy that can significantly contribute to detection, prevention and organizational intelligence.

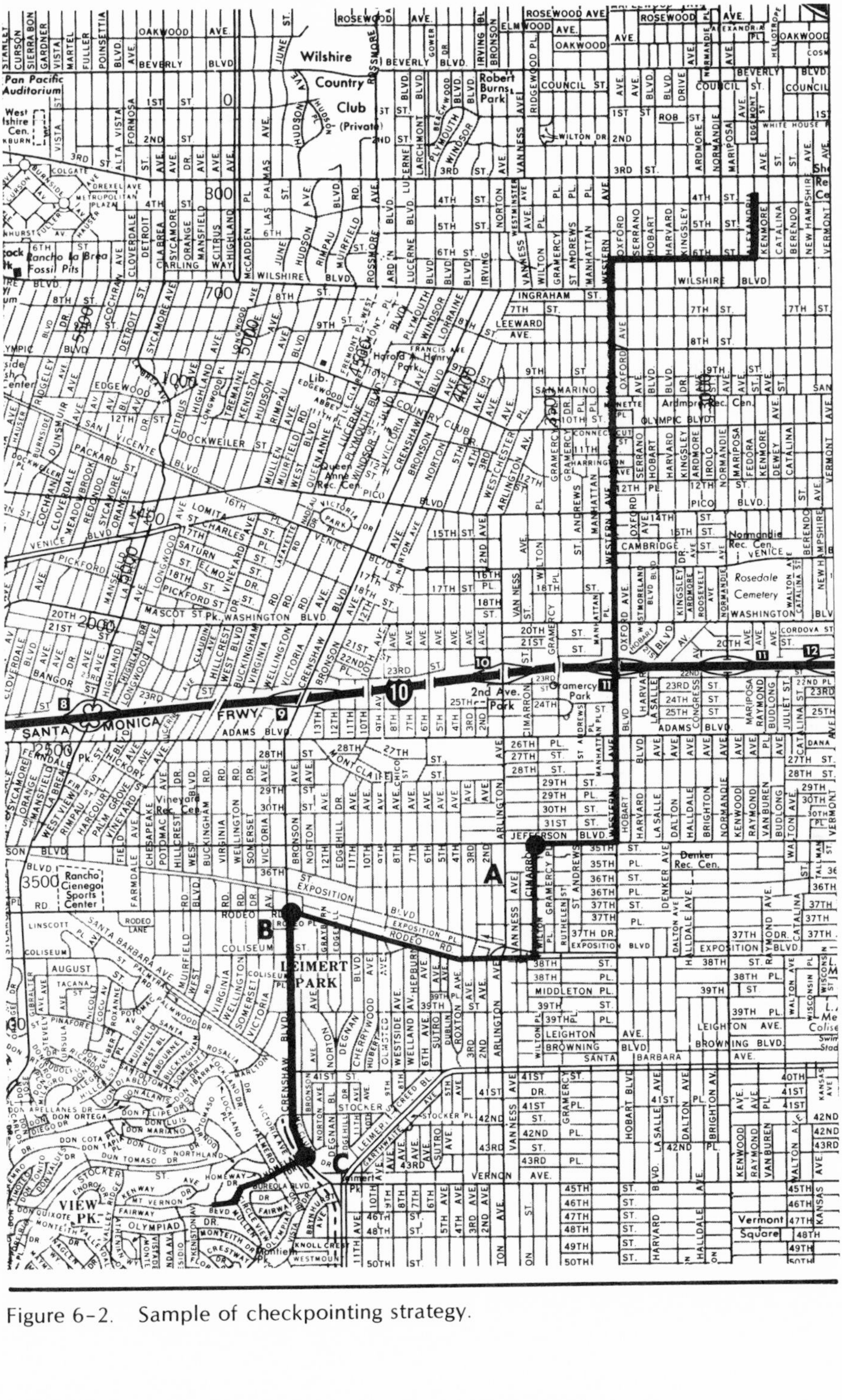

Figure 6-2. Sample of checkpointing strategy.

Chapter 7

Background Investigations

No investigative function serves the best interests of the corporate organization more than the employee screening process — the background investigation. Cases demanding investigative expertise come and go, day in and day out. Even truly exciting and significant cases involving large monetary risks or losses come and go, though with less frequency. But despite the importance or magnitude of any given case, the humble background investigation remains pre-eminent in its overall importance.

Screening applicants through the pre-hire investigation, and new employees by means of post-hire investigations, is loss prevention in the purest sense. Loss prevention *begins* internally, with the employee; only following that does it deal with the non-employee. A company-wide anti-shoplifting program, as an example, can be neutralized or otherwise made unproductive before it begins, if the very employees whose involvement in the program is essential are thieves themselves.

And theft is only one concern in determining who is employed by the corporation or seeking employment. As a case in point, a post-hire investigation by a major retailer disclosed that one of its new employees selling shoes in the children's shoe department had a criminal history of child molestation. It requires little imagination to speculate over the possible harm that might have resulted from this situation — and the potential for civil litigation. There has been an increasing tendency for the courts to extend the area of corporate responsibility for the safety and security of guests or customers. If a motel chain can be held civilly liable for not providing adequate security for its guests, and was found in a hallmark case in which a guest was raped on company property by a non-employee,[12] how much more liable would a retailer be for employing a known pedophiliac and placing him in a children's department? In similar vein, what is the responsibility of a hospital hiring a laundry employee who has a history of setting fires, a convicted arsonist or pyro-maniac? Or a financial institution hiring an embezzler or forger? Or a major oil refinery hiring an alcoholic to drive its gasoline tankers?

Do such offenders voluntarily come forward, either in the employment interview or on the application for employment, and admit that they have a propensity to molest children, set fires, commit fraud, or drink too much? Hardly. Their natural impulse is to hide what they know would disqualify them for employment. Because they must work, they will take great care to conceal such derogatory information in order to protect their own best interests.

It follows that an equal if not greater degree of care must be taken by the employer to insure that only the best candidates are selected and subsequently retained on the payroll. So-called "probationary periods" are designed, in large measure, to insure that the employer has the opportunity to examine, observe and study new employees prior to the commitment or contract of protected employment.

The marriage contract offers a useful analogy. The application for employment is equivalent to a proposal of marriage. The probationary period is analogous to the engagement period. Successful completeion of the probationary period (acceptance of the new employee as a regular employee) leads to the wedding. Once the two parties are married, separation is difficult and often painful indeed. The background investigation must complete its careful examination of the prospective bride or groom before the wedding date.

PRE-HIRE INVESTIGATIONS

Ideally, all background investigations should be conducted prior to the job offer. As a practical reality, however, there are a number of conditions that mitigate against the ideal. A prompt or timely job offer many times captures highly desirable candidates (those who apper on the surface, at least, to be highly desirable). The applicant could be lost to another company because of the inherent delay involved in background checks. In larger companies, the sheer volume of applicants for employment dictates that only the most critical positions be given a full examination prior to the job offer. Other positions, those considered less critical in terms of risk, can receive a quick initial surface check and later, after the new employee has started work, can be subjected to a closer examination. A cashier or security employee, for example, would be a high-risk position, while a dishwasher or gardener would normally be a low-risk situation.

The Master Indice File

The heart of an effective pre-hire investigative procedure would be the creation, maintenance of and referral to a *master alpha indice* (index) file. This is a negative base reference source, containing the names of dishonest or otherwise undesirable individuals, *known to the company specifically and to the industry generally*. For example, the security department of a major hospital should maintain a 3 " – × –5 " index card file on every person arrested for crimes committed on or against the hospital, its employees, patients and guests. The names of every employee of the hospital terminated for cause should also be included. Such a file would be considered the bare base, or minimum.

Ideally, in this context, all the hospital security departments in a given metropolitan area would pool their information so that the name of a ward attendant caught stealing at one hospital would end up in the master indice file of the other hospital security departments. Better yet, that attendant's name would be added to the master file in one central location servicing all hospitals in that area. All departments participating in the program would have access to that file by telephone, mail or computer.

Such central data repositories are not uncommon in the retail and horse-racing industries, to cite two quite different examples. In the former, store or mutual store protective associations serve as the central repository of all known and reported retail-related offenders, such as shoplifters, dishonest employees, credit card forgers and bad check passers. In the thoroughbred horseracing industry, files containing the names of known touts, cheats, pickpockets, "past-posters," con artists and hustlers that follow the horses are maintained. Any individual so identified is *persona non grata* at the track.

Although such files appear to be engaged in a blacklisting operation, they are, in fact, legal and in compliance with the Federal Fair Credit Reporting Act. If an individual is denied employment or terminated for falsifying either an employment application or a bonding application, based on information contained in that centralized file, the reason for the rejection is made known to the person in question. Armed with that information, the individual denied employment may challenge and/or examine any records used to justify the decision. The bottom line in any such situation is this: Is the information in the central file accurate, and does that information refute an applicant's or new employee's claim? To take a specific example, if an applicant writes the word "no" in answer to the question, "Have you ever been discharged from any previous employment?", and that answer is untruthful because he or she has indeed been discharged, the existence of the file itself is not at fault. It is the untruthfulness of the applicant that is at fault. The file did not deny the applicant a job; the applicant denied himself the job.

It should be pointed out, conversely, that many an applicant who has been straightforward with prospective employers regarding derogatory information in his background has been hired despite that information. Enlightened employers respect truthfulness, and will sometimes base a hiring decision, in some measure, on the fact that the candidate had the courage to honestly discuss problems of the past.

The central repository, or master indice file, does not contain all the details surrounding the negative information. It will include only the basic data: full name of the subject, date of birth, identification (Social Security Number, driver's license, etc.), nature of the incident, location and date of the incident, and file reference number.

Operationally, the program works in this manner. A background investigator for Company A discover's an applicant's name in the centrally maintained master file. Armed with that basic data, the investigator then phones or visits Company B, the company which had direct involvement with the applicant in question and has on file the complete information on the incident of concern. Company B's investigator confirms the derogatory information, which is contrary to the applicant's statements.

If the investigation is in a pre-hire mode, the investigator advises the personnel representative of his own company that there is documented evidence that the applicant has not been truthful, and recommends that a job offer should not be made. If the investigation is post-hire, the investigator, along with a personnel representative, interviews the new employee, focusing on the discrepancy at issue. Invariably, the employee admits falsification on his application and is then terminated. Prior to the conclusion of that interview, the investigator advises the employee that the information was discovered through a search of the central files. The employee is provided with the location, hours and other applicable conditions under which, if the employee so chooses, the relevant files may be examined. That prerogative, or option, is rarely exercised.

Past Employment Verification

A primary component of the entire screening process is the verification of past employment. Key questions that must be answered are the following:

1. Was the applicant in fact employed by the company claimed?
2. If so, was the applicant employed for the period of time claimed?
3. Was the applicant employed in the capacity claimed? For example, if the applicant claims supervisorial responsibilities, was he indeed a supervisor?
4. Did the applicant leave the company for the reason stated?
5. Is the applicant eligible for re-hire? If not, why?
6. Were the applicant's earnings as claimed? (This applies, as a rule, only to middle or upper management positions.)

In pre-hire investigations, the above questions can usually be answered by a telephone conversation with a responsible official of the past employer, such as a personnel representative, the owner or someone in the security department. The latter, if such a department exists, is preferable.

If the applicant is unknown to the industry — that is, not in the negative indice file — previous employment has been verified, and the applicant has been recommended as eligible for re-hire, the chances are that the applicant is not a high risk. In such cases this quick background check could suffice — bearing in mind, however, that more extensive checking must be done in the post-hire period.

This is not to suggest that other pre-hire work is unnecessary. The amount of effort in background screening that constitutes minimal standards is *directly* related to a given company's (or security department's) assessment of organizational needs, the sensitivity of the position in terms of risk, and the security resources available for background investigation. Take security resources, as an example. If five investigators are normally assigned to the screening unit and the company becomes embroiled in a labor dispute, it is quite conceivable that the demands and priorities for investigators could deplete the screening unit, reducing it to one or two people available. That obviously would impact on both the quantity and quality of background investigations.

Other areas that can usefully be explored in the pre-hire (or post-hire) investigation include, but are not limited to, the following:

1.   Does the applicant have a criminal record?
2.   Does the applicant have the skill or education claimed?[13]
3.   Is the applicant financially responsible?
4.   Does the applicant have a general reputation for honesty and good moral behavior?
5.   Does the applicant have good health, or the health that he or she claims?
6.   Does the applicant have a political or social bias that would mitigate against successful job performance? (Consider, for example, a member of the American Nazi Party who would be obliged, by virtue of the job, to work cooperatively and closely with blacks and Jews. Or a staunch activist opposed to nuclear energy whose job would include development of public relations materials, on a contractual basis, for a utility company operating a nuclear powered facility.)

Answers to these questions are not in themselves the determiners of employment, but they do constitute arenas for dialogue. A conviction for a misdemeanor (a petty or minor crime) would not necessarily be grounds for employment rejection (pre-hire) or discharge (post-hire) *unless the applicant lied* on the application or bonding form. The expanded dialogue or discussion would include such questions as (1) What was the original criminal charge? (2) Was the offense one involving moral turpitude? (3) Does the crime have any relations to, or in any way impact on, the position being sought by the applicant? The ultimate hiring decision would be based on the merits and circumstances of the individual case.

The Neighborhood Check

Neighbors and landlords often know a great deal more about a person than might be suspected. They are familiar with an individual's comings and goings, his sensitivity to others, his predilection for noisy parties, his drinking habits, his morality, his concern for his children (as demonstrated by involvement with scouting or other organized activities, family outings, how the children are supervised, how they are dressed, etc.), his standards of home maintenance, care for the yard or for the automobile, and so on.

If the applicant was or is a renter, the landlord can tell the investigator if rent payments are made punctually or not, and if payment is made by cash, money order or bank check. (If by bank check, the landlord can probably advise as to which bank and the branch.) Can such information as the method of paying rent be significant? What if the applicant pays by check or money order? Could this indicate that he or she has no bank checking account because of trouble with the bank? Has the bank closed the account for insufficient funds or some other abuse? These are questions which the investigator may wish to explore.

A former landlord will generally be eager to speak revealingly about a former renter who left the property in poor condition or when all accounts were not settled amicably. (It is interesting to note that most people who are compelled, for whatever reason, to speak in a negative or derogatory way about someone will almost invariably temper such comments by attempting to say something favorable as well — perhaps as a salve to conscience.)

On the other hand, the investigator will often encounter those who have derogatory information or strong suspicions about the applicant in question but are reluctant to speak unfavorably about someone looking for work. Sympathetic persons in such a situation face a real dilemma. Here is a responsible representative from a reputable company looking for "advice," asking for "my opinion." (My reputation could be on the line. I don't want to lie but at the same time I don't want to hurt Harry's chances for a job — and I certainly don't want Harry to discover that I said something that hurt him. Still, he does have a drinking problem . . .)

How does the investigator overcome this kink of problem? By giving the interviewee a way tell you what you need to know. The way is to provide an *option*. The investigator should avoid boxing the person in by requiring, for example, a "yes" or "no" answer to the question, "Would you recommend Harry for a position with our firm?" Instead, the question should provide an option. The investigator might say, "We're considering Harry for one of two positions. One is highly sensitive, with a great deal of responsibility. The other is a more average type of assignment with less responsibility. Which of the two would you recommend Harry for?" This gives the interviewee a palatable way of saying that Harry is not a good candidate. Under these circumstances, an endorsement for the so-called average job is, in reality, no endorsement at all.

The neighborhood check, knocking on doors and asking people how well they knew or know the applicant and what their assessment of his qualifications is, can be a gold mine of information — and also of surprises. A casual question may evoke the response that "The police were just here last week looking for him." Or the unsolicited revelation that "They are very generous people. Did you know they just adopted another little Asian girl, on top of being foster parents for the county's unwanted new babies?" The point is that there is often much to be learned in these neighborhood checks that can be very revealing, pro or con, and that otherwise would remain unknown.

POST-HIRE SCREENING

Once the applicant is an employee, the post-hire screening activities must be finalized as quickly as possible within the firm's probationary period. Irrespective of how thorough the pre-hire investigation has been, two important remaining steps are required. The first is the careful inspection of the bond or bonding form for content. The second, and most productive, is comparison of the bond form to the application form.

What is a bond? A bond, fidelity form or bonding form is a document provided by an insurance carrier that indemnifies employers against loss caused by employee criminal conduct, or, if the company is self-insured, it is the document completed by the employee after being hired, said document calling for information prohibited on the application for employment (such as date of birth). Note that it is legal to request such information after the employee has been hired, since there is no longer any question of discrimination in hiring. The source of the bonding form is unimportant; the important consideration is that it should exist and be used.

One important feature of this form, which is almost a carbon copy of the application form (except for the additional information noted above), is that it becomes the security department's employment record for every employee of the company. The value of this from a security point of view is self-evident. An employee's original application for employment rightfully belongs to and remains in the personnel files. The bond, however, in great measure duplicates the information in personnel files. Consequently, should the need for an investigation arise, the security department is not dependent upon the personnel department for information.

Examination of the Bond

The bonding form, which is permanently in the control of the security department after its satisfactory completion, can be examined carefully for the following indicators of possible deception:

1. Questions not answered or left blank.
   Example question: "Have you ever been convicted for an offense other than a minor traffic violation?"
   Comment: The employee who has been so convicted is often afraid to lie and will attempt to avoid falsifying the document by not answering the question.
2. Unexplained gaps in the employment history.
   Example: 10/74 to 6/75   Ace Trucking Co.
                6/75 to 3/76   Koskovich Tire & Brakes
                6/76 to 6/79   McCall & Son, Inc.
   Comment: The period from March, 1976, to June, 1976, is unaccounted for. Was he ill? Was he in jail for theft from the tire and brake shop? It must be determined what the employee was doing for that period of time.
3. Erasure or strike-outs and scratch-outs.
   Comment: To be unsure of or to change one's mind in answering a question such as the reason for leaving a job is a danger signal, an indicator of possible deception (not a fact, it should be emphasized, but an indicator worth exploring).
4. Answers that presumably cannot be checked.
   Example: Giving as a "Reason for Leaving" the answer: "Went out of business."
   Comment: This answer is a convenient and common technique of hiding employment with a firm, still actually in business, from which one was discharged, or for covering time spent in incarceration.
5. Failure to affix the required signature at the conclusion of questions (bottom of the form).
   Comment: Failure to sign the form could be indicative of a reluctance, conscious or otherwise, to perjure oneself.

There is a logic to an honest person's work history. The investigator must therefore be sensitive to the *illogical*, as demonstrated in the following case history.

Discovery of a significant amount of liquor unaccounted for from the gourmet department of a major department store prompted the re-examination of all employees assigned to that department. One female employee's bond reflected previous employment as a sales clerk for a liquor store located on Hollywood Blvd. in Hollywood. Her stated reason for leaving that job was, "Went out of business." The answer seemed illogical. If there was, in fact, such a store in that location it should have been a thriving business. Investigation determined through business and licensing records that there had been such a store. The owner was traced. He confirmed that he had gone out of business and added, "My employees stole me blind." Had out employee worked for him? "Yes," he replied, "and though I couldn't prove it, there's no doubt in my mind that she was one of the thieves." The employee was then placed under surveillance. Within a week she and two outside confederates were detected using the old "scam" in which the customer purchased an item and the employee filled the bag with unpaid-for merchandise. In this specific case, close to $100 worth of liquor was being carried out with each $6.00 purchase.

Comparing the Bond to the Application

There is an underlying strategy involved in comparing the bonding form to the application for employment. In the normal sequence of events, an applicant presents himself to the personnel department and completes an application for employment, which is a relatively comprehensive personal and work history. A few days later the applicant, after a minimal background check, is offered employment commencing the following Monday. When the new employee appears at the appointed time to begin work, a period of perhaps five to fourteen days will have passed after the original application was completed. On his first day on the new job, the employee is given the bonding form, which is, as previously suggested, closely equivalent to the application for employment document. The test is, if the applicant lied on the original application form, can that person remember, with precision, the original falsehoods and duplicate them again after a lapse in time? Experience tells us no. They will try, but the variances will stand out noticeably when the two documents are compared side by side.

Comparison, then, is necessary. If there is no comparison, the screening process is deficient. This comparison is so vitally important that consideration should be given to having the two documents as nearly identical in format as possible. If the bonding form is provided by an insurance carrier, the company could redesign the application for employment form to match the format of the bond. If the company is self-insured (either having no insurance against internal theft, or a policy with a deductible so high that it precludes practical application), the bonding form can easily be printed so that, when it is placed side-by-side with the application, the corresponding data are visually comparable. This should also be true on the reverse sides of the two forms.

Bonds received by security from personnel that reflect unanswered questions or have not been signed should be returned to personnel for further processing. Erasures or strike-outs call for no action other than deeper investigation.

Variances, discrepancies or contradictions should be handled by security, not personnel. This is done in an interview conducted by the background investigator, witnessed by a personnel representative. The thrust of that low-keyed confrontation is, simply, "Please explain." In most cases the employee will admit falsification. In some cases satisfactory explanations will be offered, removing the reason for concern. In a relatively small number of cases an employee will, out of fear or desperation, cling to the falsehood, insisting that it is true. In these instances logic will usually give the investigator direction. For example, if the employee insists that he or she worked for a company the investigator knows never existed, then the employee should be asked to bring in a W2 form (IRS earnings and tax withholding statement). If an employee swears that criminal records discovered by the investigator reflect the arrest of his twin brother, then the employee should be asked to bring in his birth certificate. An honest employee can support his claims; sooner or later the dishonest person will run out of explanations.

Employment Verification and Reference Letters

In pre-hire screening, as we have seen, verification of past employment usually is by telephone. In the post-hire peroid a rather common practice in the private sector in verifying past employment is to send out a form letter asking for employment verification and eligibility for re-hire, requesting that the form be completed and returned. This is an acceptable strategy, particularly for low-risk positions, but only if the following procedures are followed.

1. A control must be maintained, showing every letter sent out and reflecting when it has been returned.
2. Verification letters not returned in a reasonable time must be followed up by security, either by telephone or in person. An ex-employer or company receiving the verification letter, and with something derogatory to say, will often be reluctant to reduce that information to writing for fear of accusations of defamation of

character or some other repercussion. The alternative is to say nothing. This failure to respond, if properly controlled by the point of origin of the request, personnel, signals the need to make further inquiry.

3. Variances in dates of employment as reflected by returned letters should be reported to security. (There is usually little if any reluctance on the part of former employers to reflect discrepancies.)

4. "Not eligible for re-hire" responses must be pursued further, either by personnel, or if personnel is unable to obtain a satisfactory explanation, by security.

All too often this area of employment verification becomes routine and its true value is lost, primarily because these controls and follow-up procedures are not fully understood and consistently practiced.

Ongoing Investigations

Background investigations of prospective or new employees will consume the bulk of the screening effort, but such investigations should not be limited only to such employees. As the case history of a liquor department theft described earlier in this chapter indicated, a background check of a suspected employee or group of employees can be productive in specific investigations. In addition, an ongoing program of updating background information on key personnel — people in the computer, finance, personnel and security areas, for instance — should be part of the screening unit's responsibility. Only such a comprehensive and continually updated program can insure that only the best possible people come into the company, remain in it, and rise in its ranks.

Chapter 8

Discovering Covert Crimes

Criminal conduct, in most cases, is all too apparent. The corporate victim, like the individual who is attacked, is usually aware of the crime and its consequences.

The list of overt crimes is endless. Rather typical examples might include the hijacking of a company tractor and trailer, the burglary of a warehouse, an extortion attempt involving threats against the life of an executive or members of his family, a fire purposefully set in the workplace, the rape of an employee departing late in the parking facility, the robbery of a cashier, assault against an employee, the overnight disappearance of a calculator from an accountant's desk, malicious destruction of the firm's landscaping accomplished by vandals driving a vehicle through the flower beds, checks drawn on accounts with insufficient funds or on closed accounts, threatening or obscene phone calls, and so on, ad infinitum.

Even when accomplished in stealth, such crimes are quickly known. They call for a *reconstructive* investigation as a response to an historical event.

There are also a great many criminal acts, most of a larcenous nature, and other forms of unacceptable behavior that are so subtle and surreptitious in nature that the crime or offense often goes undetected, and its consequences are not immediately apparent. Some, in fact, are never known with any degree of certainty.

Such covert crimes have a number of characteristics that set them apart from overt crimes against the organization. Those characteristics are:

- They are usually committed by persons considered trustworthy.
- The acts tend to be ongoing in nature as opposed to a single, spectacular incident.
- Some of the acts tend to be shrouded in uncertainty — i.e., Was it intentional or was it an error?

This last characteristic is one of the chief problems with covert crimes. For example, consider the case of a retailer who buys 100 bottles of perfume. After an inventory he determines that he has ten bottles left in stock. Sales records, however, show that he sold eighty-five bottles. Five cannot be accounted for. Were they stolen? Did a crime occur? What happened to the missing bottles?

There are a number of possible explanations for this single commonplace situation.

1. The shipment was short in the first place.
2. Salespeople opened some bottles as samples for customers to smell.
3. Someone broke bottles in an accident but was afraid to report the loss.
4. The bottles were shoplifted by customers.
5. They were stolen by employees.
6. They were overlooked in a multiple item transaction and inadvertently not recorded as sold.
7. They were given away by salespersons paid on a commission basis who were trying to please known customers in the hope of later sales.
8. They were intentionally given by salespersons to friends or relatives.

When this range of possibilities is extended over the activity of the entire organization, it becomes clear that the problem of exposing *and properly identifying* covert crimes is enormously complex. Obviously, a number of investigative strategies must be practiced in order to surface covert activity. Because of the range and diversity of businesses and industries in the private sector, it is impossible for any list of strategies to be all-inclusive or even notably comprehensive. The strategies discussed in the rest of this chapter, however, should serve as a sound basic list. They may also serve as a stimulant to the more enterprising investigator, prompting his own adaptations and creative variations. These fundamental strategies included the following:

1. Deployment of undercover agents in the work force.
2. Taking physical inventories.
3. Refund letter circulation program.
4. Daily audit of sales registers.
5. Checking continuity of register transaction numbers.
6. Integrity testing.
7. Bank check reconciliation program.
8. Cash counts.
9. Exit interviewing.
10. Checking for "ghost" employees.
11. Vendor verification.
12. Intelligence surveillance.

13. Physical inspections.
14. Use of suggestion box or award programs.
15. Odometer checks.
16. Shoplifting surveillance.

Deployment of Undercover Agents

Undercover investigation by covert agents planted in the work force has been discussed at length in a previous chapter. Suffice it to repeat here that numerous incidents of internal dishonesty that would otherwise never be known or identified are surfaced by this strategy. In the words of Saul Astor, "Without question, the major means of eliminating internal crime has always been and always will be internal intelligence — especially through undercover investigation."[14]

Physical Inventories

There are essentially three types of inventories. The first is the annual or semi-annual inventory that should be a normal operating practice in any business that has a stock of supplies, materials, equipment or goods on hand. Simplistically stated, this kind of inventory is a comparison of the "book" inventory (what the records indicate should be on hand) with the physical or actual inventory (results of a count of what is really there). Ideally the totals should match: a recorded total of 100 units should be equalled by a count of 100 units. More often than not, however, the actual count reflects fewer units on hand, thus creating a shortage. The enlightened approach to this shortage is to assume that *at least part of the shortage reflects dishonesty*, indicating that covert crime exists. Not to take this annual inventory is to operate blind.

The second type of physical inventory is the daily accounting of specific materials or goods, such as narcotics in a health service or hospital environment. Any variation, shortage or overage, should arouse suspicion.

The third kind of inventory is clandestine. Specific items are secretly counted and, after a designated period of time, are again subjected to a secret verifying count. A truck, for example, is loaded with boxes for shipment the following morning. During the night the truck is entered and the boxes are again counted, at which time the vehicle is secured by seal, lock or both. When the truck arrives at its destination, the receiving end of the shipment, the boxes are unloaded under observation and again recounted. A shortage in the count under these circumstances would expose dishonesty, with the driver the prime suspect. Obviously this type of inventory is capable of many variations.

Refund Letter Circularization Program

In those business operations where customers are given refunds, a document must be generated by an employee that reflects the amount, date, reason for the refund, and the full name and address of the person receiving the refund. A letter circularization program is an ongoing strategy designed to verify refunds. A letter is sent to the party receiving the refund by First Class U.S. mail, return postage guaranteed. In essence, the letter asks if the transaction was handled efficiently and courteously. The exact amount of the refund is noted in the letter, and a pre-stamped return envelope is enclosed.

Ordinarily, one of four things will happen in response to the refund letter: (1) The letter will be answered, stating that the transaction was satisfactory (or even that the employee was discourteous in some instances). No dishonesty is in evidence. (2) There will be no response, which probably means that the refund was legitimate, the customer simply not bothering to reply. (3) The customer will reply to the effect that the actual refund was for a smaller amount than shown. This suggests the strong possibility that someone inside the company is manipulating the documents by raising the figure of the sale *after* the legitimate transaction — changing a $25.00 refund to $35.00, for example, and pocketing the $10.00 difference. (4) The postmaster will return your original envelope marked "No Such Address," "Undeliverable," "No Such Party at Address," etc. This also strongly suggests that the refund transaction was fraudulent.

Many cases of internal dishonesty have been exposed by this routine strategy of refund verification.

Daily Audit of Cash Registers

Among other things, a cash register is an adding maching that totals the day's receipts — all receipts, both cash and charge. Unless registers are audited daily, thefts may go undetected.

The proper audit process requires that the cash be counted by someone other than the person who made the sales. Another person, working independently, receives the register totals (in the form on an inner "detail" tape) and copies of the charge transactions. This second independent auditor adds the charges and compares this to the total sales. The sum of the charges and the independently counted cash receipts should be equal to the register tape total. *Example:* The register tape reflects sales of $436.11 for the day. The count of charge receipts amounts to $207.09. For the register to balance, confirmation is needed of a total of $229.02 in cash received and counted. The person counting cash receipts must not know what is expected. If he knew that $229.02 was required to balance but actually counted $239.02 in cash, the difference of $10.00 would be unaccounted for and readily subject to theft. If cash receipts of only $209.02 were counted and reported, the holder of the register tape and charge receipts would record a shortage of $20.00, which would have to be investigated.

Checking Register Transaction Numbers

Most cash registers are designed to imprint transaction numbers chronologically, usually in terms of up to 4 digits. In other words, the register tape imprints the number of the transaction each time the register is activated, 1 to 9,999 in sequence.

It is physically possible to reset the transaction wheel, and in some firms this is done each morning. This practice is dangerous. It creates the possibility for a dishonest employee to "steal" a given number of sales without detection, since there is no continuity in the transaction numbers from day to day. A much better practice is to have the numbers run continuously. This, if the last sale of the day on Monday is transaction 3483, the first time the register is used on Tuesday it will record number 3484. The strategy is to physically deny access to the transaction wheel and to verify the continuity of transaction numbers on a daily basis. Missing numbers will immediately suggest manipulation and dishonesty.

Integrity Testing

The most common and hard-to-detect method of theft from the cash register is for the dishonest employee simply to accept money from customers and fail to record it on the register. One way to detect this type of theft is integrity testing, commonly known as "shopping." Investigators hired for this purpose pose as regular customers making normal purchases. At the same time they are able to observe cash register practices.

As Roger Griffin, a nationally known authority in this field, observes, "The fact that the cash accepted by the employee goes into the register at the time of the purchase is of no importance. It is extremely rare when the employee fails to record and then places the cash directly into his pocket. When a person begins to manipulate his cash by not recording sales, he can make the register come out over or short, as he chooses.

"The employee keeps track of the unrecorded funds and at some propitious moment takes out the total accumulated for the day. An employee sometimes takes out an even amount (ten, fifteen or twenty dollars) while he is verifying his change fund at the beginning of the day and then makes up the shortage by failing to record an equivalent amount of money."[15]

Where the money is not taken out beforehand but accumulated throughout the day in amounts not recorded, the person on the cash register must keep a running account of the total unrecorded. This "accounting" can take the obvious form of actually writing down the amount each time in a little notebook. Since this might create suspicion, another technique is to use loose coins at the side of the register. For example, if the employee places $12.00 from a sale in the register without recording it, he places a dime and two pennies to the side. Later, if a $5.00 transaction is not recorded, a nickel is set aside. Those 17 cents in coins would not appear suspicious to an observer, but they represent to the dishonest employee $17.00 in the drawer which he can safely remove when the time is right.

In describing the shopping test, Griffin goes on to say, "It is vital to understand that the typical test performed by the shopping investigator involves payment for an article in a manner which gives the employee a *choice* of whether to ring or not to ring the payment on the register.

"A simple test is to pay for an item with exact change and casually walk away *not waiting for a receipt*. Regular customers consistently make this type of purchase.

"At this point the employee stands at the register with the money *in his hand*. He has a perfectly free choice of whether he records the money or places it unrecorded into the cash drawer."[16]

It should be added that the money does not always go into the register drawer. The method of theft depends on the kind of setting or circumstances. If the employee works alone or unobserved, for example, in a small gift shop in a resort area, and there are no customers in the store after a transaction has gone unrecorded, the money may go directly into pocket, shoe, handbag, bra or wherever it can be concealed.

Virtually everyone has been an unwitting instrument in this very prevalent type of theft. It is especially frequent when a purchase is an afterthought. After paying for his initial purchase, the customer suddenly decides, "Oh, I think I'll have a pack of cigarettes after all." He then leaves the exact change on the counter and departs. The cash register clerk is free to record the extra transaction or not.

The display window on the cash register was designed from the beginning to show the customer how much he was being charged. If the window shows "NO SALE" or an underring (the clerk records a sale of $15.88 when the actual amount was $25.88), something is clearly amiss. This may account for the number of display windows that have been covered up with advertisements, cartoons clipped from magazines, and other convenient camouflage.

Bank Check Reconciliation

The bank check reconciliation process for a business is very much the same as that used by the individual balancing his private checking account. It involves comparing cancelled checks issued against the original record. The objective is to insure against or to catch checks that have been stolen or counterfeited, or on which the amount has been increased fraudulently. This procedure should take place several times a year.

Cash Counts

There are three types of cash counts, all of which are necessary parts of an effective accountability procedure. The first and most commonly used count is one in which the responsible party is obliged to count regularly and record the amounts of funds under his control. The second is the surprise count, usually an internal audit type of activity. The last — and the one that interests us most here — is the secret count.

A common practice in business is to do what is called bulk or "bundle" counting; the money is counted on the basis of the face value of bundled or banded packs. Knowing that one way to steal from funds is to slip one or two bills from a banded pack and place that bundle (which is now short) to the rear of the vault, the investigator carrying out a secret count will count each bill in a pack, ignoring what the band indicates is in that bundle. The regular employees are not aware of this count. Banded packs that are found short present strong evidence that someone is either stealing outright, knowing that regular counts are only bundle counts, or is using company money with the intention of replacing it.

Exit Interviews

The right kind of exit interview may surface dishonesty or other conditions unknown to management. What is referred to here is not the customary final interview usually conducted by a personnel employee, but rather a multiple-page form that asks a number of questions about supervision, working conditions, treatment on the job, what needs correcting, etc. Such an interview has the potential of identifying such problems as favoritism, time-clock violations, spurious accident claims, general loafing and shirking in a given unit, safety hazards, even dishonesty.

The trick is to get the departing employee to be frank. Most employees know a great deal but feel intimidated about telling what they know. Many simply will not answer truthfully such questions as "Why are you leaving?" The usual response is "a better opportunity" somewhere else. To encourage openness in responding to the interview, the interviewer must have a solid reputation for being trustworthy or the interview must be conducted anonymously.

One effective method is to send the interview form home with the departing employee, along with a stamped, pre-addressed envelope, and request that the form be returned by mail. If the work environment has been in any way threatening, however, that procedure may be ineffective. An alternative approach is to send the interview form to the former employee a week or two after he leaves, asking in a brief cover letter, that the individual be completely frank. Assurances should be given that anything said will be held in the strictest confidence, or the individual can be invited to complete and return the form without identifying himself.

Checking for "Ghost" Employees

A "ghost" employee is simply a nonexistent employee for whom payroll checks are issued and cashed. A number of ghosts can haunt a business. One might be a fictitious name and identity, even including Social Security Number, created by a supervisor at a work location somewhat removed from the main facility. Another might be the product of the imagination of an enterprising personnel employee who has set up a file on the ghost, including name and hours of pay in the document that activates the issuance of payroll checks regularly. A third form of ghost might be an actual person who died or was terminated but for whom the necessary paperwork was not generated to stop the automatic issuance of checks. The former employee, or friend or relative of the deceased, who receives the checks either has a place where they can be cashed or simply opens a bank account under that name where the checks can be deposited.

There are two ways to check for this type of fraud. One is to have an independent person, such as an internal auditor accompanied by someone from security, intercept the checks at the point of generation. The auditor then distributes the checks to each employee in person, perhaps even requiring signatures of the recipients. Another method, used on an annual basis, is to mail all W-2 forms to employees. Fictitious addresses will cause those envelopes to be returned.

With reference to such mailings, it is important that employees should never be permitted to use a post office box as a home address on company records. The use of a post office box in itself could be indicative of a problem.

Verification of Vendor or Resource

More common than ghost employees are ghost vendors, suppliers or other resources. Again, internal dishonesty is indicated. The most common culprits are receiving agents, purchasing agents or buyers, and accounts payable personnel.

A typical theft by the receiver involves initiating a receiving document to verify receipt of a shipment and forwarding it to the person in the company who pays the bills. The receiving record is matched to a fictitious invoice mailed to the company by the dishonest receiving agent. The invoice may be very formal and legitimate in appearance, or it can be the common form available in a stationery store. It is simply a demand for payment for merchandise delivered to the company. The fake receiving document confirms receipt of the merchandise, making the bill due and payable.

The dishonest purchasing agent or buyer may claim that he received merchandise, perhaps claiming that material was delivered through the front door rather than through the receiving department, or he may act in collusion with a receiver to create a false receipt. Even more free to steal is an agent who obtains blank receiving documents, which he can simply complete and forward to accounts payable. The purchasing agent then invoices the company. The receiving document confirms the invoice and payment is made.

A dishonest accounts payable employee can, like the buyer or purchasing agent, generate his own illicit receiving documents, or he can use voided or illegible copies of legitimate receiving records to create a supporting document for the invoice.

The possible variations of this type of internal theft are almost limitless, depending on the company and its policies, procedures and controls. In each case goods or services are paid for that were never received. Payment goes to unscrupulous companies who over-invoice, knowing that receiving records will have been altered, or to nonexistent firms that are simply "mail drops" for the dishonest employee.

The strategy to prevent this kind of theft is to confirm that all companies that invoice the parent company actually exist. As with employee addresses, post office box numbers can be a warning signal. Every legitimate business has an office, plant, building, warehouse or other facility. The investigator should go to the address of every firm in question and confirm that it exists. If the address turns out to be a private residence, ownership or tenancy should be confirmed. The residence might be that of a relative or close friend of an employee.

Intelligence Surveillances

As discussed at length in Chapter 6, intelligence surveillance is the covert monitoring of a location or workplace for the purpose of determining exactly what is transpiring there.

Surveillance can be by the human eye or the eye of a camera. The human eye is more discriminating if there is a great deal of traffic and activity. The eye of the camera is most satisfactory in isolated situations — for example, when focused on a remote door which is not to be used except in emergencies. The camera used in connection with a time-lapse video recorder can tell the investigator in minutes what happened over many hours.

Physical Inspections

Physical inspections constitute a potential gold mine of interesting discoveries for the security investigator. The careful examination of a window (recall our earlier discussion of the power of observation in the investigative process) can reveal dust disturbances indicating passage of someone or something through an opening not intended to be used. A door wedged open that was supposed to be locked, a carefully concealed tear in a perimeter fence, a light bulb loosened so that an area will be dark that should be brightly illuminated — these and countless other telltale signs can alert the investigator to a potential problem.

In one case, physical inspection of a night depository disclosed that the perimeter alarm system had been defeated. A typical depository is like a closet built against the interior side of a building's outside wall. It has two locked doors, each having the key-way on the outer side of the door. One key will open the outer door from the exterior of the building, providing access to the depository, but the inner door is blank. The same works in reverse when the inner door is opened with its key from inside the building.

Normally the exterior door is not alarmed; the inner door must be alarmed. The function of the depository is for the pickup of goods, documents, etc., during hours when the building is closed. A courier service usually makes the pickup and delivery, and the courier is provided with the exterior door key. In the case in question, the inner door was equipped with alarm contacts of the plunger design. When the inner door was closed and locked, the plungers were forced deep into their receptacle. The continuous alarm circuit was then intact. With this arrangement, opening the door while the alarm system was turned on would permit the spring-loaded plunger to come out, triggering the alarm. Physical inspection revealed that someone — obviously an employee working inside the building — had taken a toothpick and jammed the plunger down in its housing, so the door could be opened without the plunger coming out.

This discovery indicated more than a prank. It meant that someone had copies of the keys to the two depository doors. It was not difficult to work out how conspirators might use those keys. One party could remain inside the building after closing, gather up all the goods desired and place them in the depository. He could then lock the door and remain in hiding until the building opened in the morning, emerging from his hiding place and sauntering out unnoticed (or appearing for work as an employee). Meanwhile, an outside accomplice could come by in the middle of the night, open the outer door, remove the stolen contents and relock the door — leaving no evidence that a theft had occurred. If it was too dangerous to remain all night inside the building, another possibility would be to enter the depository during the night, rap on the exterior door to signal waiting associates, pass quantities of stolen goods through to the outside and, when the theft was completed, simply close the inner door. Since the inner door could not be locked from the depository side, the thieves in this case would have to hope that no one would notice or regard as important the fact that the inner door was unlocked. The thieves would, of course, lock the exterior door from the outside before departing.

Inspections of any alarmed facility should include "swinging" — i.e., opening — every door and window on the system, one at a time, while the alarm system is turned on, in order to verify that a signal is actually being received on the annunciator panel or central station board. Failure to receive a signal could indicate an opening that has been bypassed and is being used for criminal purposes while the facility is closed. Since the presumption would be that no theft had occurred because there was no alarm, modest or judicious thieves would go completely undetected.

Experience will alert the investigator to signs of criminal or improper activity that might otherwise go unnoticed. This writer's years of service as a metropolitan vice investigator have made him aware of common indicators of sexual activity in public or company restrooms. While dirty words or obscene pictures scrawled on the walls can generally be ignored as the work of juvenile minds, very small messages written clearly in the grout line between tiles, usually soliciting sexual activity, are suggestive of a more serious problem. So are holes bored in the walls between partitioned toilets. Obviously, all such holes must be covered and the walls of restrooms painted or washed as frequently as necessary. More to the point of our present discussion, however, is the fact that physical inspections must be alert to any evidence of activity out of the ordinary.

Suggestion Box and Award Systems

Suggestion box and award programs are discussed at length in Chapter 12. Such programs can be a valuable source of information for the security investigator. Employees generally know a great deal about what is going on within the company, including illicit activity. Since most employees may be reluctant to approach anyone openly with such information, even when they strongly disapprove of what they observe, the key is to provide a vehicle for employees to communicate with management (and security) by some legitimate means. A variety of such programs have proved effective in exposing dishonesty by providing a structured vertical communication system. Such programs should provide assurances of confidentiality or, if necessary, anonymity for the informant.

Odometer Checks

If employees are compensated for the miles they drive their car on company business, the form used to request reimbursement should require not just the number of miles driven, but the full odometer reading before the business trip and the full reading at the conclusion of the trip. Periodic comparison of actual readings on the vehicles parked in the company lot with the mileage statements is an effective method of detecting fraud. Many a weekend trip to the mountains, desert or lake has been charged to the employer as a "business trip." For that reason the best time to record odometer readings is Monday morning.

Shoplifting Surveillance

As shoplifting is a covert crime, the action of the sneak thief, so is its detection a covert strategy. It is a very difficult strategy to learn and practice.

Good shoplifting investigators, more commonly referred to as either detectives or operatives, are hard to find. Many candidates are trained but few develop into outstanding achievers. Those who do are aware of their skills and are frequently difficult to supervise. They are typically people of exceptional courage, having been in many scrapes while making arrests. Most have seen more criminal acts performed than a police officer with the same years of work experience. They love their work, and will turn down promotional opportunities if the promotion will take them "off the floor." They are deserving of great respect and admiration.

In shoplifting surveillance, knowledge of techniques used by the shoplifter is as important as the detective's own stratagems.

Some shoplifting strategies:

1. Put merchandise on and wear it out as though it belongs to the wearer. In some cases women will come into a store wearing only underwear under a buttoned up coat. They will then put on a dress, belt and sweater after removing the price tags and wear the merchandise out of the store.

2. Put merchandise on beneath one's outer garments and wear the stolen items out concealed. A lot of swim wear and intimate apparel is stolen this way.

3. Place soft, folded items such as sweaters under the coat and armpit.

4. Push items off a counter so they fall into a waiting shopping bag.

5. Place articles in the bag of a previous purchase.

6. Carry into the store empty bags of the same or other stores and fill these bags with items while the shoplifter is shielded behind piles or racks of merchandise or in the privacy of a fitting room.

7. Hand merchandise to children who accompany you and let the children carry it out.

8. Wear special "boosting" coats that have hooks sewn on the inside to accommodate soft goods that are quickly placed there.

9. Wear special "boosting" coats that have a modified lining that makes the whole coat a huge pocket.

10. Carry booster boxes into the store. Such boxes appear to be ready to mail, wrapped and string-tied, or they may be disguised as fancy gift boxes. They are empty and have a false or trapdoor, or the bottom or side may be fitted with a spring-type hinge. Push the goods in and the false side gives way; withdraw the hand and the side snaps back to its original position.

11. Wear special "booster" bloomers, similar to old-fashioned ladies' underwear that comes down just above the knee. The legs of the garment are tied, or strong elastic is used so that stolen merchandise will not slip out. Stolen goods are pushed down the front of the bloomers, or an accomplice can push goods down the back.

12. Hide stolen items in the crotch area. Even items as bulky as a fur coat or several men's suits folded up can be hidden in this way between the thighs of a woman wearing a long, full skirt or dress, who simply walks out of the store after concealing the items. Even typewriters have been removed in this fashion.

13. Switch price tags. A garment's $50.00 price tag is replaced by a $25.00 tag from another item, and the more expensive article is then purchased at the lower price. Similar switching is often done with boxed items. For example, four cubes of margarine are removed from the package and replaced with four cubes of pure butter, which is then purchased at the price of the margarine.

14. Pick up merchandise and immediately take it to a clerk, demanding your money back.

15. Run into the store, grab items and run out to a waiting car, catching everyone by surprise (if you are noticed at all).

The foregoing list is by no means exhaustive, but it should offer some insight into the endless variety of ways retail merchandise can be stolen. To combat this highly prevalent form of loss, investigators must be as alert and imaginative as their adversaries.

Some detection strategies:

1. Dress in keeping with the store's clientele so as to blend into the crowd.
2. Watch for the customer who is more interested in what is going on around him or her than in the merchandise. A bona fide customer is interested in price, size, color, value, etc. The shoplifter is interested in who might be watching. (This is known as "eyeballing.")
3. Once a person considered a likely shoplifter appears on the scene, stay with him until absolutely satisfied that your original assessment was wrong.
4. During that continuous surveillance of a suspect, the detective must see the *selection* of the item to be stolen.
5. After the shoplifted item has been selected, the detective must then observe its concealment or he must know exactly where it is.
6. The investigator must insure that the stolen article is not disposed of before an arrest can be made. This is the most difficult part of the detective's job. People are easily frightened and will imagine they have been detected stealing even when they have not been. They will then dispose of stolen articles with as much stealth as was used in taking them.
7. The detective must be certain that the article supposedly stolen was not purchased.
8. Covert pursuit and surveillance must continue without interruption until the subject carries the stolen article or articles out of the store, where he is then intercepted and arrested. (Apprehension outside the store is not necessarily a legal requirement. It does, however, strengthen the charge that the shoplifter intended to take permanent possession of the stolen items without paying for them. Obviously, if a shoplifter is stopped while still inside the store, it is easier to claim that he had no intention of not paying for the goods, insisting rather that he wished to shop for other items or to compare the original selection with other goods to insure there was a color match, etc.)
9. Experienced shoplifting detectives will attempt to avoid a confrontation when a thief is stopped. This is usually accomplished by talking the person back into the store in a low-key, non-threaten-

ing manner. The severity of the real consequences — arrest and prosecution — should only become apparent after the shoplifter is safely inside an office of the store, where resistance or combativeness would prove fruitless.

Two final observations should be made about shoplifting surveillance. The first is that most shoplifters are not hardened criminals or professional thieves. There are professional shoplifters, but they constitute a small percentage of all those who steal from retailers. The second point of note concerns the growing acceptance and application of article surveillance, special tags attached to goods that can only be removed by sales personnel at the time of purchase. Otherwise the tags will cause activation of a sensing monitor at the store's exits when anyone attempts to leave with them. Article surveillance of this type had done more to discourage or prevent the crime of shoplifting in all types of retail establishment than any other single strategy.

III. BUILDING A CASE

Chapter 9

Interviews and Interrogations

Once a crime, act or incident has occurred, the reconstructive process has but two sources to draw on: (1) the physically observable, i.e., physical evidence, and (2) the written or spoken word of those who witnessed or in one way or another participated in the act or incident. *Example*: a forklift shears off a sprinkler head in a warehouse operation with resultant water damage to valuable goods. Under the "physically observable," we would have such evidence as:

1. the parts of the sheared sprinkler head;
2. the pipe from which the head had been sheared;
3. the point of impact on that part of the forklift that struck the head;
4. the condition of the forklift operator (if the investigator is on the scene shortly after the accident);
5. the "hard copy" of the central station receiving the water flow signal, and the time the flow stopped; and
6. the wet and damaged goods.

Now that is a great deal of physical evidence, yet we probably could not determine if the incident was an accident, an act of negligence, or intentionally done (e.g., for spite). To complete the picture, we really need the written or spoken word of those who witnessed or in one way or another participated in in incident. What the supervisor saw and heard, what the receiving clerk saw and heard, and what the forklift driver himself has to say should provide the investigator with sufficient information to resolve the matter. The obtaining of the "word" is achieved through effective interviewing and/or interrogation. This chapter will address the spoken word. Chapter 11 will deal with the spoken word reduced to writing.

Interviewing and interrogating are two distinctly different processes, although they both have essentially the same objective. They both seek insight into and information about a specific question or issue. Interviewing and interrogating are question and answer exchanges between one who seeks information (in our context, the investigator) and the individual who is believed to possess the information being sought. The key difference between the interview and the interrogation is in the person being questioned. The interview is the questioning of a witness or any party not (at that point in time) suspected of involvement in the crime or act, and the interrogation is the questioning of a person who *is* suspected of involvement. An obvious consequence of the difference is that the interrogation at some point becomes accusatory and as such strikes the uninformed as being bad, or negative, with connotations of "grilling" or administering the old "third degree." For that reason, such professionals as James Gilbert, in his fine work, *Criminal Investigation*, recommend that all police questionings be referred to as interiews.[17] Be that as it may, the investigator must understand the two processes and approach each accordingly.

INTERVIEWING

Purpose of the Interview

Let's go back to the forklift operator who sheared off the sprinkler head. We have ample physical evidence of the consequences of the act. Our purpose in interviewing witnesses in this matter is to determine specific circumstances surrounding the "accident" to better understand *why* and *how* the incident occurred. Such information may, but more probably may not, be available from any source other than a witness. For example, we want to talk to the supervisor who was on the scene to determine the following:

1. Has the operator of the forklift been properly trained?
2. Has the operator had similar "accidents"?
3. Has the operator ever been warned about how he operates equipment?
4. Did the operator exhibit "normal" behavior prior to and after the "accident" or did he appear to be hazy, loud, or otherwise uncoordinated in movement or speech?
5. Is the operator considered a good employee or have there been problems or disagreements?
6. Is the operator content with his assignment?

7. When was the forklift last serviced? When were the brakes last serviced?
8. Was there sufficient illumination for the operator to see? (The supervisor could say he has personally complained that the lighting is insufficient in that area but management has not acted to correct the condition.)
9. Has that particular head ever been struck before?
10. Did the operator act concerned and chagrined or did he think it was funny?
11. Was the pallet on the forklift overloaded, blinding the operator's view?
12. Was there a particular rush to load or unload at that time?

The answers to such questions will fill out an otherwise incomplete picture of the incident. The reader can develop his or her own scenario of what really happened by answering each of the questions a number of different ways.

The Interviewer

The effective interviewer is the security professional of good grooming and poise. Articulate but soft-spoken, gentle but firm, he clearly demonstrates, by word and action, total objectivity (except where expressed empathy might encourage additional information and/or cooperation). A good interviewer engages in "active listening." He stays with the speaker by nodding his head in agreement, raising eyebrows at a particular point of interest, emitting low, audible "uh-huh's" as the interviewee talks. Set the climate in which the interviewee does the talking. Most people enjoy an audience and like to have their say, so be a good listener!

Interviewing the Victim

Victims are difficult to interview because they are emotionally reacting to their plight. The intensity of the emotion tends to be a delayed reaction, peaking after the reality of the incident sets in, then tending to dissipate with the passage of time. And the emotional reaction should be predictable. A female employee who received an obscene phone call will be frightened; an employee whose new automobile was broken into and damaged while on the company parking lot will be angry (with the culprit *and* the company); the employee who cashed her paycheck, only to have the cash stolen from her purse before the end of the day, will be frantic or depressed.

If as an interviewer you find yourself with the victim at the peaking of emotion, then do not push for information. Instead, get him a cup of coffee or let him light up a cigarette or whatever, biding for time. If time runs out because the shift if over and the victim must catch a bus or carpools with others, put the interview off until the next day. Forcing the interview is no more or less than "victimizing" the victim again. It builds resentment against the security department. On the other hand, to show concern for and sensitivity to a victim, *after getting the basic facts,* and advising him that the interview can wait until he feels better the following day, develops good will. (It was necessary to underline "after getting the basic facts" because the victim of certain crimes must immediately share basic information.)

The interview's ultimate objective is to gather *all* the facts, every fact possible; details are important. Take, for example, interviewing a witness/victim who is the recipient of an indecent phone call from an unknown suspect pretending to be doing a lingerie survey for a well known local department store. The receiver of the call, when asked to describe what happened, will tell a "story." The "story" (not meant as a fabrication, but rather the retelling or recalling of the incident) will unvariably leave out pertinent details. Following would be a typical retelling of the incident:

"This morning, I got a call from a man from your company who said his name was Mr. Barkins and he said he was doing a survey for the lingerie department. He asked if I would answer questions to the survey and I would then receive a certificate worth $25 to buy merchandise in your store. I said 'fine.' He then asked my lingerie color preference, then my bra size, slip size, and panty size. I felt uncomfortable but answered. He then asked if I wore the brief panties or regular cut. I said brief. He then asked if I shaved to wear the briefs. I didn't think that was right so I just said 'no.' Then he asked me if I didn't shave, did hair show. I was so shocked I couldn't think of an appropriate answer and then he asked me a filthy question, to which I slammed down the phone. That's what happened, from beginning to end."

Now the interviewer must develop unstated details. For example:

1. What time exactly did the caller call? Fix the time by association with her schedule or routine. What was she doing when the phone rang? Watching a favorite TV program? Still having coffee? Husband just left for work? etc.
2. Did he use the store's name first, or at first identify himself by name, claiming he was with the store?
3. Did he say he was *Mr.* Barkins or did he use a first name also?
4. Was the phone connection clear?
5. How old a man did he sound like?
6. Did you hear any sounds in the background, such as a radio or TV, phones ringing, sounds of traffic, voices, or no sounds whatsoever?

7. Did he sound like an educated man, in terms of his choice of words, diction, delivery, or sentence structure? (Qualify the answer by asking her to compare to husband, family, or friends.)
8. Any accent distinguishable?
9. Any other characteristic in his manner of speaking, i.e., fast, slow, lisping, stutter, preceding questions with "ah," etc.?
10. Did he make any reference as to how or why he called you, i.e., did he say the local credit bureau provided your name as a good customer in the community?
11. Is your telephone listed in the directory?
12. Have you made any lingerie or other intimate apparel purchases anywhere lately?
13. If your phone number is listed, how is it listed, under your own name or your husband's?
14. Did he ever refer to you by your first name, if it's not listed?
15. Are you well known in the community, by virtue of your personal, social, political activities, or is your husband so known?
16. Is it generally known in your neighborhood that you are alone during the morning?
17. Did the caller sound like anyone, even vaguely, you have met or known?
18. Would you be able to recognize the caller's voice if you heard it again?

Obviously the answers to these questions, and more, give the investigator details. And in that detail can be the key to the identity of the caller, if not in this incident, then in another.

Sometimes, however, investigators deny themselves every detail by having, as an example, the wrong person conducting the interview. Consider the female employee who received an obscene phone call. If a male investigator were conducting that interview, some of the language during that conversation, language that could tie in with a past or future case, might not surface. A female investigator would probably obtain the entire conversation, word for word. Ideally, then, a female investigator would do the follow-up interviewing on sex-related offenses involving female victims. That is also true where children are witnesses. As a rule, small children will confide in a female more readily than in a male, and older people feel more at ease with investigators closer to their own age.

Interviewing Employees

Regrettably, many employees across the entire spectrum of business and industry tend to view the company's security department with some degree of guarded alarm or suspicion. Certainly, in some industries in which there is a relatively high incidence of employee dishonesty, fear of security is understandable. In others it may be attributable to simply identifying security as an extension of management. But whatever the case, the interviewer should be tuned in to the rank-and-file's perception of security, and more particularly, the security department's investigation unit.

There are a number of ways to substantially reduce, if not eliminate, this negative perception, but that is not for this chapter, or even this text. The point is that, if this attitude is present in a company, it poses an obstruction to good communication between security and employees, making interviewing more difficult.

There are two ways to overcome built-in resistance (asuming, of course, that the interviewer meets the personal and professional standards set forth earlier in this chapter). The first is to conduct the interview whenever possible right in the employee's work area, as opposed to conducting it in an administrative office, which in itself is intimidating to some employees. This is accomplished by having the lead person or line supervisor accompany and then introduce the investigator to the employee to be interviewed, saying something to the effect of, "Mr. Welliver of our security department needs your assistance on a company problem, so take whatever time he needs. You two can talk right here or maybe you'd be more comfortable over in the lounge. O.K.?" Standing around, or sitting, in the work area openly so all the other employees can see tends to allay the worker's concerns about his own well-being. It is then easier for him to share parts of his interview with co-workers when they ask him what it was all about — and they will! (Needless to say, this kind of interview should cover a matter other than internal dishonesty in that area.) Additionally, this kind of informal meeting tends to add dignity or importance to the employee. After all, security came to him. He wasn't summoned to their office. Lastly, that very work area and the activity the employee engages in could very well be germane to the investigation. It would therefore make sense to inspect the area with the employee witness.

The second kind of interview, particularly if the matter is internal dishonesty, can be handled in an administrative office where a supervisoral or personnel representative introduces security and remains quietly as a witness. Here again, the employee is introduced in a positive, non-threatening way, such as, "Ms. McDonald of our security department is interviewing a number of employees about a delicate matter and she needs all the assistance she can get. I know you'll help if you can. I've been sitting here so why don't you sit right over there?"

Depending upon the type of incident being investigated, the interview usually commences with the interviewer making a general statement about the case and then seeking from the interviewee his individual observations or role in the matter. *Example*: "I'm sure you're aware of our concern over the fire in the fabricating room late yesterday, Mr. Hendrix. According to my file, you played a very important role in helping extinguish that fire. In trying to put this whole thing together, I need from you what you said and what you did from the very beginning until after the firemen mopped up and left. Why don't you start by telling me *when* you realized we had a fire going."

The employee will respond with a less than detailed narration, generally no longer than one paragraph. The good interviewer will expand that first narration into many paragraphs by going back to the beginning and asking very specific questions, e.g., "Now you say you first realized a fire was in progress when returning from your break. Where were you exactly? Can you recall that?" Ask only one question at a time, and, if the answer is appropriate and intelligent, determine if that answer deserves another question.

Interviewing Non-employees

The difference between interviewing non-employees and employees is twofold. First, most non-employees feel no obligation to cooperate, and second, most non-employees do not have the same sense of dread or fear of corporate security, with the exception of sub-contractors and service organizations that rely heavily on the company as their primary sources of income. Usually, these exceptions are eager to please and their cooperation can be counted on.

In interviewing the non-employee, be it a client, customer, passerby, or what have you, the most universally productive approach to gain their cooperation is to suggest that somehow it is good for them — good as a client because service can be improved, good as a customer because prices can be kept down, good as a recipient because the neighborhood will be improved (or changed for the better), good as a citizen to carry out civic responsibility, good as an insurer because abuses can cause insurance rates to climb. And this approach need not be direct. It can be suggestive in nature. The good investigator will get cooperation.

Disciplinary and Investigative Interviews

There are two noticeable exceptions to the difference between the interview and interrogation, and for lack of better terms, we will refer to them as disciplinary and investigative. In each case, the employee is confronted with derogatory information indicting him or her but not accusing. An example of a *disciplinary interview* would be one in which the employee failed to perform as required, and that failure caused or contributed to a serious problem, but it is not possible to prove that the employee did so with intent. The failure might have involved leaving a dock door unlocked that resulted in a successful burglary. That employee could be under strong suspicion of being involved in that crime but it is unprovable. The interview would explore why and/or how he failed to secure that door, but without more substantial information, and without that employee all of a sudden blurting out an admission of involvement, the only recourse is disciplinary action, based on the admitted procedural failure. Depending upon the company and its rules, such an employee could be terminated following the interview.

In a disciplinary interview discussing an employee's failure to record a cash sale, a case in which there is substantial evidence that the employee did sell a service, goods, beverage, or whatever, but failed to record (i.e., ring it up on the cash register), the employee is asked to *explain* what happened to the transaction, the money specifically. We know the employee pocketed that money but cannot *prove* it. The employee invariably "can't remember" or insists he put the money in the register, even if he failed to record it properly. Irrespective of what the employee admits, the employee is discharged for failure to follow an important rule: All cash transactions must be recorded at the time of sale. Discharge for this procedural failure is not uncommon in the retail industry.

An *investigative interview* is a vehicle to reiterate accusations of dishonesty by co-workers. The investigator acts discreetly as a somewhat disinterested third party. As an example, the security department has identified internal dishonesty and has the culprits in custody. During the interrogation, one or more of those involved implicates someone either unknown to the investigation or someone suspected of involvement but against whom there is insufficient evidence for action. The company has two choices: (1) open an investigation into the activities of the accused (although the accused may not participate in dishonesty again because his confederates have been caught); or (2) confront the accused in an interview. That interview (preferably with a personnel representative present as a witness that the security department did not *accuse* the employee) would be handled by the key investigator as follows: "Mr. James, I suspect you are aware of the fact that Mr. White and Miss Jones are in trouble. They've told us everything. They tell us you've been involved. We'd like to hear what you have to say." If Mr. James drops his head and admits dishonesty, the interview turns immediately into an interrogation. If, on the other hand, Mr. James denies involvement and claims his associates are lying, then, in the absence of any proof, Mr. James is apologized to for the inconvenience caued by his accusers and told that the company does not take the unverified word of one employee against another. He is then sent back to work. The employee may be wary, but he usually heaves a sigh of relief. Depending on the circumstances, a covert investigation may continue.

Checking Perceptions

As an aid to judgemental determinations, such as age, weight, distance and height, ask the interviewee *your* age, weight, height, hair color, etc. This check of his perceptions will help him as well as you in putting down relatively accurate information, which is so important to the investigation.

INTERROGATION

The interrogation is the oral examination of one believed to be responsible for the omission or commission of an act considered a public offense. One definition is an accusatory confrontation betwen a person standing accused and his or her accuser, the objective of which is to induce the accused to admit culpability. It is a psychological contest between an interrogator whose purpose is to get the accused to volunteer self-incriminating statements, and the accused who seeks to protect himself from the consequences of his conduct by assuming a posture of innocence or ignorance.

The first step in "admitting culpability" is an admission of wrongdoing. Upon that first admission, the skillful interrogator will build more admissions until all is disclosed. An example of "building" on the initial admission of merchandise theft by a warehouse employee, for instance, would probably unfold as follows:

Employee:	"OK. You've got me anyhow. I put the carton of radios in my trunk just before I locked up for the night."
Interrogator:	"What prompted you to do that?"
Employee:	"I just needed the money."
Interrogator:	"How much did you get for the carton?"
Employee:	"$200.00 cash."
Interrogator:	"Who gave the $200?"
Employee:	"A guy named Willie. Don't ask me his last name 'cause I don't know."
Interrogator:	"Did you know Willie was willing to buy before you took the carton or did you take the carton and then look for a buyer?"
Employee:	"Willie and me already had talked about it. In fact, it was his idea for me to get radios because he said they're easy to sell."
Interrogator:	"When did you turn the carton over to him?"
Employee:	"That same evening, over behind Lucciani's delica-

tessen. I gave him the box and he gave me the money."

Interrogator: "What did he do with the carton, once he had it?"

Employee: "Well, he took, all the radios out and put them on his shelf. He has shelves in his van, kind of like a store."

Interrogator: "A van, like a store?"

Employee: "Yeah. He's got a step-in van, you know, kind of like a converted milk truck."

Interrogator: "Does he actually use it to sell from?"

Employee: "Oh sure. In fact, later that evening, several customers in Lucciani's came out the back door and two of them bought a radio. He's got all kinds of things, like Levi's, sweaters. One time, he had lugs of tomatoes. Never has the same stuff twice. Lots of people know Willie."

Interrogator: "What does he look like?"

Employee: (describes Willie)

Interrogator: "What does the van look like?"

Employee: (describes the van)

Interrogator: "Would you be willing to work with us, and deliver more merchandise to Willie?"

Employee: "Are you kidding? He'd kill me even if he knew I was just telling you about him. No way, man. No way!"

Interrogator: "He won't find out you're talking to us."

Employee: "God, I hope not. I'm sure your guys or the police will get him but keep me out of it. Fact is, I'm surprised he gets away with what he does. Everyone knows Willie."

Interrogator: "How did you ever make this arrangement anyhow, the arrangement to deliver a carton of radios to him?"

Employee: "He asked me where I worked. Then one thing led to another and you know the rest."

Interrogator: "How did you come to meet him?"

Employee: "I bought a leather jacket from him, from his van."

Interrogator: "When was that?"

Employee: "Just after last Christmas."

Interrogator: "Where was the van then?"

Employee: "Sitting behind Mullin's gas station. He's there a lot."

> Interrogator: "If I saw his van there tomorrow afternoon, could I buy something?"
>
> *Employee:* "Not in the afternoon. He only works at night. Besides, he'd be suspicious of you 'cause he doesn't know you."
>
> Interrogator: "How does one get to know Willie?"

It is amazing how much information can be obtained through skillful interrogation. In the above example, the interrogator is obviously interested in obtaining a full disclosure about Willie, a local "fence" or outlet for stolen goods. A great deal more information is yet to be developed concerning this case — e.g., the number of previous thefts (involving Willie or not), how he defeated the company safeguards that permitted the removal of the carton from the premises, etc.

The securing of this first admission is enhanced by the accused's sense of built — the knowledge that he or she *did* commit the wrongful act. Added to that naturally uncomfortable feeling is one's apprehension and uncertainty over just how much the interrogator knows. These factors result in an inner stress, a necessary element in any successful interrogation. Maintenance of stress will bring about an admission because of man's desire to be relieved from stress.

Invariably, unsuccessful interrogation can be attributed to a shifting of stress from the accused to the accuser! This shifting occurs when the accused perceives that the interrogator is not knowledgeable of the facts surrounding the incident, or seems unsure of the accused's degree of guilt or involvement. Such perception gives the subject confidence. With confidence comes strength and hope. The perceptive interrogator, recognizing the growing confidence and strength of the accused, tends to lose heart. His or her composure is thus undermined and the stress is shifted from the accused to the interrogator. It is almost like a game that could be called, "Stress, Stress, Who Has the Stress?" If you have the stress, you can't win!

PREPARING FOR THE INTERROGATION

Essentially, the same standards set forth for the interviewer hold true for the interrogator except that the purposeful, soft-spoken approach should be replaced by a more aggressive articulation of questions. It is important to examine oneself in a mirror, if at all possible, immediately prior to commencing an interrogation to insure that there is nothing distracting in appearance. Male interrogators should not wear lapel pins or any fancy tie tack. Female interrogators should not wear any jewelry other than one or two finger rings, a watch and a bracelet; no broach, necklace or earrings unless the necklace is out of sight and the earrings are very small and do not dangle. You do not need a subject leaning forward, pretending to be honestly curious about a lapel pin or brooch, and saying, "Oh, do you belong to the Knights of Columbus?" Or, "What a lovely pin! What kind of stone is that?"

The interrogator should be as knowledgeable as possible about the subject's personal and work history — where he was born, schools attended, occupation of parents or spouse, etc. If the interrogator knows the accused's brother is in law enforcement, a line of questioning using that fact — such as, "Your brother Fred is a Connecticut state trooper. What would he say if he knew you were in this mess?" — could come as quite a shock to an unsuspecting subject. The statement suggests that the interrogator knows *everything*.

Another preparatory activity, time permitting, is scenario development, in which the interrogator anticipates possible responses and how each should be dealt with. Responses can be verbal or physical. An example of a verbal response might be, "I quit, resign my job at this very moment. That means I am no longer an employee. Either pay me off my salary due and release me, or arrest me!" If the interrogator has not thought that possibility through, he could be caught totally off guard and, as a consequence, be unable to effectively interrogate.

An example of a physical response could be the subject fainting or going into an epileptic seizure, or uncontrolled weeping. The effective interrogator is prepared for the unexpected.

If a file on the subject does not exist, prepare one, even if it is only a "dummy file." Fill the file with numerous forms and written reports, anything to give the impression and appearance of a very comprehensive package. Have the subject's name boldly printed on the jacket or folder tab. During the interrogation such a file can be quietly "referred to." Such a file has the following advantages:

1. It gives the impression that a great deal of information has been gathered on the subject.
2. It can be picked up and examined as though comparing the subject's answer against known facts.
3. It might be used as a prop for the interrogator who wishes time to reorganize thoughts, or just to "buy" time.

Prepare yourself in terms of slowing down (be calm), feeling good about yourself and your preparation. Move forward with confidence and anticipate success (self-fulfilling prophecy, the Pygmalion Effect).

The Setting of the Interrogation

Contrary to what many of us learned while in college, a bare-walled room, almost sterile, is really not necessary for conducting a successful interrogation. Any regular business office will do, except the subject's own office, as long as it can be secured from interruptions such as a ringing phone or someone inadvertently walking in. If the room has a window to the outside, close the blinds to prevent the subject from fixing a gaze on some point in the distance or otherwise concentrating on what is happening out there.

Place two straight-back chairs opposite one another, relatively close to one another. The subject will sit in one, you the other. First, sit in the subject's chair, and look beyond where you will be. What might prove to be a distraction? A picture? A calendar? Anything that might catch the subject's fancy or attention should be removed. Now, just slightly to the right of the subject's chair, place a third chair. That will be where the partner or witness will sit, just barely discernible in the subject's peripheral vision.

Notice how the interrogator does not sit behind a desk? A desk only builds a barrier between the two principals, something the interrogator does not want. After the admissions start coming in, the desk can be used, but not until then.

Rid the room of any ashtrays, wastebaskets or any other receptacle that might be used to put ashes into.

Place the subject's "file" prominently on top of the desk or any other logical place where the subject can see it. Be sure you have the physical evidence in the room so it can be displayed when appropriate.

Be certain the room is not too cold or warm, too bright or dark. It should be normal and comfortable. The author lost a case in court based on the fact that the interrogation was conducted under spooky and intimidating circumstances, conditions which, when described in court, were true enough but to which we were simply not sensitive at the time of the interrogation. That interrogation took place in a tool-and-storage room adjacent to the public toilets in a country park at night. To heat the interior of that room we were using an antique, fuel oil burning, cylindrical-type stove that stood on three short legs. For ventilation, and presumably for appearance, there was a row of little "windows" at the height of the flame inside the heater. We purposefully kept the lights out because we were expecting another arrest, so we interrogated in the room illuminated only by the orange flickering light thrown by the heater, dancing on the otherwise dark walls. We investigators were similarly illuminated. Although the subject was caught "red-handed," and admitted his guilt, the interrogation proved his salvation and our loss.

Beginning the Interrogation

Introduce yourself and your partner (or witness) as agents of the company in a direct and pleasant manner. Seat the subject and immediately take the opposing chair. Commence the interrogation along the following lines, depending on how it fits with a particular case, but always include the questions in this suggested opening:

"Mary — may I call you Mary? Good. Mary, we have a very important subject to discuss this morning, very important to you and very important to us. In fact, it probably will be the most important discussion you've ever been engaged in. But before we get into the question at hand, I do want to ask you a couple of questions, okay? Are you in any way sick?"

Mary, with a curious expression, answers, "No."

"Do you take any kind of medicine?"

"No."

"Do you have to use the ladies' room?"

"No."

"Good."

The interrogator continues, "One more final point before we get started here, Mary, and that is my rule on lying. You have my solemn promise that at no time during our discussion will I lie to you. This is too important a matter for you to worry about me being deceptive. And by the same token, I'm asking you not to lie to me, no matter how much the truth hurts. Don't lie. This whole problem is too important to jeopardize it with lies. Do you understand that?"

Now the interrogator asks a series of relatively unimportant questions about the job and perhaps a few innocent questions about activities away from the job, all of which are designed to evoke "yes" answers. That is to establish a pattern of saying "yes"; it becomes easy to say "yes." When you get around to asking her a critical question, she may be in the mood to tell the truth.

Now if Mary gets a dry throat or says she has to use the toilet, the interrogator says, with raised eyebrow, "Why, Mary, just a very short time ago I asked you specifically if you were thirsty and you said you weren't. Why is your throat now dry? I can tell you with absolute certainty that the dry throat is a sure sign of guilt." The point is that asking those four questions at the outset of the interrogation precludes the possibility of an interruption that otherwise you would be unwise to refuse. Such interruptions are obviously designed by the accused to relieve stress.

If the subject starts looking around for an ashtray while trying to extract a cigarette, tell the subject there is no ashtray in the room and that, during the discussion, you would appreciate it if he would not smoke. Don't tell him he cannot. *Ask* him not to. Why this request? Because smoking soothes stress. A smoker denied a cigarette becomes distressed, adding to the very condition the interrogator wants. And there is nothing immoral or illegal in prohibiting smoking in certain areas at certain times.

If the subject starts to use profanity, admonish him immediately. Profanity is used as a substitute for other words. The individual who has difficulty in expressing himself tends to resort to the use of profanity, and such use makes him feel good about himself, intellectually or socially. Take away the "cuss words" and his vocabulary is dramatically reduced, or so it seems to him. That is also *stressful.* That is exactly what the interrogator wants. The "admonishment" would go something like this: "Please don't use profanity during our discussion here. This is too important an occasion to mar with profanity. I don't use it. I expect you not to use it."

Constantly observe the subject for indications of stress and for reactions to questions. If the subject starts picking at a fingernail, ask him to stop and concentrate on your questions and his answers. The eyes do two things: (1) your constant eye contact penetrates the guilty man's consciousness and creates stress; and (2) your eyes tell you when to ask the same question again; when to suddenly stand up and look down on the subject, then walk around the room and return to your chair; when to remain silent.

Other physical indications of stress include dry mouth, a bobbing Adam's apple, a paling complexion, beads of perspiration on the forehead, the onset of a tic (e.g., uncontrollable shaking, usually of the hands), inability or unwillingness to look the interrogator in the eye, and uncontrolled elimination of body waste.

To stand up and look down on a subject tends to subjugate the one seated. It is a way to re-emphasize, if necessary, who is in control. Unquestionably, there are some theatrics involved here. Let us say the subject contradicts himself and realizes it. Upon hearing the contradiction, that could be an excellent time for the investigator to rise and, looking down, say, "Do you realize what you just said?" Or to rise and walk around the room while saying, "Well now, *that's* interesting! First you said the supervisor was in his office and *now* you say he was on the dock. Why would you change your story?" The stress is magnified because, in the mind of the subject, he is in more trouble than before and is "locked" into the chair, whereas the righteous person (the interrogator) is "free" to get up and walk around, as well as to look down on him (the unrighteous).

Could you imagine a blind man or woman conducting an interrogation? Highly unlikely!

Do's and Don't's of Interrogation

Following is a list of other *Do's* and *Don't's* that can be helpful to the security interrogator:

1. Do use silence as a weapon. Ask a direct question and then wait for the response. The silence may seem like a long time, but it is thundering in the mind and ears of the accused, to whom it seems like an eternity.
2. Do keep questions short.
3. Do ask only one question at a time.
4. Do question the answers.
5. Do guard yourself against giving away information.
    and...
6. Don't make promises of any kind.
7. Don't threaten an accused with discharge, police involvement, or violence.
8. Don't show surprise at any answers.
9. Don't use profanity. Some still believe the only way to communicate with tough employees or outsiders is to speak "their" language. Don't lower yourself to them; rather, raise them up to you.
10. Don't be a big shot. Arrogance and pomposity close communication lines, which defeats the interrogator's purpose.
11. Don't lie. It may be unwise to tell all. What you do tell must be truthful.
12. Don't ever lose your temper. If you lose your temper you "got the stress" and lose the interrogation.

Remember, the person being interrogated is, after all, a human being who is psychologically and emotionally suffering at your hands. Most people want to confess. The interrogator can relieve that suffering by his genuine concern for the accused and the final resolution of the matter at hand. As a result, the accused senses that concern and wants to share with the interrogator. If that seems odd, it is closely parallel to the equally odd but well-documented phenomenon of kidnap victims becoming attached to their captors. The professional security investigator, functioning as an interrogator, is sensitive to human behavior and emotional needs, and by his behavior and attitude wins the confidence and respect of the man or woman in trouble. Once the subject respects and has confidence in that professional, the confession follows.

Chapter 10

Evidence

Evidence is variously defined as (1) the state of being evident; (2) something that makes another thing evident; a sign; and (3) a statement of a witness, an exhibit, etc., bearing on or establishing the point in question in a court of law.

Regrettably, the dictionary definition of evidence in the legal sense unduly limits the scope of the definition by specifying "a court of law" as the only body before which witnesses make statements and exhibits are presented. As a matter of fact, in the private sector, a great deal of evidence is developed, presented, weighed and decided upon in any number of settings other than a court of law.

Take, for example, internal disciplinary action by a company where an employee was discovered consuming an alcoholic beverage on the job and was under the influence of such beverage. Before the personnel department acts, they require evidence to prove that the employee was in fact consuming and under the influence. Evidence would include the empty or partially empty container of the prohibited beverage, the statement of a witness or witnesses, and anything else that would tend to "bear on or establish the point in question..." For instance, upon taking the bottle away from the employee, the security representative could quickly prepare a handwritten statement concerning the taking of the employee's property for safekeeping and have the employee sign such a statement. The scrawled signature of the intoxicated employee is but another piece of evidence.

The personnel department, after examining and listening to all available evidence, then acts in this particular case, terminating the employee. Later, the company could receive notification from a state or federal agency alleging that the terminated employee was not fairly treated by virtue of his (or her) sex, age, race, color, or creed, and an administrative hearing may be held to determine if the company's action was justifiable. Without the original evidence used to prove the accusation, it is not far-fetched to envisage the employee being reinstated and "made well" by receiving all back wages lost due to termination. Evidence is obviously essential not only in the court but in business and the industrial community as well.

DEMONSTRATIVE EVIDENCE

There are four kinds of evidence:

1. Judicial Notice (that which comes to the knowledge of the court, e.g., the exact time the sun set on a given date).
2. Parole Evidence (oral testimony).
3. Documentary Evidence (writings).
4. Demonstrative Evidence (physical objects).

For the purpose of this work, our primary focus will be on demonstrative evidence and, to a lesser extent, documentary evidence.

Most physical evidence is found at the scene of the incident in question, be it a pried-open desk drawer in an executive's office; a stolen shirt discovered in an employee's locker while the employee is being taken into custody for the theft of items on his person; the little nook in the corner of the warehouse where the employee was "sacking out" and imbibing; or the smashed plate glass window of the store through which burglars entered and/or exited during the middle of the night. Whatever the case, the scene is carefully examined for whatever evidence it has to offer. Preserving that scene is critical. No one should be allowed to enter or otherwise disturb that scene until the investigator is satisfied that all the evidence has been identified and collected.

If possible, the scene should be photographed before anything is removed. If photography is not possible, a sketch of the scene and its relationship to the rest of the area is recommended. Physical evidence removed from that scene can be so noted on the sketch.

Rules Involving Physical Evidence

There are four basic rules surrounding physical evidence:

1. Get all evidence that can have any bearing on the case.
2. Mark it.
3. Properly wrap, package, or preserve to protect the evidence from contamination or destruction.
4. Establish a chain or continuity between the discovery of the evidence and its subsequent presentation.

Get all evidence that can have any bearing on the case. The emphasis belongs on the word "all." Put another way, get *everything* that can have a bearing on the case. If everything really boils down to enormous quantities, such as a freight carload of goods, take a sampling as evidence, treat it as evidence, photograph the rest, and simply recover the balance and return it to its proper place. The strategy of getting everything simply insures that nothing is overlooked or left behind, because once the investigator leaves the scene, unless specific arrangements have been made to preserve that scene, evidence left will be lost, more often than not, forever. Too much is better than too little. From that overabundance one can pick and choose what should be presented in a hearing or in court.

Mark it. The marking of evidence should ideally occur when and where it was discovered, within reason, of course. That is to say, if a crowbar was left on the ground beside the forcibly entered boxcar, the investigator is not obliged to stop in his tracks and mark the crowbar right then and there, but it should be marked prior to its removal back to the office.

Minimally, the marking should be the initials of the investigator and the date. If possible, the case number could be included. This marking must not (1) in any way affect the evidenciary value of the object; or (2) damage or deface or take away from the value of the object.

Avoiding such damage may require some care. In one shoplifting case, an expensive ladies' handbag had been recovered as evidence. It was lined with a light, melon-colored silk fabric. The investigator noted her initials and date with blue ballpoint pen on that lining, rendering the handbag a total loss. Proper identification of the evidence is simply a matter of using some imagination when applying the markings. See Figure 10-1.

Figure 10-1. Marking physical evidence.

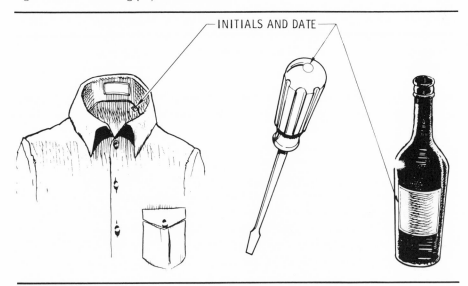

If it is not possible to mark on the items, then attach a label and mark on that. If the item is too small to mark on or to attach a label to, put it in a small container, seal the container and mark on it.

Marking serves the obvious purpose of making it possible to positively identify the object later, during an administrative or judicial hearing. The investigator may be asked, "Is this the shirt you way you found in Mr. Martin's locker?"

The investigator responds, "Yes, sir."

"Are you positive this is the shirt and not one like it?"

"I'm positive it is the shirt."

"Absolutely positive?"

"Yes, sir."

"How can you be so positive?"

"When I found this shirt in Mr. Martin's locker, I took my pen and placed my initials and the date right here inside the washing instructions tag in the neck of the shirt. Here it is, right here."

Properly wrap, package, or preserve to protect the evidence from contamination. If the evidence is of a fragile nature, such as glass or a plaster of Paris cast, or if the evidence is easily destroyed, such as a plastic or latent fingerprint, great care should be taken to insure that when the package is reopened the evidence has not been destroyed. Common sense gives direction here. If there is a question, seek advice.

Establish a chain of continuity between the discovery of the evidence and its subsequent presentation. Accounting for the uninterrupted control of the evidence is referred to as the "chain of custody" or the "chain of evidence." The so-called "chain" is the inked documentation of each person's possession of that evidence by name and time and date. The shorter the chain (or the fewer the people who handle it), the better. Ideally, the chain would be only one person, the one who discovered, collected, marked, packaged, carried and locked it in the vault, and subsequently retrieved it from the vault and carried to the hearing. The inked documentation (so as to avoid erasures) should be on the outer container or package as well as noted in the investigation file itself.

Reading Physical Evidence

The condition or state of physical objects can have a great deal to tell us if we come to understand how to read their messages. Look at the story left behind by the Indians in Chapter One, a story told by physical evidence. From the presence or absence of sap (or moisture) at the fracture side of a tree exposed to the sun, natural laws offer valuable information. And the natural

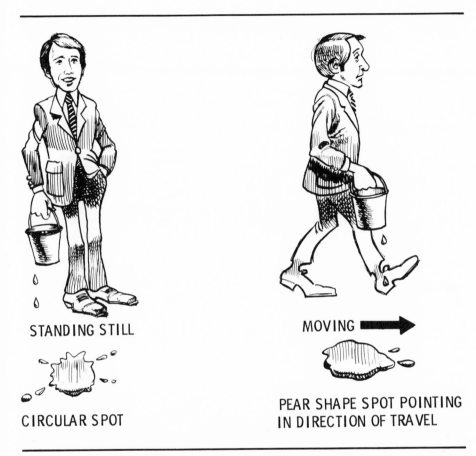

STANDING STILL

MOVING ▶

CIRCULAR SPOT

PEAR SHAPE SPOT POINTING
IN DIRECTION OF TRAVEL

Figure 10-2.   Liquid spots.

laws are not restricted to wilderness areas. They are in play all around us. Take, for example, the dropping of a liquid substance on the floor. The marking of the substance will tell us if it fell at 180 degrees from its source straight down, or if it fell at less or greater than 180 degrees from its source at a slanting angle. If the liquid struck the floor or pavement at 180 degrees, its source was motionless, standing still. If the liquid struck at an angle, its source was moving, and the marking tells us in which direction the source was moving. See Figure 10-2.

Direction of movement on foot is ascertained by one of two types of footprints. A *plastic print* is an actual depression of the print, such as in mud or snow, which can be preserved by taking a casting, preferably a plaster of Paris casting. A *surface print* is visible due to a shade or color contrast, such as the print made with a wet, bare foot on a dry surface or the prints left on a dusty surface. The only way to preserve surface prints is to photograph them

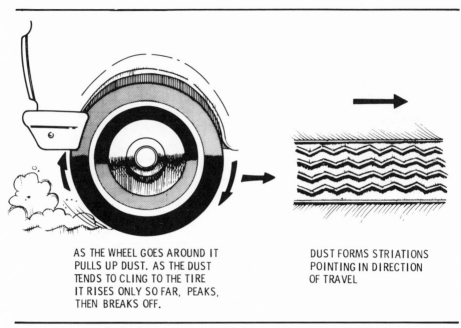

AS THE WHEEL GOES AROUND IT
PULLS UP DUST. AS THE DUST
TENDS TO CLING TO THE TIRE
IT RISES ONLY SO FAR, PEAKS,
THEN BREAKS OFF.

DUST FORMS STRIATIONS
POINTING IN DIRECTION
OF TRAVEL

Figure 10-3.   Vehicle direction.

with oblique lighting to highlight the contrast.

Two ways to determine the direction of a moving vehicle are shown in
Figure 10-3.

Investigators in the private sector are frequently required to investigate
incidents on company property which involve damage to glass. The following
points could be helpful:

1. Due to the tensility of glass, high velocity projectiles (bullets) make a
    hole generally smaller than the bullet that passed through.
2. Bullets create a cone, without radial and concentric fractures, and
    that cone is on the opposite side of the glass from the entrance of the
    bullet. See Figure 10-4.
3. The faster the projectile, the smaller the hole — e.g., a .22 caliber
    hole will be larger than the hole made by a 30.06 bullet.
4. Larger and slower-moving projectiles knock out portions of glass
    and leave radial and concentric fractions. See Figure 10-5.
5. Examination of a side view of a broken piece of glass will reveal
    which side of the glass was struck. See Figure 10-6.

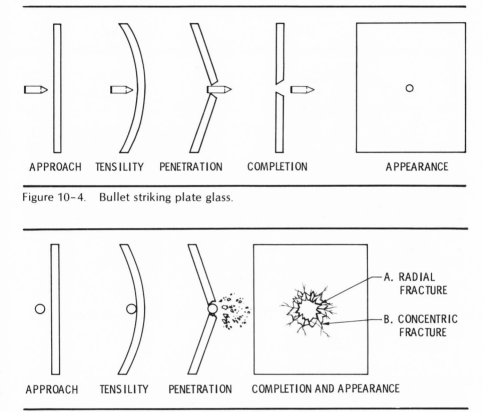

Figure 10-4.   Bullet striking plate glass.

Figure 10-5.   Non-bullet striking glass.

Fingerprints

The evidenciary value of fingerprints has long been established and de-serves a word here. There are three types of fingerprint impressions:

1. The visible print.
2. The plastic print (physically imprinted into a material such as putty or paint).
3. The latent print (not clearly visible or discernible until dusted with contrasting powders).

Some investigators in the private sector are very knowledgeable about the science and mechanics of fingerprinting, and can dust, raise, photograph, lift, classify and make comparisons and identify prints, and they do so in their

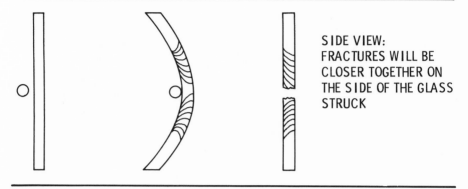

Figure 10-6.   Determining which side of glass was struck.

security roles. This specialized field is, in actuality, in the realm of the public sector. When and if a technician's services are needed, the security department's role should be to safeguard the area and call on the public sector to do the job. If the nature of the investigation does not warrant police involvement but a fingerprint technician's services would be helpful, then hire one on a part-time basis.

What kind of case would *not* warrant police involvement but would warrant a fingerprint technician's services? One example could be the discovery that some unauthorized employee is getting into files which contain sensitive or otherwise confidential information. A very clean obstacle could be placed in a position which blocks access to the files of concern. At the end of the day, or the following morning, that obstacle could be carefully removed and dusted for latent prints. There are any number of such non-criminal problems that must be solved in the work organization, and the evidence of fingerprints can be one of the many strategies used by the security department.

Creativity and Physical Evidence

If there are no tree limbs, saplings, or brush of any kind that can be trampled or broken, signaling that someone has passed through, or no stones on a path that can be disturbed, then create your own signals. Have you ever folded up a very small piece of paper and pinched it into place between the door and jamb, exposing a tiny piece so that, when you returned later, you could tell if someone had opened the door or not? How about running a thin thread a foot high off the floor, tacked down or in some other way secured in place? Someone passing through or entering would inadvertently break that thread and never know it. The odds are against ever having taken regular baking flour and gently blowing it over a surface with the intention of returning later to inspect that surface with a flashlight. The oblique angle of the light would highlight footprints of whoever walked on that surface. We are too often limited by our own imagination, or the lack of it.

The Case of the Rainy Day Burglar. An interesting example of observable evidence was a case in which a burglar barely escaped apprehension inside a ten-story department store late one night. The building was surrounded, and for the trapped man to exit the store would have resulted in capture. It became apparent to all that the burglar would wait it out until the store opened its doors to the public at 10:00 a.m.

At about 5:00 a.m., just befor the housekeeping crew arrived at the store to start their day's work, it began to rain. All the employees who arrived for work carried umbrellas or wore raingear. Customers started arriving just before 10:00 a.m. They too carried umbrellas and wore raingear. The burglar had been in the building hiding for over 12 hours. He would want to get out as soon as possible. He probably did not know it was raining and would not know it until he left his hiding place. If he did not have rain gear when he entered the store, he would be conspicuous once he mingled with the customers. If he did have raingear, it would be dry.

Every exit was covered by security. Five minutes after the store opened to the public, a man attempted to exit the store wearing a bone-dry coat. It had to be the burglar. It *was* the burglar.

DOCUMENTARY EVIDENCE

In our commercial society, paper work in all its many shapes and forms lends itself to a variety of manipulations requiring security, if not police, involvement. The three most common problem areas in documents are:

1. *Anonymous communiques* such as extortions, threats, sexual invitations, sexual harassments, accusations, or notes informing on someone within (or out of) the organization.
2. *Counterfeited or altered documents and negotiable instruments* such as company bank checks and payroll checks, severance vouchers, raised money orders, gift certificates, etc.
3. *Forged signatures* of customers, in credit card cases, of company officers in payroll or accounts payable sections, etc.

The one thing these three areas have in common is the question of *who* is responsible.

Anonymous Communiques

Anonymous letters or notes are usually typed or handwritten. "Cut-outs," i.e., messages made up of words or letters cut out of magazines and pasted onto a blank sheet of paper, are not common in the private sector. The typed anonymous letters are usually sent to management, and the handwritten notes are more often sent to specific individuals of the company, not necessarily to someone in management. The typed letters tend either to be demanding — i.e., unless the company does so and so, something bad will happen — or they are informative, i.e., "I think you should know...." Handwritten letters tend to be threatening, abusive (usually sexually abusive) or sexually suggestive.

In terms of evidence, the letter and its envelope usually have been handled by at least two or three people before they ever land on the desk of the responsible investigator. If a series of letters arrive from the same source, the handling can be reduced to the investigator. Depending on the nature of the case, he may choose not to open the envelope but rather transport it to the public sector authorities for examination by the crime laboratory and fingerprint technicians.

There is a three-phase process in anonymous letter investigations:

1. Examination of the material used.
2. An analysis of the content of the message.
3. Comparison of suspect handwritings or suspect typewriters.

Examining the material.   Careful examination of the envelope flap after you gingerly unseal it and the reverse side of the postage stamp may reveal traces of lipstick. If the letter is sexually abusive to a female, and lipstick is on the envelope, it could be a jealous co-worker who is hiding her identity by pretending to be a male author. Other examples of evidence include the postmark (i.e., where it was mailed from), the kind of paper used, and where that same paper can be found. Is it available in the office? Is the paper a quality paper with watermarks (easily seen if the paper is held up to the light)?

Analyzing the Content.   What is the author of the letter trying to do? Is the intention clear or disguised? If we understand the intention, the objective of the letter, does that narrow down possible authors? Does the language of the letter, in terms of style, choice of words, sentence construction, etc., give any clues? Do the grammar and spelling reflect a poor or good education? Is the author revealing information that only a very few would know? Is the general message realistic (possible) or a fantasy?

Comparing handwriting or typed samples.   By the time you get to the third phase of the investigation, one or more possible suspects will have been identified. If the letter is handwritten, then handwriting samplers of the suspects wil be compared against the letter. A good source of samplers (known writings of a given person) can be the security department's employee bonding file. If more handwriting is necessary, the personnel department's file on the employee or the employee's immediate work area could prove productive. If the suspect is not an employee of the same company as the investigator, the security department of that suspect's employer might prove helpful. If the suspect is unemployed, then perhaps one or more educational, financial, or retail sources may have his handwriting on record. If handwriting samplers are needed, they can be found.

Because our handwriting, our penmanship, is learned early and practiced regularly, it develops very specific and identifiable idiosyncrasies by way of habit. Even if we try to hide our writing (usually done by writing with the opposite hand or writing very small), habit creeps in. In a way, handwriting is like fingerprints: no two are identical. The good investigator need not be a questioned document examiner or expert to make comparisons between the sampler and the suspect letter and find identical characteristics on both. That is not to say that analyzing handwriting is simple. It is to say, however, that anonymous letter authors are relatively easy to identify, primarily because there is a good deal of material in the letter to compare. Forgeries are another matter altogether.

Typewritten anonymous letters are more difficult in terms of identifying the author. What usually happens, once possible suspects are identified, is that the typewriter on which the letter was typed is located, especially if the machine is on company property. Determining who typed that letter on that machine may not be possible. But the knowledge that a given area of the company is discontented, or that someone in that area is trying to tell management something, can be helpful.

Typewriter comparison, preferably done with a low-power microscope, is more exact than comparing handwriting, because the identifiable characteristics are mechanical in origin. The flaw in the letter "W," as an example, be it caused by accident, during repair, or at the time the particular key was cast in the factory, will consistently be there. And the likelihood of other "W's" having the same flaw and striking the paper at precisely the same pitch and with the same spacing before and after it, when it strikes, is more than remote.

Most anonymous communiques in the private sector are not reported to the authorities. The exception is letters of extortion. The police or F.B.I. will take the letter(s) and envelope(s) as part of the documentary evidence for their case. Security files should contain copies of those letters.

All other anonymous letters should be retained in a specific "Anonymous Letter" file. If the author is identified and the case is classified under some other category for record–filing purposes, a copy of the original anonymous letter should still be in the Anonymous Letter file with a reference to the case number. Upon receipt of an anonymous letter, it can be compared to others that have been received over the years. The person who sends an anonymous letter this year may do so again next year.

In one such case, the letter-writer, who openly admitted employee status with the company, sent four letters to management over a period of about seven years. These letters were usually complaints about facility conditions or specific supervisory practices; one was information about internal dishonesty. The anonymous employee felt duty-bound to report conditions to management. The interesting thing about that case was the ease with which we could identify the letter as yet another from the same person, even after a lapse of one or two years. The author used the same typewriter, misspelled the same words, used the same format, underlined words and used the same exclamation mark with the same frequency, etc. Although we never identified the employee, we came to trust the author and took seriously his complaints or information.

Counterfeited or Altered Documents and Negotiable Instruments

The best evidence in a counterfeiting or altered document case is, again, in the comparison of the good against the bad. The whole array of commercial documents subject to counterfeiting or alteration is beyond the layman's imagination until it is pointed out. Redeemable coupons, scrip notes, refund forms, gift certificates, expense vouchers, payroll checks, accounts payable checks, tickets for passage and admission tickets are some of the documents or instruments that can be altered or counterfeited.

Although it is not directly related to the discussion of evidence, a word must be said about the necessary strategy in this area, which is threefold: control, comparison and reconciliation. *Control* includes quality controls in the printing process, e.g., ink colors are stable and consistent so that variations are conspicuous; control by serialization (if appropriate); and control by distribution, i.e., metering out given quantities to specific individuals on a need basis with the balance protected by lock and key, use of indicia or signature, etc. Comparison can be effected by way of samplers appropriately displayed where the media can be easily compared against such samplers. Counterfeiting or alteration can also be detected by *reconciliation* of the negotiated instruments against the disbursement record, e.g., gift certificates numbered 0001 through 0100, all cashed for $100.00, should be reconciled against 0001 through 0100 as issued for $100.00 each.

Forged Signatures

In my wallet are six credit cards, all of which have a place for my signature. I refuse to affix my signature on any one of those cards. Why? If I should lose one of those cards, why should I provide a sample of my signature for the criminal user to copy?

Credit cards probably constitute the bulk of forged signature problems in the private sector. The forged salescheck or tab is documentary evidence itself. Further evidence is the handwriting of the forger, in terms of those peculiarities of his handwriting which tend to surface even when writing someone else's name.

Another interesting bit of evidence is found in those cases where the forger inadvertently signs his own full name, or own first name, or starts to write his own name and then corrects it to the forged name. If the true party's name is Mrs. Donald Crossen and the forger starts to write a capital "B" instead of "D," habit has forced her to commence writing her own first name, which in this example could be Barbara, Betty, Beverly or any other such name. That is certainly an important investigative key, but more importantly, it is powerful evidence.

Once the forger is in custody, a handwriting sampler, at least a full sheet, should be taken. Contained therein would be the name forged, as many times as possible. If the forger is willing, a whole vertical column of the forged signature would be desirable. A handwriting expert could testify that the signature on the document was written by the same person who wrote the sampler.

SOME RULES AND DEFINITIONS
OF EVIDENCE

Not only must be investigator appreciate and understand the importance of evidence as a tool of the reconstructive process, he must also be sensitive to its ultimate value as proof of culpability. Further, there is invariably some misunderstanding or confusion over evidential terms. Let's consider the following shoplifting scenario as a means of illustating common terms for better understanding.

A young woman, a college graduate, enters a store and a store detective observes the following: The woman approaches the handbag department, tears the price tag off the handstrap of a new bag, drops the tag on the floor after wadding it up, then places the items from her old handbag into the store's bag and sets her old bag among the display. She then selects four blouses and enters an enclosed dressing room. She comes out of the dressing room, carrying only three blouses, and hangs those three on the rack. A quick check of the dressing room reveals an empty hanger.

At this point the woman is carrying another store's paper bag which appears to contain merchandise. When she entered the dressing room she was only carrying the handbag (plus the four blouses on hangers). She leaves the store without paying for the handbag, and the detective is confident she also stole a blouse. She is approached and detained. She admits the theft of the handbag and one blouse.

The case described involves direct evidence, circumstantial evidence, physical and material evidence.

Direct evidence is also known as parole evidence, i.e., oral testimony. It is always a result of the witness's direct observation or what that witness heard, felt or smelled. Testimony of the detective's observation of the purse switch is direct evidence. It is a powerful form of evidence because it tends to prove a fact, in this case the fact that the woman took merchandise without paying for it.

Circumstantial evidence is just as potent as direct evidence *if* the accused fails to provide contrary evidence. In our shoplifting scenario, the theft of the blouse is circumstantial evidence because the detective did not actually see the theft. The circumstances strongly indicate a theft occurred.

Indirect evidence and *presumptive evidence* are the same as circumstantial.

Physical evidence is any object connected with the matter at hand. In our example, physical evidence would include (1) the stolen purse, (2) the abandoned purse, (3) the crumpled price tag that was removed from the stolen purse, (4) the blouse, and (5) the paper bag used to conceal and remove the blouse.

Real evidence and *demonstrative evidence* are the same as physical evidence.

Material evidence is that which tends to prove *part* of the issue. It is material that the culprit assumed unlawful ownership of the purse by transferring her personal effects from the old bag to the new one.

Immaterial evidence is considered to be unimportant and not germane to the issue. The fact that the culprit is a college graduate has nothing to do with the issue of shoplifting. How much money she had in her wallet is also not germane and is immaterial.

Competent evidence is responsible evidence, sufficient to prove a given fact has a bearing on the issue — e.g., the removal of the price tag by the woman.

Relevant evidence is that which relates directly to the matter — e.g., the culprit's admissions of theft, the discovery of the empty hanger, the sudden appearance of another store's bag with contents. Obviously, materiality, competency and relevancy are very similar.

"Best Evidence" applies only to documentary evidence, or writings. Sometimes there is confusion in applying this term, for example, to having the actual purse or blouse in the hearing room, instead of a photograph, because the objects are the "best evidence." Best evidence means the actual documents, not facsimiles or copies.

A Final Word About Evidence

In his text on criminal investigation, James Gilbert makes a point that underscores the thrust of this chapter and is worth repeating here: "Evidence is anything properly admissible in a court, that will aid the function of a criminal proceeding in establishing guilt or innocence. There are many different types of evidence, having different degrees of importance. In general, evidence that is inanimate, or nonhuman, is valued more highly than evidence involving human beings. This is due to the fallibility of the human condition (e.g., loss of memory or purposely altering the truth)."[18]

Bearing this reality in mind, the effective investigator, while seeking out anything and everything that bears upon a case, will place the strongest emphasis and reliance on his own direct observations and on hard physical evidence.

Chapter 11

Written Statements
and Confessions

There is no question that an admission of guilt or a full confession, when reduced to writing and signed, is impressive evidence. In most cases, that single piece of evidence is and always will be *the* deciding factor. Conversely, its absence has undoubtedly served the culprit's best interests in many cases, much to the chagrin of both public and private investigators.

As a matter of fact, the *admission* (a relatively brief statement admitting culpability with no reference to intent) and the *confession* (a comprehensive written narrative with details of the offense, including intent and sometimes motive) are so potent, in terms of their damning impact on the accused, that the United States Supreme Court and a host of lesser judicial bodies have come to focus on these documents, with particular attention directed toward *how* they were obtained. In detecting what would constitute abuses of one's constitutional rights, the Supreme Court has laid down specific guidelines for officers and investigators in the public sector. Such guidelines — to repeat, for the public sector at this point in time — must be complied with to quality admissions or confessions as legal and admissible items of evidence in criminal courts of law.

HISTORICAL BACKGROUND

At the beginning of this writer's career in law enforcement, in the early 1950's, trickery, coercion and even strategies that were psychologically or physiologically abusive were common in obtaining confessions. One technique which struck us as the epitome of deceit was having the investigator pose as a priest; we can recall a discussion in one of our college classes of an actual case of this type. But in those days there were simply no constraints upon law enforcement officers in this area. Deception — and worse — were accepted practices. The same unconstrained "freedoms" were similarly enjoyed in the private sector.

Early Court Decisions

It became evident in mid-1955, with the California Cahan decision, that the pendulum had commenced its swing away from this gathering of evidence through deceit. That landmark case made evidence inadmissible if illegally obtained. In its Cahan decision, the court reacted to what it considered an abuse, the "bugging" of the defendant's bedroom. Cahan was suspected of bookmaking.

Thereafter, the public sector of law enforcement became increasingly more limited in its power to search for and seize anything of evidential value. However, those constraints were on the public sector, which "represented the sovereignty of the state," and did not in any way constrain search and seizure in the private sector.

In 1963, the rights of the private sector were challenged but ultimately upheld in yet another California case, *People v. Victoria Randazzo,* 220 Cal. App. 2d.768, which said that the rule that evidence obtained in violation of constitutional guarantees against unreasonable searches and seizures is inadmissible does *not* apply to evidence obtained by a private person unconnected with government law enforcement agencies. This meant, of course, that investigators in the private sector had a great deal more freedom in gathering evidence than did their cousins in the public sector.

Then, in 1964, in *Escobedo v. Illinois,* the United States Supreme Court took the position that when an investigation changes from a general inquiry into an interrogation, the suspect must be advised of his constitutional right to remain silent and must be given legal counsel if it is requested. The evidence of incriminating statements and confessions was placed under new constraints — but again, not for the private sector!

The 1966 *Miranda v. Arizona* decision went even further than *Escobedo* by requiring the advisement of constitutional rights at the time of arrest, certainly much earlier in the law enforcement process than the formal interrogation. The 1967 Supreme Court decision in regard to *Cault* extended the right to legal counsel to juveniles.

The private sector's immunity from the "Miranda rule" has been tested but the position has remained essentially the same: If the private sector investigator is a private citizen and is not deputized or in any other way affiliated with governmental authorities, he need not advise a subject of his rights.

The Zelinsky Decision

At the time of the Cahan decision in 1955, it was not possible to see clearly the outline of things to come on the horizon. There has been a new California decision, however, which dramatically impacts on the private sector. This time the future seems more predictable. The case in question is another California Supreme Court decision, *People v. Zelinsky,* 24 Cal. 3d. 357, handed down in 1979. Because of the magnitude and potential impact of this case, the facts, as well as some of the court's language, should be of special concern to private security.

The facts of the case were commonplace enough. The defendant, Virginia Zelinsky, was observed by Zody's security personnel to place a blouse in her purse, put a pair of sandals on her feet and a hat on her head, and then place her purse inside a straw bag. The defendant then purchased a pair of shoes and left the store without paying for the other items. She was detained and brought back to the security office, where she was subjected to a pat-down search for weapons by Zody's security. After the pat-down, her purse was opened and the blouse retrieved by a security agent. A pill vial, later discovered to contain heroin, was also found. Zelinsky was convicted of possession of heroin and appealed that conviction to the California Supreme Court.

The language of the court in commenting on the case deserves close attention.

> The people contend that the evidence is nevertheless admissible because the search and seizure were made by private persons. They urge that *Burdeau v. McCowell* (1921), 256 U.S. 465, holding that Fourth Amendment prescriptions against unreasonable searches and seizures does not apply to private conduct, is still good law and controlling.
>
> Defendant contends, on the other hand, that only by applying the exclusionary rule[19] to all searches conducted by store detectives and other private security personnel can freedoms embodied in the Fourth Amendment of the federal constitution and article 1, section 13 of the state Constitution be protected from the abuses and dangers inherent in the growth of private security activities.
>
> We have recognized that private security personnel, like police, have the authority to detain suspects, conduct investigations, and make arrests. They are not police, however, and we have refused to accord them the special privileges and protections enjoyed by official police officers. (See *People v. Corey* (1978), 21 Cal. 3d. 738.) We have excluded the fruits of their illegal investigations only when they were acting in concert with the police or when the police were standing silently by. (*Stapleton,* supra, 70 Cal. 2d. at p. 103.) We are mindful, however, of the increasing reliance placed upon private security personnel by local law enforcement authorities for the prevention of crime and enforcement of the criminal law and the increasing threat to privacy rights posed thereby. Since *Stapleton* was decided, the private security industry has grown tremendously, and, from all indications,

the number of private security personnel continues to increase today. A recent report prepared by the Private Security Advisory Council to the United States Department of Justice describes this phenomenon in the following terms: "A vast army of workers are employed in local, state and federal government to prevent crime and to deal with criminal activity. Generally thought of as the country's major crime prevention force are the more than 40,000 public law enforcement agencies with their 475,000 employees. While they constitute the . . . most visible component of the criminal justice system, another group has been fast rising in both numbers and responsibility in the area of crime prevention. With a rate of increase exceeding even that of the public police, the private security sector has become the largest single group in the country engaged in the prevention of crime." (Private Security Adv. Coun. to U.S. Dept. of Justice, LEAA, Report on the Regulation of Private Security Services (1976) p. 1.)

The court's conclusion, with but one dissenting vote, was that the evidence (the heroin) was illegally seized and therefore inadmissible. Zelinsky's conviction was reversed. *This means the exclusionary rule now applies to private security agent searches.* It is only a question of time before "the second shoe drops," and private sector representatives will be required to follow the same guidelines as the civil authorities in order to submit, as evidence, admissions and confessions.

Ourselves to Blame

How did we in the private sector reach the point where the court system feels an obligation to protect the citizenry from us? Because, intentionally or otherwise, we have abused our prerogatives. As a case in point, also a California case, in *People v. Haydel* the court held that security agents acted improperly in holding an employee and the employee's wife, caught in the act of theft, for a period of 5½ hours. The couple's small child was with the mother at the time she was taken into custody, so the child was, literally speaking, also in custody. During this period of time, the security investigators obtained four written statements from the employee. One document suggested that the wife and child would be set free in exchange for continued cooperation. Such was not the case.

Although the employee and his wife were caught "red-handed" in the act of theft, and additional stolen goods were recovered from their home, the court reversed their conviction of larceny, using the following interesting language: "A confession's inadmissibility may stem from civilian as well as police coercion. . . . He signed the second statement after being tricked into the belief that it would free his wife and child from captivity. Section 847 [referring to the California Penal Code Section that spells out the private person's authority to arrest] directs him to take the arrestee to a magistrate or peace officer without unnecessary delay ... the well-trained and well-financed private security forces of business establishments are heavily involved in law enforcement.... The entire process of arrest, detection, incommunicado interrogations and extraction of signed confessions was the indissoluble product of the arrest under color of state law. The exclusionary rule applies here...."

An otherwise excellent piece of investigative work was irrevocably lost in this case because the investigators held their subjects too long and used some deception in gaining the employee's signature to statements. The lesson is clear: Abuses lead to constraints.

TYPES OF CONSTRAINTS

Constraints on Public Sector Investigators

Investigators in private security should be fully cognizant of the constraints, as they pertain to admissions and confessions, under which those in the public sector must operate. They are as follows:

1. Confessions may not be obtained through the use of threats or violence. They must be free and voluntary.
2. Confessions may not be obtained through inducements or promises of leniency.
3. Persons from whom confessions are sought must be informed of their right to remain silent and of the fact that anything they say may be used against them in court.
4. A person suspected of a crime has the right to obtain the services of an attorney, retained or appointed, before making a confession. He must be informed of this right. Interrogation must not be started until the arrival of the attorney if the suspect indicates that he wants legal counsel.
5. A suspect who decides against an attorney may, nonetheless, refuse to answer questions, in which case the interrogation must cease.
6. Police who claim that a suspect has waived any of his rights prior to making a confession must be able to prove that the suspect was fully informed of such rights, that he understood them, and that he or she did knowingly and intelligently waive those rights. The waiver should be written if at all possible. The waiver should spell out the warnings that were given, and should include a statement that the suspect understands and is voluntarily waiving the warnings.

Constraints on Private Sector Investigators

Constraints on representatives of the private sector are currently limited to only two:

1. Confessions (and admissions) may not be obtained through the use of threats or violence. They must be free and voluntary.
2. Confessions may not be obtained through inducements or promises of any kind.

We consider such so-called constraints to be absolutely necessary as well as reasonable, a position most professional investigators in the private sector would agree with.

The problem and danger we see on the scene today is the growing tendency of private sector investigators to go beyond these constraints. Specifically, many are now applying the Miranda rule to subjects in their custody. *This must not be done.* We should not "Mirandize" anyone unless we are legally obliged to — i.e., security personnel who are deputized, commissioned or have peace officer status. For us to Mirandize now, when it is not legally required, will only set unnecessary, unwanted and confusing precedent which could accelerate or otherwise cause legal imposition, on those of us in the private sector, of all those constraints now in force in the public sector.

Imagine what problems would surface if we were obliged to advise every person of his constitutional rights! If an employer (and security is the employer's representative) catches an employee with his hand in the company till, in the act of a crime, must the employee be advised of his constitutional rights? Would such constraints preclude the private sector from handling criminal activity as a crime? What of employees caught in borderline criminal behavior, such as padding their expense accounts? Must they also be advised of their rights? Would not the advisement of rights somehow interfere with the normal, necessary and expected communication between management and employees? If an employee's misconduct is grounds for discharge under company policy, such as the consuming of alcoholic beverages on the job and being under its influence, must that employee be advised of his rights? If an employee wants an attorney, who is to provide one? If an outsider is in the custody of security and that outsider wants an attorney, who provides one? Must security advise people of their rights if criminal prosecution is not considered necessary or desirable?

These and other questions could be paralyzing issues, opening a Pandora's box of problems we do not want or need. The self–imposition of all the public sector's constraints in our private arena is truly foolhardy.

CONFESSIONS AND ADMISSIONS

The Written Confession

Complying with the existing two constraints on private security in the matter of confessions and admissions is simple. Don't threaten, don't use force, don't suggest dire consequences, don't make deals, don't "trade" a concession for a confession. Do solicit absolutely free and voluntary admissions and confessions, and build in the *proof* in the subject's written admission or confession.

Following is an example of a typical written confession made to an investigator in the private sector. Note the choice of words that set the tone.

STATEMENT OF JACK J. DOE

I, Jack J. Doe, employee of Ruiter Air Service, make the following statement of my own free will, without duress, threats of any kind or promise of any reward or immunity, this 19th day of December, 1980.

This evening, at about 9:00 p.m., December 19, 1980, I was in the process of filling my car's gasoline tank from the Ruiter Air Service's pump located in the service yard when I was approached by Mr. Christman of the Security Department. He asked me what I was doing and I told him he caught me taking gas that was not mine to take. At that point, I had taken eleven (11) gallons. We then came to Mr. Christman's office where he asked me about previous incidents in which I took gas from the company. I told him the first time I took gas was in the middle of 1979, during the very beginning of the big gas crunch. I remember that first night I took exactly five (5) gallons because I was low and had a date over in Middleton. I was afraid to alter the pump record because it could easily be discovered. I just cleared the pump reading each time with my key.

I've taken over five (5) gallons a week ever since July of last year. Mr. Christman asked me to compute that loss. I figure at the most, five (5) gallons a week for eighty (80) weeks, which comes to 400 gallons. I understand our cost is presently $1.29 per gallon. My calculation is I've taken $440.00 worth of gasoline from the company and if given the opportunity, I'd like to make restitution.

I know I'm going to lose my job and I deserve to. I truly regret what I have done, but at least I feel better now that it has all come to light and is over.

This typed statement was the result of my conversation with Mr. Christman. He then typed it up. I've read it and it says what I want to say. Again, this is my statement which I voluntarily offer and Mr. Christman has been very fair with me tonight.

(Signed)   Jack J. Doe, 10:40 p.m., 12/19/80

Witnessed: Sidney R. Christman, Asst. Security Manager
                   19 Dec 80

Such a statement should withstand the test of scrutiny in any judicial or administrative hearing. Consider how much this statement tells:

- The author.
- The date it was written.
- The time it was written.
- Who actually composed the words.
- How it came about (subject being caught in the act).
- When he first got involved in trouble.
- His estimate of the frequency of similar incidents.
- His estimate of quantity taken.
- His calculation of the financial loss to the company.
- That the relationship with security was positive.
- That the statement was made and signed freely and voluntarily.
- That no threats or promises were made.

The tone of the statement, which is sincere, is a true reflection of the subject's attitude at the time the statement was made. This usually does not change appreciably. If he later challenges his statement, he will have an uphill struggle because of its tone. It would be hard to perceive a villainous security investigator behind this statement. To add to its voluntary quality, we suggest that a word be omitted in one sentence and that another word be misspelled. Have the subject correct these errors in his own hand and initial the corrections. If the statement has more than one page, have the subject sign his name in the bottom right-hand corner of each page, including page 1, and write "page 1 of 2" and "2 of 2" to show clearly how many pages are included.

The sample confession by Jack J. Doe printed above is narrative in format. Another acceptable format is the question-and-answer. For example:

Mr. Christman: "Think back. Can you recall for me the very first time you took gas?"

Mr. Doe: "Yes, I remember it was at the very beginning of the big gas crunch in the middle of last year. I remember the first time. I had a date in Middleton and was low on gas. I took exactly five (5) gallons."

The writer personally favors this format over the narrative. It does, however, require the presence of either a stenographer or tape recorder, with subsequent transcription.

Typed Statement vs. Handwritten

Typed statements are preferable if the subject makes corrections and initials them. Why this preference? Typing is easier to read, has a more professional impact, and suggests that time was not a factor (because typing is quick). It also allows the investigator to assist in composition, which is acceptable as long as it is so noted in the statement.

The Written Admission

The written admission may be the only signed, self-incriminating document the investigator can obtain. Whereas the written confession is usually signed at the conclusion of the interrogation, and is frequently reduced to a typewritten document, the admission is taken early in the interrogation, in the handwriting of the subject, and is limited to a simple statement of guilt.

Its advantages include these factors:

1. It is secured right after the verbal admission of wrongdoing, which is an emotional peak for the subject. In the eyes of the subject, the simple written sentence or two is no different than the oral admission, so there is less reluctance to sign.
2. If, after some time passes, the subject decides he or she does not want to sign a confession, the investigator at least has the admission, as opposed to having nothing.
3. Once the admission is secured, its existence tends to mitigate against any later reluctance to sign a full statement, or confession, the logic being, "I've already signed once, so what's the difference?"

Typically, an admission comes about in the following manner. The investigator, while on surveillance, observes an employee take a $20 bill from the cash register and put it in his shoe. The employee is taken in custody to the executive offices. Upon being advised that he was observed stealing, he produces the folded bill from his shoe.

Investigator: *(Unfolding the bill)* "I appreciate your sensitivity to the problem, Bill, and also appreciate your spirit of cooperation. You said you took it, but you don't know why. That's an important statement. Would you please make that statement here for me? (*He hands Bill a tablet of paper and a pen.*)

Bill: "You want me to write that down? Here?"

Investigator: "Please. Just the way you said it to me."

Bill: "Why do you want it?"

Investigator: "I want it as part of my investigative file. I'm not asking you to write down anything that's not true, or anything you didn't say or do, am I?"

Bill: "No, that's what I did and said, all right."
Investigator: "Okay. Just put down what you said, but start with the word 'tonight,' because it did happen tonight, right?"
Bill: "Right."

Bill then writes out in long hand or even prints his brief admission, which reads, "Tonight, I took $20 from the register and I don't know why." Bill shows the statement to the investigator.

Investigator: "Good. Now date it. Today's date is June 10, 1980." (*Bill dates it.*) "Good. Now sign it for me if you will, please."

Bill signs the admission and hands it to the investigator. The investigator signs the document, dates it, and affixes the time of day after the date.

The investigator now has a signed admission of a breach of company rules (improper removal of company funds), the primary concern of the private sector investigator, as well as an admission of theft (a public offense), which may or may not be a matter placed before the judiciary.

Value of the Confession

There is divided opinion over the value of confessions. Charles E. O'Hara, a noted authority and author of the fine text *Fundamentals of Criminal Investigation,* says, "There is a tendency on the part of even professional investigators to exaggerate the value of such a confession and to misinterpret its significance. The written confession does not, for example, prove the matters to which it pertains."[20] He goes on to point out that confession is difficult to get into evidence and that the normal defense is that the confession was obtained by duress, etc.

That controversy or difference of opinion over the value of confessions rightfully belongs in the public sector. In the private sector, there is no question whatever of the importance of signed statements admitting misconduct or dishonesty. A statement taken from one private person by another private person is an entirely different matter from the situation in which an officer of the law takes a statement from a citizen. In the public sector, such statements serve but one objective: to help sustain a criminal conviction in a court of law. In the private sector, such a statement supports and justifies the action of the company — e.g., discharging employees, terminating contracts, arresting customers — and *may or may not* be used to help sustain a criminal conviction in a court of law.

How many times has a shoplifter, for example, having been found Not Guilty in a court of law (where conviction requires evidence *beyond a reason-*

able doubt, the determining factor in criminal law), then turned around and sued the store for false arrest or false imprisonment? In many such cases, the existence of a signed admission of guilt has either discouraged pursuance of the action, or in the action has weighed heavily in the *preponderance of evidence* (the determining factor in civil law) on the side of the defendant (the store).

Written admissions and confessions, then, are an offensive strategy in the public sector where the objective sought is a conviction. In the private sector they are defensive (with offensive capability), and are thus a necessary and valuable strategy.

Chapter 12

The Use of Informants

In a later chapter devoted to the "Where" in investigations, our focus is primarily on sources of information in both the public and private sectors. Just about anyone has access to information available in the files of the Department of Motor Vehicles, the Registrar of Voters, Municipal Court records, Bureau of Vital Statistics, etc. A variety of data in privately held files is also readily available to any legitimate investigator.

As valuable and indispensable as these general sources of information are to the investigator, private and confidential sources are even more important. Such confidential sources are commonly referred to as "contacts." Who are they? According to Fuqua and Wilson, "Contacts are people willing to provide information which the investigator would not normally have access to."[21] That distinction alone separates confidential sources from the generally available sources.

There are other important differences. Investigative sources such as those described in Chapter 15 will provide data that could lead to locating a suspect. A private source, or contact, can tell the investigator where the suspect is. The information contained in certain records might well suggest the motive for an act or crime, such as arson, but the contact can tell the reason with absolute certainty. Records and documents might indicate or even prove that a given incident occurred after or before a specific date; the contact can advise as to the precise time. General sources of information might unfold a pattern upon which an investigator could predict future acts, such as thefts occurring while the supervisor is on a day off, but the informant can provide the specifics of the next planned crime. A contact or informant, furthermore, can advise of individuals who are actively engaged in misconduct or theft when such activity is unknown to management or security.

Suffice it to say that the development and maintenance of good informants has great value for the private investigator as well as the public law enforcement counterpart. O'Hara speaks not only of the pure value but of the productivity of such sources of information: "One informant in the San Francisco area is responsible for an estimated 2000 arrests a year, mostly in narcotic offenses."[22]

PROFESSIONAL CONTACTS

The first category of private sources are professional contacts. They are, for the most part, other investigators or security personnel and security executives. As a rule they provide confidential information only when it is solicited directly.

At first blush it may seem inappropriate to classify other investigators as "private sources," but the validity of this premise becomes clearer when it is held up against the Fuqua-Wilson definition cited above. On examination it should be evident that an Investigator A, working in the public transportation industry, will not automatically obtain the information he desires simply by calling Investigator B, who works on the opposite side of the country in the heavy manufacturing industry. There is a very real and legitimate professional restraint that inhibits the passing of information. And Investigator B, not knowing Investigator A on a personal basis, may very well be hesitant about providing information which the inquirer "would not normally have access to."

On the other hand, there is an equally powerful, unwritten professional code that requires Investigator B to assist if possible. How does he resolve this dilemma? More often than not he will refer to a professional publication, such as the American Society for Industrial Security's membership directory, to verify Investigator A's identity and status. If no listing is found, Investigator B may refer to the cross-referenced listing of A's employer to determine if any member of that company belongs to or is listed in the directory. If he locates another name, B may call that individual and confirm A's identity. He may even go so far as to advise A's associate of the request for information and inquire if such information is necessary and should be released. Then, and only then, B may provide the information sought. The point is that not many people normally have access to what B has in the way of information; it isn't "readily available."

Where individuals or companies are known to each other, the sharing of information on a private basis is more readily accomplished. An investigator of one company may come into possession of valuable information he will wish to share with another company. For example, during the course of an investigation in Company A, information is developed that an employee has a boy friend who is employed as a receiving clerk in Company B. That boy friend is discovered to be working in collusion with a driver of a trucking firm. The employee of Company A is selling to co-workers, at a very low price, merchandise stolen by her boy friend from Company B. An investigator in Company B ends up as the recipient of some very valuable and sensitive information from an investigator in Company A — a professional source of private information.

INFORMANTS

The second category of private sources are private contacts, more popularly known as informants. It is possible to classify at least seven kinds of informants:

1. One-time informants
2. Occasional informants
3. Employee informants
4. Anonymous informants
5. Criminal informants
6. Personal informants
7. Mentally disturbed informants.

The One-Time Informer

The one-time informant usually has very specific information and is anxious to see that information acted upon. The motive behind providing the information is commonly based on moral grounds: what is happening is wrong.

These informants give a lot of thought before acting. They are usually nervous about what they are doing, and they seek assurances that their identity will not be disclosed. Some see the act of informing as a civic duty or in keeping with their religious convictions. One-time informers may be employees (who are discussed later as a separate general classification of informants), and if so they tend to view the passing of information as good for the welfare of the company. This is particularly true if the employee has a vested interest in the success of the enterprise. Another variation on motivation for the one-time informant is revenge. The informant may be seeking to get even with someone for a slight or a wrong; evening the score is viewed as "the right thing to do."

In most cases it is difficult to gather additional information from the one-time informant after the initial contact, although not impossible. The difficulty lies usually in the informant's "second thoughts" about involvement.

This is not always true. A few such informants are so committed to seeing the matter resolved that they become quite participative. In one case an informant, a female resident of a nearby community, went through the typical soul-searching. She initially called and stated that one of our employees, whom she identified by name, lived on the same block as her own residence. She stated that the employee in question was using and dealing in marijuana. According to her testimony, the employee was also stealing goods from the company and had a quantity of stolen merchandise in his garage.

What bothered this informant most was the fact that she had two impressionable sons who had always looked up to the employee, who was now bragging about his newly acquired wealth and how easy and profitable it was to steal. Although the informant's fear for her own safety was secondary to her concern for her children, she felt strongly that, if the employee discovered she had informed on him, violence would follow. She was reluctant to stay in touch and provide additional information until she caught her younger son with marijuana. The mother then was fiercely determined that the employee should be brought to justice. Thanks to her, the thief was apprehended and convicted.

We never heard from this informant again, although it was later learned that the convicted man moved out of the neighborhood after he got out of jail. The occasion and the circumstances prompted the woman in this case to become a one-time informer.

The Occasional Informer

The occasional informer is an opportunist who will pass along information from time to time, usually if and when it satisfies some need. This is the person who will inform on a supervisor if the supervisor's demise offers an opportunity to advance. Or he may be one who secretly envies the investigator's role in the organization (and in life) and seeks recognition and praise from the investigator or security administrator. Becoming an informant is a way of identifying with the security organization. One clear example of type time of informant was a young college student who had been shunned by a fraternity. He liked to hang around the campus police office and would occasionally provide information about illegal or improper conduct on the part of that fraternity or its members. He acted not so much for revenge as for the acceptance he felt he received from the campus police chief for that intelligence.

Whatever the motivation — which is rarely financial — the occasional informant should be quietly encouraged and praised. He or she should be made to feel like part of the investigative team. That encouragement alone will go a long way.

The Employee Informant

While it is true that an employee may be a one-time informant or an occasional informant, employees as a group deserve very special attention and consideration because of their potential as sources of intelligence. This is one category of persons who can effectively be solicited to inform through a structured program.

In any given work force there are employees who either strongly suspect or definitely know of dishonesty in the organization. Some of these employees do not approve of co-workers who steal or condone their dishonest activities. In many cases the frustration experienced by the honest employee who sees others getting away with theft leads to resentment against company management for its failure to stop the thievery. Yet management may be completely ignorant of the existence of any wrongdoing. This type of situation quickly erodes morale. It is not uncommon for the honest but frustrated employee to reason, in effect, "What the hell, if others are doing it and no one cares, I might as well get some for myself." Theft is contagious.

Why do such honest employees not promptly report internal dishonesty, thus avoiding all the frustration, resentment and possible involvement? There are two principal reasons. In the first place, many employees are unsure of whom to go to with information. Should they report to their immediate supervisor? Perhaps the supervisor is involved in the dishonesty. Should they go over the supervisor's head to someone higher in the company? Going over the boss's head is frowned on in most organizations. Uncertainty holds these potential informants' tongues and adds to their frustration. A second and equally strong deterrent is the fact that the thought of being identified as a company stooge is quite unpalatable to most people. In the vast majority of organizations such a reputation would either make working conditions intolerable or dangerous for the informant. Fear of discovery and its consequences thus leads to silence and continuing frustration.

The problem is that there is no *legitimate* or structured way for the honest and well-intentioned employee to tell the company what is happening, except by means of an anonymous letter or phone call. Therein lies a golden opportunity for management: Provide a legitimate and structured program for information to be passed up to management.

A number of firms across the country have developed formalized programs aimed at encouraging employees to report dishonesty in a confidential way. Protected anonymity is the key. J. Kirk Barefoot cites one such loss prevention reward program in his book, *Employee Theft Investigation.*[23] A program designed by this writer, which has since been adopted by a number of companies, is called the Silent Witness Incentive Award Program. Its preamble reads, "The Silent Witness Incentive Award Program provides employees of this company with an opportunity to share in substantial awards and at the same time help reduce our losses caused by thieves.'' For information leading to the detection of a dishonest employee the program paid 10 percent of the value of recovery with a minimum award of $100.00 and a maximum of $2,500.00.

This program, which is discussed with all new employees, is spelled out in detail in pamphlet form. The pamphlet is distributed to all employees. It reads, in part, as follows:

> When you have any information regarding internal theft, call the Director of Security on his private line (phone number is listed here) and describe to him, or in his absence the Security Manager, what you have observed. Your information will be treated in strict confidence.

> If you prefer to remain anonymous, you should outline the complete details of the matter in a letter. Mail the letter through the U.S. postal system to:

> > Director
> > P. O. Box 0000
> > Midtown Station
> > Middle American City, CA 90009
> > "Confidential"

> It is not necessary to sign your name; simply write any six digit number or code in the upper right and lower right corners. Tear off the lower right corner and keep it for identification purposes.

> A special bulletin will be published periodically and code numbers eligible for awards will be in such bulletins. If your number appears, you may present the torn off portion of your letter containing the number, either in person or through an intermediary, to the Director of Security (or designate) and receive your award.

The pamphlet goes on to describe eligibility to participate, which includes all employees except internal auditors, senior management and security personnel.

How effective was this program? In the first year after it was instituted over 20 employees were apprehended as a direct result of the program. In the second year over 50 employees were caught! These results are startling indeed in view of the fact that, prior to implementation of the award program, not a dozen such cases were referred to security by employees over a comparable period of time.

The Anonymous Informant

Anonymous informants obviously seek to protect their identity. As we have seen with the employee informant discussed above, the desire for anonymity may come from the fact that the informant is in or closely connected with the firm and does not want to be known as an informant. If the informant is not connected with the firm in any way, he or she may still wish not to get involved in any way beyond passing along information. What this outside informant is saying, in effect, is, here is some information, do with it what you please.

A third category of anonymous informant may or may not be connected with the firm, but what they pass on is not true. It is spiteful, degrading or disrupting, aimed at causing suspicion, fear or hostility in the organization.

If a formalized informant program is in force, the number of anonymous calls or letters from those in the first group cited here will virtually disappear except for tips received through the structured program.

Outside informants may, in fact, provide good information while insisting on remaining anonymous. However, because of the inherent possibility of false information from members of the third group, anonymous information must rank low in terms of credibility. There is always a greater chance of receiving false or biased information from an anonymous source than from an identifiable informant.

The Criminal Informant

The criminal informant is more commonly identified with the public sector of law enforcement than with private security. Prostitutes, petty thieves, narcotics users, those on parole and other assorted "street people" frequently pass information to the police. Often they are bartering information for freedom from prosecution, lengthy imprisonment or a return to prison, although money is the prime motive for some informants. One must wonder how many times hapless and amateurish purchasers of narcotics have been seized by officials because of a tip from the very party who sold the drugs — who then collects a reward.

Although generally considered essential by police and other law enforcement agencies, the criminal informant is not a major source of information to investigators in business and industry. When they do appear on the scene in the private sector, however, as they do from time to time, they are worthy of attention.

In one such case, a caller asked if my employer paid for information. After some discussion of the nature of that information, the caller agreed to a meeting. He then put his cards right on the table. He was a professional forger with a lengthy criminal record including state prison time. He claimed to be currently involved with a forgery ring. He produced nine fraudulent documents for my examination. Three were bank checks of the company, the type prepared by the accounts payable department to pay company bills. The other documents were three California Department of Motor Vehicles Operator Licenses and three Social Security cards. The checks were made payable to three different persons, with addresses included. The same three names were contained on the driver's licenses and Social Security cards. The informant's own photograph was on each license. He had three sets of identification to support the checks, each of which was made out for a sum around $2,500.00.

According to the informant, the plan was for him to go to three separate banks and establish checking accounts, using the company's checks in each case as the initial deposit. After enough time had elapsed for the checks to have cleared the company's main bank, a member of the gang of conspirators would call each bank branch where an account had been established and determine whether or not the forged check had successfully cleared. He would do this by pretending that he was a service station owner who had a customer wishing to buy an expensive set of tires and wanting to pay by check. Did the customer have enough in his account to cover a $400.00 check? If the bank said no, the fraud had failed. If the answer was yes, the depositor (who was the informant) would withdraw all the money from the three accounts. The company would remain ignorant of the theft until either an audit or a regularly scheduled bank check reconciliation occurred. The only potential flaw in the plan was the magnetic coding on the checks. The checks were masterfully reproduced, genuine works of art.

The informant sought to sell information on the location where the checks were being printed and the identity of the other members of the ring. He had reservations about his associates and wanted enough money to leave the country and spend an extended vacation in Europe. Our company, it turned out, was not the only intended victim. Other nationally known firms were also in the process of being victimized, and the informant was dealing with them as well as with us. After pocketing the money he was to receive for his information, he would then work with the police until arrests of the conspirators were made, along with the seizure of printing equipment and other materials used in the scheme. His plan was to be en route to Europe while his associates were en route to jail.

Bank and company accounting executives, believing that the magnetic coding on the checks could not be duplicated, were confident that the threat described by the informant was not as great as the security department claimed. However, the informant insisted that the coding had been successfully duplicated. The police were involved in the case. The plan unfolded. A number of people were arrested, equipment was seized, blank checks were recovered — and the informant winged his way across the Atlantic.

Oh yes, the checks did clear, in spite of the magnetic coding. Had this informant not approached us, a serious financial loss would have resulted without discovery for a matter of months.

Criminal informant situations, then, do occur in the private sector. They include, but are not limited to, shoplifting arrests where the person taken into custody will offer to deal with the security people, offering to inform on others or revealing such vital information as where stolen merchandise is "fenced." (A fence is a person or organization that knowingly buys stolen property from thieves and sells the goods at a profit.)

The Personal Informant

The personal informant is one who will deal with only one investigator, refusing to provide information to anyone else under any circumstances. Such relationships will often commence with something the investigator says or does. It could be the result of assisting a person whose car won't start, solving someone's problem by composing a letter he is unable to write, exhibiting concern for an individual's family, or even treating the janitor who cleans the investigator's office with respect. The recipient of any one of these actions, knowing what the investigator does for a living, may choose to return the kindness by providing information.

One personal experience offers an illustration of the sometimes unpredictable motivation of the personal informant. He was my first such informant, a man named Lacey. I received a call one night while doing some paper work in the Vice Detail headquarters. The caller identified himself as Lacey and asked if I remembered him. I did not. He told me that I had put him in jail for pimping. When he related some of the details surrounding his arrest, I recalled him. He told me that his arrest landed him in jail for six months. He had just been released that day. He wanted to meet me at midnight at an intersection in a rough area of Los Angeles.

"Why do you want to meet me?" I asked.

"I want to talk to ya."

"We can talk on the phone."

"Nope, I want to see ya and talk to ya."

I agreed to the meeting. Several of our brother vice officers deployed in the vicinity at the appointed time, not knowing what to expect. I parked my car near the intersection and approached with some apprehension. Lacey stepped out of a darkened area and said, "Betcha remember me better now, don't ya?"

"Sure, I do," I said, thoughtfully clutching the .38 caliber Chief Special in my jacket pocket.

"Well now, I got two whores lined up for you tonight. Wanna bust two whores?"

"What?"

"Your job is to bust whores, ain't it? And I gotcha two for tonight."

"How come you want to be so good to me, considering what happened the last time we met and serving six months?"

"Well, it's this way," Lacey answered seriously. "I sat there for six months thinking about me and you, and how you caught me. And I said to myself, of all the times I've been arrested, nobody ever treated me as nice as you did. It made me feel so good that I decided when I got out I was gonna help out the best way I know how. So I lined up two broads for tonight, and I hear there's a guy with a still makin' whiskey over near Compton. I'll line that up for ya in a couple of days or so. I like ya, man, just plain like ya."

Writing this account many years later, we can still see his smile and recall our mutual friendship — and the many cases that one personal informant steered us to. But Lacey would talk to no one else. When we left the vice detail, there was no way we could "transfer" that valuable informant to another officer. He simply disappeared after that — voluntarily, we hope.

That was a lesson not to be forgotten.

The Mentally Disturbed Informant

The last category of informant to be discussed here is, in fact, not a genuine informant at all, at least in our experience. Such people do exist, however, and for the investigator they are a tragic nuisance. They are tragic because they are sick and do not know it, a nuisance because, after your first meeting with them, usually a clandestine one at his or her request, you cannot easily get rid of them. That usually happens, paradoxically, because the investigator, upon recognizing that the supposed informant is actually a disturbed person, will try to be gentle, understanding and sympathetic as a strategy to end the meeting. The sick person, for whom rejection is a more typical experience, will latch onto that kindness as a sign of acceptance.

Sooner or later every professional investigator will, by virtue of the work itself, come into contact with the individual who purports to have information but is in fact mentally disturbed. Strangely enough, some of these persons are quite convincing at first. That may be because the investigator wants to believe what he or she is hearing. But in due course, usually quite quickly, it becomes apparent that the informant has a distorted sense of reality. Their "information" is worthless.

Treatment of Informants

The investigator who speaks scornfully of informants in all probability has no informants or, should one appear, will never be able to keep him.

Avoid using such words as "snitch," "fink," "stoolie" or "stool pigeon." Such jargon should be left to the cops-and-robbers of television. It has no place in the professional investigator's glossary of terms. Refer to an informant as a "contact" or a "confidential source."

Irrespective of an informant's motive, always treat him with the same courtesy and respect you would show anyone else. To treat all people with dignity, no matter who they are, has its rewards. That kind of philosophy somehow attracts people with information. To treat people with disdain or disrespect, no matter who they are, also has its consequences, and they do not further the investigative purpose.

The Need for Corroboration

As a general rule information received from an informant is not directly actionable. That is to say, if an informant reports that the head cashier of the firm is embezzling funds and has just purchased a new Cadillac for her boy friend, the investigator does not set up an interrogation of the suspect. The information received needs corroboration. Does the cashier have a boy friend? Did she in fact purchase a new Cadillac? How is she embezzling funds? Should the internal auditors do a cash count under the ruse of a routine check? These and many other questions have to be answered before information received from an informant can lead to a confrontation. What information does is provide the direction for further investigation.

This point is well expressed by Gene Blackwell: "Remember that the investigator seeks at all times to upgrade the status of the information he receives by having it verified and corroborated from additional sources whenever possible."[24]

Information from informants that is not verifiable in one way or another has limited value. Where such information can be corroborated, however, it can prove an invaluable aid to investigation. The use of informants, with prudent regard for their limitations and motivations, can be a productive tool for the investigator in the private as well as the public sector.

Chapter 13

Report Writing and Note Taking

It is remarkable how quickly the human mind loses a considerable part of its ability to recall the details of events. This phenomenon applies not only to events merely witnessed but even to those directly experienced. The importance of recording events in writing is clear: If an event is not recorded, it will soon be forgotten entirely or in part, or it will be distorted with the passage of time.

Everything else being equal, the difference between a good or competent investigator and one who is considered excellent is reflected in the superior investigator's report-writing skills. Furthermore, there is a direct relationship between the efficiency of a security department or an investigative office and the quality of its records and reports.

Report writing is not a peripheral activity which has little to do with real business of investigation. On the contrary, the individual who argues that he can investigate a problem and solve it but he cannot write reports is comparable to an auto mechanic who says, "I can remove and repair your engine but I can't install it back in your car." If he cannot finish the job, he is not what he claims to be. Report writing is a natural and necessary part of the very job description of an investigator. The investigator who avoids or puts off writing reports — and some do — is in the position of a fireman who avoids fires or puts off arriving at the scene of a fire. Such people are in the wrong business.

Defining the Investigative Report

In the absence of a generally accepted formal definition of an investigative report, the following is offered: An investigative report is *a clear, comprehensive, written documentation of facts, presented chronologically, which is*

an objective, first person recording of the investigator's experiences, conver-
sations and observations regarding a specific assignment, and from which the
events of the investigation can be reconstructed even after a lapse of time.

The investigative report reflects, in writing, the investigator's work on a
case. As suggested in our definition, it should be able to withstand the test of
time. A good report, when read by a stranger five years later, will make as
much sense as it did to the author on the day it was written. The ultimate test
of a good report is simply this: If the reader of the report has a question, the
report is deficient.

NARRATIVE REPORTS

A report is most easily understood when presented in the first person
narrative style, and the heart of any investigative report is the narrative body.
In many organizations, in fact, the narrative comprises the entire report.

An effective narrative report must include the key elements of our definition. Extracting those elements, a good report must be

- A writing
- Told in first person narrative
- Objective
- Factual
- Chronological
- Easily understood
- Comprehensive
- Able to withstand the test of time.

A Writing

There is no substitute for the written word when it comes to the investigative report. Despite the availability of videotape recordings, audio recording
capabilities or any other item of hardware, the report must end up on paper.
Even if the investigator dictates his report, the net result will be the written
word on paper. No other kind of report can be as quickly reviewed, and no
other so successfully meets the requirements of being both comprehensive and
readily understood.

Since the final version of the report is in writing, it follows that correct
grammar, spelling and punctuation as well as legibility will reflect either favor-
ably or unfavorably on the author — the investigator. He does not have to be a
consummate stylist, but he does have to be able to organize and present his
facts clearly. Lapses in grammar, spelling and punctuation often have the

troublesome result of making things unclear. So, obviously, does an unreadable scrawl.

Told in First Person Narrative

The use of the first person narrative is recommended because, for the average person, a report flows more naturally in this style. If we write as we think and talk, the material tends to become both easier to write and easier to read. The following, for example, is both stilted and unnatural: "The undersigned then asked the victim's supervisor if he recalled the time of the phone call. The supervisor advised undersigned that the call was approximately 3:00 p.m." A more natural first person rendition of this report might read, "I asked the victim's supervisor if he recalled the time of the phone call. He told me it was sometime around 3:00 p.m." The use of such expressions as "this writer," "this investigator" or "the undersigned" is not wrong or bad per se, but it does tend to become awkward and cumbersome.

Again, write as you think, and write for the reader.

Objective

The investigative report is no place for speculation, hypothesis or opinion (the investigator's judgment or prejudices). If the reader of the report engages in any of the above, as a result of the facts presented, that is his prerogative.

This is not to say that the investigator should not have opinions or engage in speculation. But any such subjectivity should not be included or reflected in the report itself. If there is any need for subjective expression, it should be made in another or a different report, such as a memorandum to the investigator's supervisor.

Factual

The problem of an investigator reporting non-factual information in his report does not, as a rule, occur intentionally. The common mistake is for the investigator to *assume* the facts are there when they are not. *Example:* "Employee Jones then clocked out at the end of his shift, 4:00 p.m., and went home." Maybe Jones went home. Maybe he went to the Red Rooster Bar & Grill. More factually the investigator's report should have read, "Employee Jones then clocked out at the end of his shift, 4:00 p.m., and left the company property." At a later date that "fact" concerning Jones going home could come back to haunt the investigator.

Consider another example: "Jones left the Red Rooster Bar & Grill at about 9:15 p.m. and drove off in a rented Cadillac, further description and license plate number unknown." The information about the rented car was obtained from a waitress. Factually the report should have read, "According to the waitress, Jo Dennis, Jones left the Red Rooster Bar & Grill at about 9:15 p.m. and drove off in a Cadillac that Jones claimed he had rented. At this time we have no further description of the car or the license number." The difference between these two statements is obvious. In the first, the investigator includes a conclusion or assumption about the car, based on the waitress's input, but it reads like a fact. The second statement is indeed a report of facts. It is a fact that the waitress gave certain information. There may be some question about her telling the truth, but there is none about what she reported. The reader of the report would unquestionably view the information about the rented car differently, depending upon which report was read.

Chronological

The investigator's report is a record *of his own work*. The chronology of the report, then, is concerned with the investigative process, not with the crime or incident under investigation. The chronologically structured report is the unfolding, in order of time, of what the investigator did. The following report offers a typical example:

> On Tuesday morning, November 16, I interviewed subject Jones' landlady, Miss Rose Hovely, who told me that Jones rents a small room in the rear portion of the garage for $35.00 weekly. She said that Jones moved in during the 4th of July holiday weekend earlier this year, and every week pays his rent with rolled coins, mostly quarters and dimes. She said she personally didn't like to handle the coins, they were heavy to carry to the bank. When she asked Jones why all the coins, she said he told her he was a coin collector. "Some coin collector he must be," she said. "Whenever he comes home after too much drink, there's coins lying around the driveway and grass by his door."
>
> I returned to the General Offices and met with the head cashier, Mrs. Rubin Angelo. She produced for my examination the history of daily vending machine receipts for 1979 and 1980 by machine, location of machine in each facility....

How the report unfolds will coincide with the investigator's verbal testimony concerning the same events as it might be given in an administrative or judicial inquiry. Observe the chronology unfolding in the following testimony:

Q.   Now, after taking the report of an unexplained decrease in vending machine revenue and after conducting a second and more thorough investigation into the newest employee's background, Mr. Smith, then what did you do?

A. I went to Mr. Jones's residence and spoke to his landlady.

Q. Why?

A. I wanted to determine how Mr. Jones paid for his rent. If it was by bank check I was hopeful the landlady could tell me which branch. Once I knew the branch I hoped to learn if he made deposits with coins.

Q. Did you discover his bank and branch?

A. No, I didn't.

Q. What did you discover, if anything?

A. I learned that Mr. Jones has always paid his rent with rolled coins.

Q. After learning that, what did you do?

A. I returned to our General Offices and . . . .

The chronology of the crime under investigation will be pieced together and presented, either in summary form as an introduction to the report itself or in a summary of a suspect's confession. That chronology, however, is secondary to the sequence of events in the investigation itself.

Easily Understood

The report must be written so that it is easy to understand. Small, familiar words are better than words of many syllables. Short, clear, direct sentences are preferable to long compound or complex sentences. The *Security Investigator's Handbook* recommends sentences of no more than twenty words, a good rule of thumb.[25] If technical terms must be used in the report, define or explain them. The report is not meant to be a literary materpiece, but rather an accurate and easy-to-understand story of the investigation.

Comprehensive

A report is comprehensive when it has both scope and depth in terms of specific and pertinent facts. That is not to suggest the report should be wordy; on the contrary, it should be as brief as possible. But some space must be devoted to detail when detail is germane. Take, for example, the description of a person who is considered the responsible party in a crime. A comprehensive report would include all of the following in the description:

- Name, including aliases and nicknames
- Address and phone number
- Sex
- Race
- Age

- Height
- Weight
- Hair color and style
- Color of eyes
- Build
- Complexion
- Beard
- Teeth
- Unusual mannerisms or voice accent
- Dress habits
- Birthplace
- Amount of education
- Occupation
- Avocation or hobby
- Relatives and friends

In one recent case, a number of people were meeting during evening hours in the back room of a public restaurant. As part of an investigation under way it was important to identify those in attendance. Because all participants in the gathering had to arrive by vehicle, the logical approach was to identify them through the vehicles, by running the license plate numbers through the Department of Motor Vehicles.

There was an inordinate delay in getting the desired information. Finally we called for the responsible supervisor. We were advised that the name of one party obtained through the vehicle license records was a mysterious name. The investigators could not account for it, resulting in the delay. We asked to see the report. It read essentially as follows:

"Surveillance teams in position on N, S and E sides of the lot at 1830 hours. Suspect vehicle arrived at 1915 hours, followed by below listed vehicles:

Time	License No.
1915	DDC 768
1918	JPR 098
1922	BVD 432
1925	EXS 101"

On the following day the investigators took that list of licenses and followed through on them. Most vehicle license information comes back from motor vehicle departments as follows: License #FFE343, 1979 Ford, Joe and/or Mary Henn, 8424 Camelback, American City, Nebraska. Comparison of vehicle and owner identities indicated that a mistake had been made. It was finally determined that two numbers in one of the license plate identifications had been transposed.

The failure of the investigators in the listing of autos during their surveillance was one of comprehensiveness; the report lacked the necessary depth of detail. The human error that always creeps into detail work — in this case the error of transposing numbers on a license — would have been detected immediately if the initial listing of numbers had been done in something like the following fashion:

Time of Arrival	License #	Auto Make	Approx. Yr.	Color	Style
1915	DDC 768	Plymouth	77	Yellow	2-door
1918	JPR 098	Buick	78	Maroon	Regal
1922	BVD 432	Ford	72	White	Pickup
1925	EXS 101	Chev	75	Blue	4-door

Had an investigator then transposed the numbers of the second car's license plate, the vehicle license information on record might have shown "JPR 098, 1974 Toyota, etc." A comparison of the two reports would immediately have disclosed the error and given direction for further investigation to resolve that error. Such is the value of comprehensive information.

The Test of Time

As our definition of an investigative report suggested, the report should be so written that the events of the investigation can be reconstructed from the report even after a prolonged lapse of time. Consider whether this is true of the following example:

> John McCall from Headquarters called Mr. Switzer, Senior Investigator, on September 19, 1979, and reported his suspicion that a cashier in Unit 33 was slipping twenty dollar bills out of banded bundles. Thus daily bulk counts failed to reflect shortages, but when bundles were broken for use such bundles were short.
>
> On Sept. 22, 1979, I observed Catherine Goltz slip a bill from a banded bundle just after opening the safe at 8:00 a.m. She was removed from the cashier's office and taken to the Personnel Office, where she admitted to me her theft of this day as well as numerous prior thefts, as listed below. . . .

At the time this report was written, it might well have been quite clear in its record of events. At that time there was no question whatever about the who, what, where, when and how of the matter under investigation. But that report will not necessarily stand the test of time, as a closer examination will show.

At the time of the report, we may assume, every security supervisor and investigator knew John McCall; he was an upcoming internal auditor and very pro-security. In fact, John passed on more information to security than the rest of the internal auditors combined. It was also well known that internal auditors worked out of the Headquarters operations. And everyone knew that Unit 33 was the numerical designation for the facility in Stanton. But in the course of five years a number of things change. Perhaps McCall left the company for a better position the same year the report was written, and the chief internal auditor was promoted and transferred to another division of the corporation. Three years after the report, the internal audit function was part of an organizational realignment, and was moved out to the data processing facility. At the same time unit number 10, an old and unproductive part of the operation, was closed down. Following that, the numerical designations for other units were abandoned. And finally, as luck would have it, the investigator who wrote the report and his supervisor both moved on to other jobs.

In the short span of five years, this report obviously leaves much to be desired. It would have been dramatically improved if the original writer had simply included John McCall's title and department, and if he had avoided using a code number instead of the proper name of the location cited in the report. Eventually, it is true, the information given in the report can be tracked down, but that is not the point. The content of an investigative report should not require research later. It should not require questions.

Nor are the omissions already cited the only missing pieces in this sample report. Consider that part of the report about observing the theft. How was it observed? The report does not offer a clue. At the time the report was written it may have been common knowledge that cashiering operations had built-in surveillance grills in the ceiling. Investigators would lie concealed above the ceiling and observe the employees handling money. But what if, two years later, a court determines that procedure is an invasion of privacy and, as a result of that decision, surveillance positions overlooking work areas become a thing of the past? We are personally aware of similar surveillance arrangements that were later a source of astonishment to new investigators.

Many things change with time. The investigative report written today should not cause confusion or be incomprehensible a few years later.

STRUCTURED OR FORMALIZED REPORTS

The heart of the investigative report, the narrative body, often constitutes the entire report, as previously stated. Some organizations, however, make use of a more structured form that includes a heading section, the body or narrative, and an ending or conclusion. The latter is simply a statement of the status of the investigation, no more and no less.

The heading portion of a preprinted investigative report form usually calls for answers or information that fits into boxed spaces. Almost anyone can fill these out without difficulty. An exception might be the type of form sometimes used in the private sector that includes the nine parts of a *modus operandi*. Here some confusion can set in about the kind of information required. The following breakdown suggests the type of answers required to those nine basic questions.

Question	*Answer*
1) Time of attack	Date and time the offense was committed.
2) Person attacked	Type of person attacked, e.g., female child.
3) Property attacked	Type of location where the offense took place, e.g., single story retail store.
4) How attacked	The way in which the person or property was attacked, e.g., theft of goods.
5) Means of attack	Instrument, tool, device, trick or method by which the person or property was attacked, e.g., placed goods in lining of jacket designed to accommodate stolen items.
6) Object of attack	Why the crime was committed or attempted, e.g., to sell stolen goods for money to support drug habit.
7) Trademark	Any peculiarity which may serve to distinguish the offense or offender from others, e.g., crawls behind counters in the store to avoid detection.
8) What the suspect said	What and how the suspect spoke to victims or witnesses, not to the authorities, e.g., upon discovery claims he's looking for the men's toilet.
9) Transportation used	Description of vehicle used. If no vehicle seen or heard, so note.

NOTE TAKING

It is difficult to imagine an investigator writing a formal comprehensive report, whether in a structured format or as a complete narrative, without referring to notes taken during the course of the investigation. Good note taking is as important in the investigative process as it is in college courses. It is essential.

There are three specific needs for on-the-spot notes by the investigator. These are

1. *Recording times.* It would require a very superior intelligence to recall accurately all the dates and times that are so important in the investigation.
2. *Recording full name.* Besides full names of witnesses, including their proper spelling, notes should list their title or rank, address, home and business phone numbers. The investigator cannot rely on securing printed business cards from everyone connected with the case.
3. *Recording quotations.* Quotations can be a powerful part of the investigative report. If a person is to be quoted directly in the report, however, those words will lack credibility unless backed up by the investigator's notebook. That is because the report is frequently not written until the case is finalized. Days or even weeks may have elapsed, and it is a difficult challenge to try to explain how you can recall someone's exact words days or weeks later.

The notebook should be small, pocket-sized, and bound so that pages cannot be added or removed. A 3″-by-5″ notebook will fit conveniently into a breast pocket of a man's coat or jacket.

In a formal hearing, attorneys will often attempt to authenticate or discredit the investigator's report, and his memory of events, by determining the time differential between the date of the incident or conversation and the time when that incident or conversation was written in the formal report. Invariably the investigator called as a witness will be asked something like the following: "Your report (or testimony) is very explicit about what Miss Hovely said about the coins, yet you wrote the report six days after that conversation. Did you make any notes during or immediately after that conversation?" If the investigator says no, his report (or testimony) immediately loses credibility and force. If the investigator says yes and is able to produce those notes when asked to do so, his report (or testimony) becomes credible and impressive.

The fact that, as indicated in this example, the investigator's notebook can be asked for and examined by an adversary attorney or hearing officer is an important consideration. The investigator should not write anything in that book which might mitigate against the case. *Example:* One investigator who was interviewing neighbors about a suspect employee made a personal note in his notebook that read, "Employee must be queer." Such a comment could raise all kinds of claims of bias and lack of objectivity about the investigation and unnecessarily discredit the real, objective work of the investigator.

SUMMARY

The finished investigative report is a reflection of the skill level of the investigator. Effective report writers will observe and remember these basic principles:

1. Use a personal notebook which will serve as a basis for your report.
2. Write as though you are telling someone what happened.
3. Use small, easy-to-understand words. Avoid technical or professional terms if possible. If that is not possible, define or explain the terms.
4. Be impartial and objective in what you report.
5. Only report what you know to be a fact; do not report assumptions.
6. Write the report as a chronological unfolding of events.
7. Be certain the report is understandable in terms of what actually happened.
8. Be certain that important information is not omitted.
9. Be prepared to support quotes with notes. Quote exactly. If offensive or obscene language is used, quote it, don't soften it.
10. Be sure the report raises no unanswered questions.

IV. APPLYING INVESTIGATIVE STRATEGIES

Chapter 14

Identifying Suspects:
The Who of Investigation

The first of the basic questions in investigations is directed at establishing *who is responsible for a given act.* It should be understood that there are many other questions of identification that might be asked in any investigation. Who can be trusted to keep the inquiry quiet if confidentiality is needed? Who can provide technical information or assistance? Whom should the investigation be assigned to? Who might know who did it and be willing to inform? Considering the type of investigation, who might be the most effective interrogator after the responsible party is caught?

But the most important and popular question asks, Who is the responsible person, or culprit? That question is the very stuff of which mystery novels are written, the reason such stories are called "whodunits." After determining what happened, which is usually (though not always) apparent, all minds immediately commence the speculative process designed to discover who could have done it.

The Process of Elimination

In the fanciful world of mystery novels, the suspect is usually one of a small cast of clearly defined characters. It had to be the butler, the disinherited nephew, the brother-in-law, the wife in the wheel chair, etc. Interestingly, in most cases in the private sector dealing with internal problems there is also a relatively small cast of possible suspects. Take, as a typical example, a series of thefts from a cash register. If a total of seven employees have access to that register, it is from that small cast that we must identify our prime suspect.

As in the murder mystery, the first steps are designed to eliminate *who it isn't*. The disinherited nephew is the most likely candidate but he could not possibly have killed the old man because he was locked up for drunk driving in the city jail at the very hour the crime occurred. This process of elimination is applied until only a few suspects — or preferably one — are left.

In our register theft case, we would plot or chart the history of the losses and compare that history to be record of the seven employees' attendance, as illustrated in Figure 14-1. This graphic chart tells us that employee Leland can be eliminated because he was off work when a theft occurred on February 23; Beutok because he was out ill when two thefts occurred on February 19 and 20; Daniels because he was off duty when three of the thefts occurred, on February 1, 8 and 15; Sanchez, because he was on vacation during one week when three of the losses occurred; and Rundstedder, because he was sick on Friday, February 5, when $40.00 was taken. Only Wagner and Morton remain as suspects and deserve watching. The process of elimination has reduced the number of suspects from seven to two, greatly simplifying the investigation.

The Case of the Anonymous Letter.   In one actual case a college student received an anonymous letter concerning his fiancee. The letter was obscene and luridly graphic in describing the alleged sexual orientation and history of the young woman the student loved and was about to marry. Although he did not believe the charges in the letter, the student was deeply disturbed to know that someone who knew both him and his betrothed would write such a letter. He did not wish to involve the police or postal authorities, but he did ask for my assistance as the chief of campus police.

We listed on a piece of paper everyone who knew the young man and his fiancee. That list constituted our cast of characters; on that list was the suspect, the author of the letter. Since we were in possession of a typewritten letter, the next task was to obtain, secretly, samples of typed material from the typewriters owned or used by all those persons on the list. The sample was to be one full paragraph taken from the offending letter so that a direct comparison could be made.

Typewriter after typewriter was eliminated because the samples could not match the original letter. Finally, all of the student's friends and work associates had been eliminated, at least in terms of typewriters known to exist. There were only three machines left to be checked — the three in his parents' home. Somewhat reluctantly at this point, the student brought in sample paragraphs from two typewriters, one in his father's study and the other in his brother's room. In each case the type did not match the original.

I asked about the third and last typewriter in his home. Where was the sample from that one?

"Oh, you can forget that one," he said. "It's my Mom's. Besides, it's in her bedroom and she spends a lot of time up there. I don't think I can get to it anyhow."

FEBRUARY	Mon 1	Tue 2	Wed 3	Thu 4	Fri 5	Sat 6	Mon 8	Tue 9	Wed 10	Thu 11	Fri 12	Sat 13	Mon 15	Tue 16	Wed 17	Thu 18	Fri 19	Sat 20	Mon 22	Tue 23	Wed 24	Thu 25	Fri 26	Sat 27
Cash Shortages	$20		$20		$40	$40	$20		$40		$40		$40				$50	$50		$40	$50			
Wagner				X						X						X						X		
Leland		X						X						X						X				
Morton		X						X						X					X					
Beutok				X						X						X	X sick	X sick				X		
Daniels	X						X						X						X					
Sanchez		X											⎯ V A C A T I O N ⎯							X				
Rundstedder				X	X sick					X					X							X		

X = DAY OFF

Figure 14-1. Cash register timetable

After some persuasion the student brought in the typed sample from his mother's typewriter. It matched! The student refused to believe it, becoming very upset and defensive of his mother. I did not accuse her but simply told him that, in my judgment, the original offensive letter had been typed on his mother's machine. He wanted proof. Through the low-powered microscope he was able to note the same distinctive type characteristics that I had found.

Several days later the young man's father came to the office, quite angry. He calmed down after making the same microscopic comparison. Shortly after this discovery the student and his father confronted the mother with my findings. She then admitted authoring the letter. She did not want her son to marry for fear of losing him. The drama-packed emotional confrontation and confession brought recognition of the mother's need for medical help.

No chart was feasible in this second case, but the same process of elimination was applied to determine which of the suspects were innocent, until only the guilty one remained.

Reading the Physical Evidence

In some cases, either through chance or circumstance, the elimination process is not necessary. A proper reading of the physical evidence will point the investigator toward the offender.

The Case of the Missing Eyeglasses.   One night several students scaled a main building on campus and draped over the facade an uncomplimentary message aimed at the school's administration. Lying on the roof after the escapade was a pair of eyeglasses. The cleanliness of the glasses indicated that they had not been exposed to the elements for any length of time but had been left there recently. The obvious conclusion was that they belonged to one of the students who had hung the sign.

The thickness of the lenses made me wonder how their owner had ever got down from the roof without them, let alone climbed up to the roof while wearing them. It was reasonable to assume that the owner could not go very long without a new pair of glasses. If the local optometrists could not identify the owner through the lens prescription, they could be alerted to notify me if and when anyone showed up seeking new glasses with the same prescription.

Those eyeglasses were like a calling card. Before the day was out, the student's identity was known. A local optometrist recognized the glasses. I called the subject and told him that I had his glasses and he could pick them up at my office. He wanted to know where I found them. When I informed him, there was a long silence on the phone. I asked him about that silence later. He said, "I was just thinking to myself ... what if I'd done something *really* bad?"

A Case of Red Paint.   The semester was about to end. Summer vacation was a matter of days away. I was called at about seven in the morning at my home by a member of the administration of Scripps College, frantically reporting that a great deal of damage had been done during the night to statuary and Shakespearean reliefs at the college.

At the scene I found that someone with a bucket of red paint had prowled the inner courtyards and passageways, applying the paint to the genital areas and breasts of a large number of wall reliefs and statues. The removal of the paint would be very costly; moreover, it could well cause the loss of some of the details created by the artists.

By carefully examining the paint droppings on the tile and stone flooring, I was able to follow the route the vandals took as they moved from art object to object. Partial sole markings left in some of the paint droppings also established that there had been more than two persons involved.

The last object painted was near the front and side of the building complex, adjacent to a broad expanse of lawn that separated Scripps from the neighboring men's college. By crouching close to the ground it was possible to track the red drippings on blades of grass across the lawn. The trail brought me to the wall of the home occupied by the men's college president. Painted on the wall in letters three feet high was a lurid, two-word obscenity. In terms of how we think in the private sector, the damage done to the statuary was a misdemeanor, but the writing on a president's house changed the case to a felony!

I continued to follow, at times on hands and knees even though dressed in a business suit, the trail of infrequent drops scattered on the leaves of grass. It led back across the lawn to a clump of bushes at the side of Scripps College. There in the bushes was the paint can and brush. The can was not really a paint can but a container used to package candy. The brand was unfamiliar. It was a product manufactured in Phoenix, Arizona. The paint brush, too, was not really a paint brush. It was a wadded up portion of the *New York Times,* of a recent date.

Who composed the cast of characters for this offense? The evidence pointed to immature students of the men's college. Why immature? My experience with the upperclassmen of Claremont Men's College, an outstanding academic institution, convinced me that none of these older students would be involved in such a foolish and destructive episode. Female students at Scripps, on the other hand, would not be likely to deface their own campus. Moreover, they had no quarrel with the president of the men's college.

Given this conclusion and the evidence I had tracked down, my task then was to identify those freshmen and sophomores at Claremont Men's College who (1) came from the greater Phoenix area and (2) subscribed to the *New York Times,* or any two young men who roomed together at the college and who together would meet my twin criteria. Within an hour those few students whose homes were in the greater Phoenix area were listed. Shortly after that the mailroom provided me with the names of those students who received the *New York Times.*

One freshman met the criteria. His dormitory room was empty when I called there. The door was unlocked and I went in. The chrome handles of the bathroom sink were sticky with red paint. The soap bar and the white interior of the wash bowl were pink and also sticky with red paint. The balance of the New York newspaper not used as a paint brush was still in the room.

I left the building and went to the parking lot set aside for that school. The student's automobile, parked in the lot, was examined. Red paint drippings were visible on the ground behind the car, as though a can had been opened there and the paint transferred from one can to another.

The physical evidence gathered within a few hours was enough to lead to the identity of several young men, who were subsequently dismissed from college. The trail of red paint and the evidence were able to point to the culprits, but only when that evidence was read accurately and the judgment was made eliminating older Claremont students and Scripps College students. Finding the physical evidence that is there is only the first part of the investigator's challenge. He must also be able to interpret the significance of what he finds.

The Investigative Interview

Often the available physical evidence alone is insufficient to point to the "who" of an incident. In such cases the investigator must track down every possible detail that might be relevant. One of his tools is the careful and thorough questioning of any person or persons affected, whether victim or witness, as the following case illustrates.

A Case of Kidnap and Rape.   Late one spring evening I received a call from a house mother, the resident manager of one of the girl dormitories at Pomona College. She reported that she had a serious problem and insisted on my presence. When I arrived, there was a campus police unit as well as a local city police unit parked in front of the dormitory. Both units advised me that a campus unit had been requested and the city unit had acted as a backup. When they reached the scene they were informed by the house mother that a girl had been raped, but the manager then refused them admittance to the dormitory.

Once inside the building I had a brief conversation with the reported victim about what had happened. Although she seemed to be in a state of shock or near-hysteria, she told me that she had gone to the basement of the building, where the coin-operated washer and dryer were located, to do one load of washing. When she pushed through the double swinging doors of the washroom, she was startled to see a young man standing there, brandishing a knife.

According to the girl's story, the attacked forced her to crawl out of the basement through an open transom window. He followed her out. After climbing over a wall that surrounded the dormitory area, she was forced into the back seat of a four-door sedan. There she was trussed up, lying on her stomach while wrists and ankles were bound behind her back. With the girl helpless on the floor of the car, the man drove up into the nearby mountains. There he raped her.

After the attack he drove back into town, releasing the girl at the intersection closest to the dormitory. She could not get in because it was past lockout time, the hour when every girl had to be inside. She pounded on the door until the house mother heard her and let her in.

Immediately after this initial interview I had the girl transported to the hospital for (1) a vaginal smear for evidence of semen, (2) a medical douche and (3) medication to calm her. Before she left I told her that we would meet again in the morning, along with the local police, and talk more in depth.

After the girl left I examined the scene of the alleged attack, carefully inspecting the basement area. Lying on the floor just inside the double swinging doors was a box of detergent, some of which had spilled on the floor; two quarters; and a few items of intimate apparel. Nearby was an open transom window; beneath it was a bench. While standing on the bench I was able to peer outside. I could see clear foot impressions in the flower bed. I set a cardboard carton over those prints. (I would take plaster of Paris casts of those footprints the next day.)

At the hospital the following morning, a representative of the police and I sat with the girl to get more details about her experience. The report of the attending doctor had confirmed that there was a seminal deposit.

The girl described her attacker. During the course of the questioning a number of details were gone over carefully. She had been wearing a "baby-doll" nightgown when she went to the basement, a sheer, loose, short-sleeve pullover top with matching briefs. She did not attempt to run, even though she was out of the building first through the transom, because she was afraid. She scaled a six-foot wall, although she probably could not do it again. She had no idea what kind of car was involved. She did not fight or resist the man because he threatened her. While up in the mountains, the attacker at first had tied her wrists to separate trees, her arms stretched out in a spread-eagle position. Later he had untied her, and she admitted that, during the drive back into town, he had left her untied and sitting up on the front seat of the car.

It became apparent that the police representative was skeptical of her story. He became aggressive in his questioning. To one question she admitted that she was not a virgin. For my part, I continued the interview with the belief that she was telling the truth — in which case I needed specific details, as suggested by the following exchange.

"Can you recall if the rear-view mirror hung down, came out from the windshield, or came up from the dashboard?"

"I don't remember."

"Was the front seat and seat back cold or warm?" It had been evening, and the answer would indicate a cloth or synthetic seat covering.

"Cold, come to think of it."

"Was there a radio in the car?"

"Yes, I remember music, and I remember him saying he wanted to hear a news flash if there was one ... about us."

Of the many minutiae included in the questioning about the car, the following proved invaluable: "Did you see any words, numbers or symbols on the dashboard?"

"One time I put my foot up on the dash, and I remember the word 'Eight' was right by my toes."

"Printed or in script?"

"Script. And in chrome. The word went up at an angle like this." The girl motioned with her finger.

"Did he smoke?"

"Yes, cigars."

"Cigars!"

"Yes ... in fact, I remember, on the way back, he put the stub of his cigar in the ashtray and it started to smolder. I was choking on the smoke so I reached over to close the ashtray. He yelled at me, 'Don't push in that ashtray. You'll put out the light!' Then I realized there was some kind of light connected with the ashtray, and the light shone down around my legs."

In interviewing a victim or witness, it is important to get every detail possible. In searching questions about the suspect rapist, I asked the girl to recall everything he said to her, sometimes repeating questions in the effort to learn absolutely everything she could remember. As I continued to probe she suddenly said, "Oh! I remember one thing he said that I didn't understand at all. He said, 'The landscaping at Pomona College stinks!' "

When I left the girl at last I had a considerable amount of information about the "who" of this case. I set about locating a man about twenty-five years old, blond, stocky, about 5'8" tall, whose choice of words coupled with his coarse, rough hands suggested that he was a blue-collar worker or laborer. I knew also that he had an opinion, for whatever reason, on landscaping. Additionally, he drove a two-toned, light-over-dark, 4-door sedan that did not have cloth seats and had very dirty, uncarpeted floors.

The search in this case was complicated by the fact that the police were of the opinion that no crime had in fact been committed. They believed that the girl had been out having fun and was caught by the dormitory's lockout policy. To protect herself against any disciplinary action, she contrived the kidnap and rape story.

Believing otherwise, I asked the maintenance people of the college to provide me with a list of every contractor and subcontractor who had worked on or around the institution. At the same time automobile manufacturers were queried in an effort to identify the auto used in the crime. Was there any model auto equipped with a light switch connected to the ashtray and also a chrome script "Eight" that ran at an upward angle on the passenger side of the dashboard? The answer came back: there was one such car, for only two model years, the 1952–53 Pontiac.

I requested that the police ask the Department of Motor Vehicles for a listing of all 1952 and 1953 Pontiacs registered in Los Angeles and San Bernardino counties. They felt that was asking too much. I then asked if they would assist in obtaining auto registration information for all the license plates on such cars that I could come up with. They agreed, despite their belief that I was on a wild goose chase.

Meanwhile, contractor after contractor hired at one time or another by the college failed to throw any light on the search. About the fifth day of this full-time effort, I called a water sprinkler contractor who had sub-contracted an installation at the college the previous year. I made the call just before lunchtime, asking the now routine question: "Did you have a young man working for you while here on the campus, someone in his mid-twenties, about five-eight, with blond hair?"

"Sure did," came the answer. "His name's Bob Greene."*

"Where's Bob now?" I asked, attempting to sound calm.

"Gee, I don't know. Haven't seen Bobby in a year, I guess."

"Don't you have his last known home address?"

"No."

"You must have some kind of records for tax withholding purposes, workman's compensation and the like."

"Oh, I don't keep those kinds of things. My bookkeeper keeps all that."

"What's her name?"

"It's a him."

The contractor gave me the name and phone number of the bookkeeper. I called him immediately, explaining that the contractor had given me his name, and asked if he could provide me with Bob Greene's home address. Within a few minutes I had the suspect's home address, which was in a neighboring city.

---

*The name is fictitious for the purpose of this work.

I went home for lunch but could not eat. I left the table and drove to the address on the note tucked into my shirt pocket. Parked in the driveway of the house, which was in a somewhat run-down residential area, was a dirty, two-toned, light-over-dark, 4-door 1953 Pontiac sedan. On the back seat of the car lay a rope. The seats were covered in vinyl, the floors uncarpeted and dirty. Cigar butts were in the ashtray.

Later that afternoon, Bob Greene was picked out of a police lineup as the assailant by the victim of his attack. Before the day was out Greene admitted the abduction and rape of the girl. He was convicted for his crimes and served time.

SUMMARY

Investigation is a very inexact science which we must nonetheless approach as a science. My intriguing aspect of the cases cited in this chapter is that these cases were solved more by common sense and persistence than by sophisticated skills. Check every possibility, get others to assist, follow up on the most minor piece of evidence, obtain every possible detail, and stay with the search tenaciously — these are the laws of our "science."

In seeking to identify the "who" of a case, remember. . . .

- Eliminate those who could not have played a part in the incident.
- Collect and analyze all available evidence.
- Look for relationships between evidence and possible suspects.
- Where possible, obtain the assistance of law enforcement.
- Make full use of available information sources (e.g., automobile manufacturers).
- Do not jump to conclusions or pre-judge the case.
- Make full use of the investigative interview.
- Persist, persist, persist.

Chapter 15

Finding Information: The Where of Investigation

In attempting to determine who was involved in a crime or incident under investigation, the emphasis is on the search for identity. When attention turns to the question of "where" in an investigation, the emphasis is one of discovery. The question of "who" is people-oriented. The question of "where" is location–oriented.

As with the first question, there can be a number of location questions that might be relevant to a given case. Where is the offender? Where is the evidence? Where are the fruits of the crime? And where can information be found that assists in the investigative process? Locating individuals, physical evidence or stolen goods, when they are not discoverable through the routine of physical search, is often a matter of knowing where to look for the right information.

The effective investigator knows where to find the information he needs, just as an effective lawyer knows where to research case law. Sources of information are all around us. Some may be so conspicuous and familiar that their potential is not realized, as the following two investigations illustrate.

The Case of the Missing Mascot.   The student body president of Claremont Men's College reported that someone had stolen the school's mascot from an unlocked building over the weekend. The issue was an emotional one. As a rule, students take a dim view of the theft of their mascot.

The prize in question was a life-sized stag deer, poised on a platform, that could be carried by from four to eight men on their shoulders. The size and weight of the mascot made it obvious that several people had to be involved in carrying it off, and that a truck or trailer had to be used to remove it any considerable distance from the college.

Security officers who had patrolled the area over the weekend were asked if a truck or trailer had been seen near the building that housed the stag. One officer had observed a Chevrolet car pulling a yellow, tandem-wheeled trailer in that immediate area. The auto was occupied at the time by what appeared to be college students, and nothing particularly suspicious was observed by the officer.

Even though the possibility of finding any physical evidence was remote, I checked the area carefully. My search came up with a wing-nut lying in the gutter of the street alongside the building from which the stag was removed. The wing-nut had yellow paint on it. The wing-nut appeared to be of the type that is used in pairs to hold the rear gate of a trailer in place.

Turning to the first basic investigative question, I asked myself who could steal a college's mascot. College students from a rival school, of course! What would be the motivation for absconding with their rival's prized possession? Again an obvious answer suggested itself. The thieves probably intended to parade the captured stag, with something less than decorum, at the next football game in which the rival schools met. If that premise was true, the potential for a small riot was clear. The stag had to be recovered before the game in question. Where was it?

The telephone directory held the answer. I obtained a phone book for every city in which a rival college was located. I began with the book for the city in which was the college that was scheduled to play Claremont the upcoming Saturday. Using the yellow pages of the directory as a guide, I telephone every trailer rental agency in that city, asking, first, if their trailers were painted yellow and, secondly, if they had a tandem-wheeled trailer. In my calls to the third city on my list, which was the home of the University of California at Riverside, I received affirmative answers to both of my questions. Riverside was scheduled to play Claremont Men's College in a football game in three weeks. I then asked if the four-wheeled trailer had been rented over the past weekend. It had been. I asked the man on the telephone if he would check the tailgate to determine if the trailer was missing one wing-nut. There was a short wait until he returned to the line. He said, "Why yes, it is. How did you know?" There was a puzzled note in his voice. "I have it and I'll bring it over," I said. "I'll be there in an hour and a half."

The rental agency was a Riverside service station. When we returned the wing-nut to the tailgate of the tandem-wheeled trailer, we then examined the rental agreement. It contained the name of the renter, his driver's license number, address and automobile license number.

I took my information to the University Police at Riverside. The renter of the trailer was a registered student. When confronted with the evidence, he admitted his involvement and told us where the stag had been hidden. As we had guessed, the thieves intended to use the mascot to put down their Claremont rivals during the forthcoming game.

The student body president of Claremont Men's College and several other students triumphantly returned the stolen stag to their campus — thanks to one wing-nut and a telephone directory.

The Case of the Stolen Calculators.   Another case that hinged on locating stolen property involved the theft of ten expensive small calculators from a Broadway Department Store. One of the company's many stores specifically ordered the calculators from the manufacturer. The shipment arrived in that store accompanied by an invoice. The invoice was approved and forwarded to the accounts payable department of the finance division for payment. The calculators were placed in a locked stockroom behind the camera department. The manager of that department saw the calculators in their original shipping carton on several consecutive days. Then the calculators disappeared.

Security was advised that the calculators were gone. An investigator from the main office was assigned to the case and dispatched to the particular store. A search revealed the original shipping carton in a trash deposit. Several key employees of the store, including members of management, were questioned about the calculators. One member of management seemed unduly nervous. There was, however, no evidence against him or anyone else.

Two weeks passed and the case remained unsolved. Only one possibility suggested itself. The nervous management employee, whom we will call Mr. Dunbarr, was conspicuously upset each time the investigator reappeared at the store. The conclusion was reached that Mr. Dunbarr was the thief, despite the fact that he was known as a very religious man and a leader in the community. If he stole the calculators, what did he do with them? If they could be found, we could possibly connect them with Dunbarr. But without them there was no evidence against him, only suspicion.

In thinking the matter through, it became apparent that the special order for the calculators must have been put through to satisfy a request. An order for ten units would have come from a commercial source rather than a private party. Further, it was concluced that Mr. Dunbarr would be one of the few individuals who could walk out of the store carrying a large box or parcel without arousing suspicion. He must have carried the calculators out and delivered them to the party who had placed the initial order. It seemed probable that that party might be ignorant of any wrongdoing. The calculators might have been paid for in cash or a personal check made out to the executive under suspicion.

If this hypothesis was correct, the next logical assumption was that the purchaser would naturally have acted to protect his legitimate investment by forwarding the product warranty cards identifying each calculator to the manufacturer.

We pulled the serial numbers from the invoice. The next morning a call was placed to the manufacturer, located in another state on the other side of the country. All ten warranty cards had been received. They had been mailed to the manufacturers from a travel agency in a community near the Broadway store.

A team of investigators went to the travel agency. The stolen calculators were observed in use on various desks. The owner was asked to talk in the privacy of his office. There he openly discussed his interest in and eventual purchase of the calculators from the Broadway. He had dealt with one of the store's executives, a gentleman who was a friend and a member of the travel agent's church, Larry Dunbarr.

"How did you pay for the calculators?" he was asked.

"By check. I would never carry that much money around on me."

"To whom was the check made payable?"

"To Larry. He said he'd take care of it back at the store."

"Do you have that cancelled check back from the bank?"

The agent was becoming agitated. "There's obviously something seriously wrong or you wouldn't be asking me these questions."

"That's why we're asking questions. It appears you may be the innocent victim of receiving stolen goods."

"How could they be stolen when I got them from your company?" he protested.

"You may have made payment for the calculators, but that payment was never received by the company. As far as the company is concerned, the calculators are missing from the inventory. Stolen, if you please. And you have them. That doesn't look good, does it?"

"But I paid for them," the agent cried. "One thousand dollars!"

"Mr. Green, you got a real bargain for a thousand dollars, and you know it. The truth of the matter is, either you were in collaboration with Mr. Dunbarr and knew these calculators were 'hot,' or he took advantage of you. We tend to think the latter is true and we expect your cooperation. We want the calculators — we'll give you a receipt for them — and we want your cancelled check."

We received the travel agent's cooperation.

If such simple and readily available sources of information as a telephone directory and the warranty files of a manufacturer can make the difference between success or failure in an investigation, imagine the almost unlimited number of sources that are ignored, unknown or untapped.

The detailed listing of private and governmental information sources on the following pages is by no means all-inclusive. Nor does listing here always imply easy access. In some areas the information is extremely difficult to obtain. In others the information is there for the taking. The important point is to appreciate the vastness of the sources of information available to the investigator. How one accesses these sources is essentially a matter of skill, ingenuity, personal contacts and tenacity.

SOURCES OF INFORMATION
IN THE PRIVATE SECTOR

In seeking to discover the "where" of an investigation, the diligent investigator will familiarize himself with the wealth of files and records in non-governmental sources containing information pertaining to persons, companies, personal property and real property. Not all personal records are equally accessible, but a great deal of information *is* available.

Banks

Savings accounts can provide information regarding the balance in the account, dates of deposits, whether deposits were made in cash or by check, and amounts of deposits. Amounts and dates of withdrawals are also on record. Checking accounts contain the same information regarding deposits plus check activity, including the number of checks written during a given period, to whom and for what amounts.

Loan Companies

Loan applications reflect employment data, primary income and other sources of income, property owned and its location, state of indebtedness in terms of amounts and to whom owed, and a variety of personal and family data.

Credit Reporting Agencies

Most trade, professional and business entities have their own credit reporting agency, such as retail credit agencies. They have information in detail about customers by name, marital status, spouse's name, number of dependents, present and former addresses, how long at address, credit rating, companies that have dealt with customer before and that history. The major business (as opposed to personal) credit reporting agency is Dun and Bradstreet, which maintains historical data on businesses and the principals connected with the business.

Title Insurance Companies

Title insurance company records identify the owner of a given piece of property, latest address of that owner, date property was purchased or sold, and the amount of that transaction.

Telephone Companies

From just a phone number in the telephone directory one can determine where the phone is located and the identity of the subscriber. Other phone company records contain information on the length of service at that address and where previous service was located, monthly billings and an itemized record of toll calls. There are also "reverse guides," listing subscribers by address as well as the alphabetical listing. Unpublished telephone numbers are on film.

Other Utility Companies

Applications for water, power and gas service will reveal some personal information on subscribers, as well as where they had previous service, when service commenced and a history of usage. Most utility companies maintain records by address, so occupants of a given address can be identified (except for rental property where the landlord pays the utility bills).

Van and Storage Companies

Moving and storage records will reveal where an individual came from and when, or where he is going. If goods have been stored, it may be possible in some circumstances to examine the goods in storage.

Insurance Reporting Services

Your firm's counsel or risk management executive can direct you to the agency that maintains files on bad risks and histories of claims filed against carriers.

National Auto Theft Bureau

An example of one kind of insurance reporting service, the National Auto Theft Bureau publishes a directory with all state license plates, in color, as well as location of each state's motor vehicle licensing agency. The NATB also maintains files on all known auto thieves, experts on auto identification, and methods of theft.

Funeral Directors

In addition to financial data on the deceased and facts about the estate and survivors, funeral directors are often privy to a great deal of gossip and other casual information about the survivors as well as the deceased.

Taxicab Companies

Cab companies maintain records of trips, including the time and location at which a taxicab took on a fare, the passenger's destination and amount of fare. Some packages are also sent by cab. Some individuals will have cabs pick up liquor and deliver it to themselves.

Auto Rental Agencies

The records of car rental agencies will reflect driver's license information, local address of the renter, mileage driven, and the names of others authorized to drive the rented vehicle. The same records will also have a description of the car rented.

Drug Stores

Prescription files of drug stores will reflect, for each prescription, the doctor's name and address, date prescription was written and date filled, type of drug (from which it may be possible to determine the ailment), and patient's name and address. Drug stores also maintain a poison register that records type of poison purchased, the quantity, to whom sold and reason for purchase.

Film Processing Company

A neglected source, film processors may be able to provide photographs of a subject, his family, friends and surroundings.

Real Estate Offices

The records of realtors will include the asking and selling price of a given property, names of seller and purchaser, amount paid down, name of the mortgage company holding the first trust deed, and a description of the property, often quite detailed.

Hospitals

Hospital records contain patient information, including their treatment and medical histories with that particular facility, as well as insurance data and other personal information.

Newspapers

Newspapers, like any other business, maintain files on the names and addresses of subscribers and advertisers. In addition, the newspaper "morgue" file is a cumulative file on every person whose name has ever appeared in the paper, including a photograph if one was used in a story. Newspapers also maintain a library of every issue in the paper's history.

Schools

School records include the name and address of every student, with date of birth and place of birth. Personal data on each student will include name and address of each parent, the parent's occupation and place of employment, whom to call in the event of an emergency, and the family doctor's name and number.

Colleges and Universities

In addition to personal data similar to that found in schools, college and university records may provide such information as extracurricular or off-campus affiliations and activities, academic objectives, grade point average, major field of study, financial status of the student and work history while attending school. Class yearbooks include student photographs. Some *alumni associations* also have up-to-date mailing lists of graduates, with a current history of each.

Housing Projects

The administration offices of housing projects maintain files on tenants by name, address, age, number of children, former or forwarding address, place of employment and salary (if salary is a determining factor in residing in the project, which is normally the case), rent payment history, and history of complaints by other tenants, if any.

Better Business Bureau and
Chamber of Commerce

The Better Business Bureau keeps files on all scam operations and operators in the community. The Bureau can provide information on the business reputation of local or distant businesses or can report that no derogatory information about a business has been recorded. The local Chamber of Commerce can provide a map of the community with an overview of climate, growth, primary industry, population and other data. The Chamber of Commerce will also have information on local businesses, and will have copies of back issues of the city directory.

DIRECTORIES AND PERIODICALS

The telephone directory cited in a case history earlier in this chapter is only one example of an almost inexhaustible quantity of printed matter available to the investigator as sources of information. As one small example, take three publications in the security industry: *Security Management* magazine, *Security World* magazine and the American Society for Industrial Security's membership listing by member's name and by the member's company's name. These three publications are a mine of information about who we are, where we can be found, what we do and how we go about doing our work. The same kind of information is available about almost every occupational specialty in this country, from accountants to zoologists.

The following list suggests some of the most common and useful directories. No attempt is made here to list the enormous number of periodicals available covering every field; in this connection the directory of periodicals is a valuable source.

City Directories

Each city publishes a directory containing the name, address, occupation and sometimes the place of employment of residents of that city. Back issues can provide the same information covering previous periods.

American Medical Directory, Foreign and Domestic

The *American Medical Directory* lists presidents and secretaries of all county medical associations. Also included are lists of all hospitals and all medical doctors by the cities in which they work. Individual listings give the doctor's date of birth, medical school attended and date of graduation, year of license to practice, home and office address, and his or her area of specialization. There is also an alphabetical name index.

Directory of Newspapers and Periodicals

This directory is a guide to newspapers and periodicals printed in the United States, with a description of the city or town in which they are published. Each listing gives the name of the periodical, frequency of issue, political posture, date established, size, price of suscription and circulation.

Reader's Guide to Periodical Literature

As opposed to data concerning the periodical itself, the *Reader's Guide* lists magazine articles by author, name of magazine and title of article. The articles are also listed under their general subjects.

Cumulative Book Index

As the *Reader's Guide* provides an index to magazine articles published, the *Cumulative Book Index* lists all books published each year in the English language. Both the *Reader's Guide* and the *Cumulative Book Index* are standard reference works in libraries.

Who's Who

The *Who's Who* contains biographical information on prominent persons. Similar biographical compilations are available covering prominent individuals in different fields of endeavor, including authors, scientists, etc.

Hotel Red Book and Directory

The "Red Book" lists hotels in the United States, Canada, Mexico and some other countries. The listings are alphabetical, according to the city, by name, address, number of rooms, type of plan, rates and innkeeper's name. Similar information can be found in a variety of travel guides for hotels and motels.

Baird's Manual of American College Fraternities

Baird's Manual provides a complete listing of fraternities and sororities, both active and inactive. Data for each organization include the history, objectives, numbers and locations of each, and their individual publications, if any.

Mallett's Index of Artists

This index provides a listing of painters, sculptors, illustrators, engravers and etchers by name, birth date, place of birth and address.

INFORMATION SOURCES IN LOCAL GOVERNMENT

Government agencies at every level often seem to be in the business of collecting and maintaining files and records of every description. While privacy limitations may restrict access to some personal information, most of the data accumulated in such files is a matter of public record and available to anyone. Municipal and county records useful to the investigator include the following sources.

Tax Collector

Records of the local or county tax collector include the names and addresses of property taxpayers, legal description of property, amount of taxes paid on real and personal property, and the status of taxes — whether delinquent, for example. Tax records also include the names of all former owners of a given piece of property.

Building Department

Building permits record the name and address of applicant, location of construction, amount and cost of construction, and blueprints and diagrams showing details of the building.

County Recorder

The County Recorder's office is the repository of such records as all papers pertaining to real estate transactions, mortgages, certificates of marriage, wills, official bonds, transcripts of judgment, births and deaths and bankruptcy records. The detail included in some of these records is quite extensive. The birth certificate, for example, includes name of infant, sex, date and hour of birth, exact location of birth, if the birth was premature or full term, the parents' names, ages, addresses and occupations, length of time in the occupation, mother's maiden name, the condition of the infant and the name of the attending physician.

The death certificate is even more striking an example. It gives the name, address, sex, age, race, birth date and birthplace of the decedent; place, date and time of death; how long the decedent had been in the community, the country, the hospital (if death occurred herein); whether the decendent was a veteran and, if so, what war; the Social Security Number; marital status, with name and age of spouse; occupation of decedent; parents' names; mother's maiden name; and the name and address of the person who is reporting the death. If death occurred while under a doctor's care, the medical certificate will reflect the doctor's name, how long the decedent was under treatment, the last time seen alive and the doctor's statement as to the cause of death. If the decedent died while *not* under a doctor's care, a coroner's certificate will reflect whether death was accidental, suicide or homicide, date and location of death, whether death occurred at work or not and, finally, the disposition of the body, including information concerning burial, cremation or removal (with place and date), and funeral director's and embalmer's names and license numbers.

This kind of exhaustive detail is common in most governmental records. Marriage license applications and divorce filings similarly offer much information to be searcher.

Registrar of Voters

The affidavit of registration reflects the name of the voter, age, address, occupation, political party affiliation, state of birth, where and when naturalized if foreign-born, any physical disability that prevents registrant from marking his or her own ballot, and the last previous place of registration.

Welfare Department

Very complete files in the Welfare Department include information on where and when a person worked, salary, what property the recipient owns, property owned by relatives, state of health, criminal background information, and detailed data concerning immediate members of the family.

County Recorders Civil
and Criminal Indexes

The Civil Index lists all civil actions, usually alphabetically by plaintiff and defendant, and by date with a reference file number. Criminal actions in the Superior Court are listed alphabetically in the Criminal Index by defendant with a reference file number to the Criminal Files. (See below.)

County Recorders Criminal Files

In addition to reflecting the type of crime, the County Recorders Criminal Files include a transcript of the testimony given in the Preliminary Hearing, which in turn provides names of all officers and witnesses, and a copy of the Probation Department's report on the defendant's background.

County Recorders Probate Index

The Probate Index lists actions alphabetically by the name of the estate or petitioner for causes of action relating to adoptions, incompetency, insanity and termination of probate.

INFORMATION SOURCES IN
STATE GOVERNMENT

Various state departments maintain voluminous files on individuals and corporations. Many are either open to inquiries by ordinary citizens or will provide information for a small fee. In addition to the specific officers and departments noted here, most states have a regulatory relationship over vocations such as doctors, dentists, athletes, pharmacists, barbers, optometrists, veterinarians, chiropractors, contractors, embalmers and nurses. Personal data would be available in these and other vocational files, in some states through a department of professional and vocational standards.

Secretary of State

The Secretary of State has records of all articles of incorporation of businesses, associations and churches. The same source also has a record of all names which have been legally changed, and maintains records on election returns and candidates for elective state offices.

Controller

The State Controller keeps an account of all warrants drawn on the state treasury, examines and settles accounts of all persons indebted to the state, and inspects the books of persons charged with receiving, safekeeping or disbursing state funds.

Department of Agriculture

As might be expected, the Department of Agriculture controls weights and measures and performs other tasks related to agricultural activities within the state. It has information on dairies, state licensed veterinarians, stallion registration and cattle brand registration, among other agricultural data.

Department of Motor Vehicles

Records of automobile ownership, past and present, are maintained by the state's Department of Motor Vehicles. Files include licensed operators of vehicles with a history of moving violations and accidents. In many states, photographs of licensed drivers are available. In general, files may be accessed in two directions. If the driver's name is known, data can be provided on make and model of vehicles owned and operated, and the license numbers. If a vehicle license number is known, its owner can be identified. In most states motor vehicle information is available to ordinary citizens for a small fee, usually by mail. Law enforcement agencies have direct and swift access.

Department of Industrial Relations

This department maintains files on industrial accidents and, usually, oversees trade apprenticeship programs. Its files may also include records on unfair labor practice problems based on charges of discrimination.

Department of Natural Resources

The Department of Natural Resources maintains complete files on such matters as mining operations, parks, forestry activities, fish and game licensing and violations, and oil, coal or gas operations within the state.

Department of Alcoholic Beverage Control

Files kept by the Alcoholic Beverage Control Board include information on licensees reflecting name, addresses (both home and business), marital status and detailed background history.

OTHER SOURCES

With respect to sources of information at the federal government level, very little can be said of current value to the investigator, simply because very little information is available. This is primarily a result of Right to Privacy legislation.

This is not to say that a one-on-one relationship with a representative of any given federal agency would not be useful and productive. The opposite is true. If, as an example, a Post Office Inspector and an investigator from a major corporation had a case of mutual interest, undoubtedly there would be an exchange of information. The same applies, of course, at the state and local government level as well.

In the same vein, no attempt has been made to list as potential sources of information the many law enforcement agencies at every level of government. Again, the one-to-one personal relationship, based on mutual need and respect, can produce results that otherwise would not be possible.

Chapter 16

The Time Factor:
The When of Investigation

The question of "when" in the investigative process is obviously time-oriented. The question seeks to isolate and identify a significant time factor, be it a time before or after a known event, a span of time between known events, or a specific time.

Known time can eliminate possibilities — e.g., a bus could not make it from the east side of town to the west side in ten minutes. It can also eliminate suspects — e.g., when the fire started, Harry was on his day off. Further, the determination of when an offense occurred or is occurring gives direction to the detection strategy. If money is being pilfered from a given location regularly, for example, it simplifies the investigation to determine that the pilferage must be occurring between 5:00 a.m. and 7:30 a.m.

With regard to criminal offenses, the entire issue of the statute of limitations revolves around the time factor. The perpetrator of the crime must be identified and moved against within one year after the commission of the offense (the general rule for petty or misdemeanor offenses) or within three years (the general rule for major or felony offenses). Consequently, if the discovery of a crime takes place months or years after its commission, the task is to prove that the offense occurred within the period specified under the statute of limitations.

Through this text, in citing examples and case histories, both actual and hypothetical, there have been a number of references to the time factor. In many of these examples the times determined are only approximate, but even such approximations can be valuable, as this review suggests.

1. Placing the hand on   Reveals the car has *recently* been driven if
   the hood of a car: hood is still warm.

2. Horse chips: The degree of hardness tells *when* horses passed this way.
3. Coals in center of fire: Reveals *when* the fire was last fed.
4. Post mortem lividity: Reveals time of death.
5. Rigor mortis: Helps determine time of death.
6. Sap in tree limb
   fracture: Suggests *when* the branch was broken.
7. Damp side of stone
   turned to the sun: Shows *when* stone was disturbed.
8. Dry clothing of suspect Reveals amount of time suspect has been
   when it is raining: inside the store.
9. Cash register "plot   Establishes which employees could or could
   chart":   not have committed thefts, based on the time factor.

Just as much energy and imagination may be expended to determine the significant time factors in an investigation as are devoted to determining who did it. And again, as in other aspects of the investigative process, much can be achieved through the application of common sense and the power of observation.

METHODS OF ESTABLISHING TIME

Self-Evident Time

Perhaps a classic example of establishing the precise point in time when an incident occurred is the case of the smashed watch on the wrist of the dead driver of a vehicle which careened off a mountain road, an accident unobserved.

More often than not there is no way to determine time with such precision, but there are a surprising number of what might be called self-evident time indicators. The simple situation of a tea kettle boiling on the fire is one example; it could not have been at the boil for long or the water would have evaporated in steam. Among literally thousands of such examples that could be cited is one involving a typed document dated in the 1960's which had been typed on an IBM Selectric typewriter — prior to the production of the Selectric. The evidence speaks for itself.

A minor incident offers further illustration. It occurred when, by chance only, I noticed a quantity of rubbish and trash that had been illegally dumped along an isolated dirt road in a remote area reserved for nature studies. The trash appeared to have been recently dumped, as indicated by the fact that the papers were not weathered in any way.

Personal trash is often an interesting source of information in any investigation. In this case I wished only to identify the person who chose to litter this protected natural area. Among the trash was an envelope addressed to a resident of a neighboring community. It was postmarked three days prior to my discovery. Also found among the rubbish was a personal note addressed to the same individual.

I telephoned the party in question, a woman, and instructed her to get back in her car, drive out to the area and retrieve her trash. At first she feigned ignorance, claiming that she had just walked in the door upon returning from a two-week vacation. She could not possibly have done what I accused her of. It was not difficult to convince her that she should clean up the mess she caused. Had there been no way to pinpoint the time factor in this matter, however, her story would have been more difficult to shake. As it was, the evidence of "when" was impossible for her to overcome.

Significant Time Variations

Relevant considerations of time can frequently be determined by noting a variation in an established process or pattern of activity.

Theft of money is a typical problem in the work environment, whether the victim is the company, an employee or guest, a client or customer. Usually the discovery of a loss requires an immediate assessment of when the theft could have occurred. Determining the time factor is usually a key to identifying possible suspects.

A typical example is theft from cash registers that hold money overnight when the premises are closed. In the usual procedure, all the money in the register is removed temporarily at the end of each working day. From that total quantity, a daily "bank" or working fund is subtracted from the total and replaced in the register. The drawer is then closed. The balance of the money removed from the register represents the day's receipts from that register, which are deposited. The following morning a person other than the one who closed the register the previous night opens it and counts the "bank" (which is always the same amount, such as $100.00). If there is a variation from the established amount, that variation must be reported.

Most registers have the feature of an inner or "detail" tape that records each transaction as the day progresses — e.g., the thirty-third time the register was opening on April 16th was a sale in the amount of $23.46 by employee Smith. Additionally, in a normal operation, some member of management will clear each register, usually with a special key, at the start of the day's business. This clearing allows for the daily audit of sales, and each day starts back at the zero transaction number. Put another way, a series of "No Sales" are rung on each departmental and clerk's key, erasing the previous day's totals. The register then awaits the new day's business. The first time it is activated, it will record that transaction as number one.

When the employee opens the register in the morning to verify the bank, that entry constitutes the first transaction. If on that entry the bank is found to contain only $80.00 instead of the established amount of $100.00, there is a $20.00 shortage. In determining who could possibly have stolen this money, the investigation must first determine, if possible, when the theft occurred. Did it happen at night during the closing procedure? At night after the closing procedure? In the morning during the clearing procedure? After the clearing procedure but before the first regular transaction? Or during the first normal transaction?

As a rule, such thefts do not begin and end with one act. They tend to occur with growing frequency until the culprit is caught. Given the circumstances outlined, the investigator would take the detail tapes for days on which no losses occurred and compare them with the tapes for days of loss. If the person who opened or closed the register took the money, the tapes would show no variation. The same would be true if the management or security representative who cleared the registers was the thief. (In fact, these three persons would be unlikely to steal *from this particular source.*) The tape comparison frequently will reflect an additional entry for those periods when theft occurred. If a night crew remains in the building for housekeeping or maintenance purposes, the culprit's entry will be a "No Sale," and it will follow the last legitimate entry made during the closing procedure. In effect, the tape will show two closings. If, on the other hand, the thief enters the register after it is cleared in the morning or at night, the tape will reflect two number one entries. The legitimate initial entry is actually the second of the day.

In this example, as in many other situations, a variation from the established norm can help to pinpoint the time factor.

Determining Time by Incidental Documents

The time an incident occurred can sometimes be determined by an examination of incidental documents, as in the following cases.

In one case, while working as a vice investigator, we seized a pornographic film that portrayed felonious conduct, an unnatural sex act. Before the District Attorney would issue a criminal complaint, it was necessary to establish that the unlawful action occurred and was photographed within the past three years. The act in question was being performed on a living room sofa, in front of which was a coffee table. On the table was a newspaper. Enlarging the picture made it possible to read the headline on the newspaper.

A check of all the newspapers in the metropolitan area disclosed which paper had carried that headline — and on what date.

In a very similar case, empty beer bottles were in some of the scenes photographed. At that time a popular California beer packaged its product with a large gold-and-red "X" as the dominant part of the logo on the label. The brewery referred to its beer as "age-dated," and indeed each label bore a black printed date in the very center of the X. In this case, the frame of the motion picture including one of the beer bottles was enlarged to a size where the date on the label could be read. As in the case involving the newspaper headline, the photographs could not have been taken at an earlier date. Filming had to have occurred on or after the dates established, making it possible in both cases to establish that the incidents occurred within the period covered by the statute of limitations.

Another example of determining time by way of an incidental document was the discovery of a store receipt in the pocket of a dead man. The time of death was unknown. The dated receipt established that he had to have died on or after that date.

As a final illustration, there was an incident in which a customer of a retail store complained about the quality of help she received while shopping for a bedspread. Her note sharply criticized store management for permitting horseplay at the expense of good customer service. The complaint concluded with the statement that the customer had made her purchase in spite of, not because of the employees in the department. She insisted, moreover, that she would never shop there again.

The customer did not mention the day or hour of her experience. However, her charge account reflected the purchase. The cash register certification on the sales check showed not only the date but the transaction number. The detail tape on the register certifying the sale showed that more than sixty transactions had occurred that day; the customer's purchase was next to the last one. The documentation revealed that the incident occurred on a Wednesday at the very end of the evening. Armed with that intelligence, store management was able to take corrective action.

Determining Time by Events

Many events play an important role in our lives. These events tend to be time benchmarks. They may be daily events, if the focus is on recent times, or they may be of an annual nature, such as Christmas or one's own birthday. The effective investigator is able to use events to help establish the time factor when it is relevant.

The Case of the Telephone Tap. In one investigation, a manager was asked when he first noticed his phone acting strangely.

"Oh, maybe three or four months ago," he answered vaguely. "I don't recall exactly."

"Well, this is October. Do you think it was in the middle of summer?"

"Yes, I do know it was in the summer."

"Maybe you can associate that first suspicion with something that happened during the summer. Did you take a vacation this summer, for instance?"

"Right! And it was just after I got back that I noticed something funny. I remember now, we went to Nebraska to visit with my wife's folks, and to spend the Fourth of July in their town. We got back the third Monday in July, and that's when I got the first funny feeling."

The vacation was a significant event that made it possible to establish when something else began to occur.

The Case of the Customized Bed.   In this pornography case, felonious sexual activity recorded on film was performed on what appeared to be a large, customized bed-divan. The motion pictures were obviously shot in the home in question and on that bed. The people were identified. But there was nothing in any of the footage that offered a clue as to when the filming occurred. If the time of the offense could not be established, there would be no complaint and no prosecution.

Investigators came upon this case unexpectedly and made the arrests without a warrant, based on our observations. While still in the house following the arrests, two investigators drew the owner of the home aside and engaged him in conversation. He was implicated in the crime and was at that time under arrest. The conversation was light, however, and in due course came around to his nice home and its furnishings. Noting the oversized divan, one investigator commented, "Man, that is one beautiful sofa."

"Thanks. It's custom-made. Makes into a bed."

"A bed! You're kidding."

"No, a king-size bed. Here, look at this." He started to remove the cushions to show us how it worked.

"Where could a guy get one like that?"

"Like I already told you, it's custom-made. You gotta have it made up special."

"It must be expensive."

"Yeah."

"Mind if I ask how much?"

"You gotta talk to the guy who makes 'em. The price could be anything, it all depends on the fabric for covering, the size, the quality of the mattress. If you're serious, I'll give you the manufacturer's name and address. He's in Culver City."

"You know, I'm so impressed with the one you have, I'd like to have one just like it," said the investigator. "Will he remember yours?"

"Absolutely. Mine he'll never forget because it's the biggest one he ever made, and my check was the biggest he'd received, at least up to last year."

At this point of the conversation, the subject produced from his desk drawer his receipt for the bed-divan and handed it to the investigator to record the name and address of the company which had made the unit. The date of purchase was recorded on the receipt. The "when" of this case (which was successfully prosecuted) was established at the moment the receipt was produced.

HOW TO PRE-ESTABLISH TIME

A number of steps can be taken prior to the occurrence of any incident that will help to establish the time factor when something does take place that requires investigation. The following suggestions are basic:

- Add a date and time generator to your CCTV recording surveillances.
- In still photography surveillance, or in CCTV or motion picture surveillance that is triggered by action, have a clock in the field of focus.
- In a basic and rudimentary intrusion detection system, aimed not at apprehension but at determining when the intrusion occurs, have a trip device that stops a clock.
- In any alarm receiving hardware, or in any access control program, add or modify the system so as to receive hard copies showing the times of the breaks or passages.
- Use sealing devices to secure envelopes, packages, entryways, vehicle compartments or storage areas. Sealing devices include metal "railroad" seals, wire and plastic seals that look like small padlocks, tape or even staples. Inspection of the seal when the item is sent and again when it is received should show the seal intact. If it is damaged, you know when the damage occurred (i.e., en route). If seals are placed on stationary locations, they should be inspected on a regular basis. If the seal is found damaged, you know the time frame in which entry occurred.

  (*Note:* Sealing wax could and should be more widely used. We have seen many cases, for example, in which money was sent from one floor of a building to another in a plain enveloped stapled shut. When the envelope arrived there was less money and two sets of staple holes, the original holes and the new set made when the envelope was re-stapled. A seal would expose this type of theft — anything that would show damage or destruction if the sealing agent was defeated.)

- Implement count systems. Count the number of items at the end of the day; recount them in the morning. If a dozen steaks have disappeared from the refrigerator, you know when the thefts are occurring.

The Case of the Missing Furs.   In one case we secretly implemented this kind of counting system in a warehouse fur storage area, a locked room, as a result of reports of missing furs. The counts revealed a shortage on a Sunday. Only one person was on duty that day: the security officer. A television camera was installed to monitor the interior of the locked fur storage room. The lens was disguised behind an electric appliance wall receptacle, the type you plug your toaster into. The following Sunday the camera was activated. It was monitored in another building a short distance away. Before much time passed, the security officer was observed entering the storage room, which he had no reason to enter. He removed a very expensive full length mink coat, boxed it and left the room. He carried the box from the building and placed it in his car — at which time he was apprehended.

An enterprising security management will find other ways to build the time factor into established operations and procedures. And when incidents take place out of his control, the effective investigator will be alert to physical evidence, variations in patterns of activity, incidental documents or evidence, and significant events that will help to establish or at least to limit the time factor so critical in many investigations.

Chapter 17

Crime and Solution:
The How of Investigation

There are two primary questions of "how" in the investigative process: How was the crime or act accomplished and how can the crime be solved or the culprit be caught? Both questions deal with strategy — the strategy of commission, on the part of the criminal, and the strategy of solution or correction adopted by the investigator.

To some extent, the detection strategy is often dependent on the strategy of commission; that is to say, you cannot catch an embezzler until you know *how* the embezzler is diverting funds. It does not automatically follow, conversely, that once you know how the crime was committed you will know how to solve it. The crime and its solution remain separate issues, despite the fact that one must follow the other, as the following case illustrates.

The Case of the Telltale Flour. In a processing unit of a warehouse operation, a serious morale problem had developed. An undercover agent was placed in the unit to determine the cause of the problem. The agent soon reported that the male supervisor of the unit was showing favoritism to one female employee to the point where she worked only if she felt like it. It was further rumored that her favored treatment — which was causing resentment among other employees — was the result of her generosity in bestowing sexual favors on the supervisor, an activity that was taking place somewhere on company property during the shift.

An investigator's search of remote and likely areas of the property revealed irrefutable evidence of sexual intercourse taking place in a dark and rarely used stairwell behind some barrels stored on the bottom landing. The illicit activity and the "commission strategy" were now apparent. How to catch the supervisor in the act was not so clear. The investigation to this point had revealed what was happening, where it was happening, who was involved, why it was going on and how it was occurring. One unknown factor remained: When was it happening? Until that answer was found, the case could not be resolved.

A number of solution strategies were possible. Some were tried or considered; most were rejected. The solution strategy required catching the couple in the act. It was not possible or practical to place an investigator on that stairwell landing and wait for the supervisor and the employee to arrive, because they would discover the investigator. It was not feasible to surveil the landing with a television camera, nor was it possible to use cameras to cover all the various doors that provided access to that stairwell. A hard-wire microphone (a microphone and recorder-amplifier physically connected with a cord or wire that conducts the sound) failed because the wire picked up the radio signals of a nearby public radio transmitter. A wireless microphone with its own transmitter could not penetrate the concrete and steel stairwell enclosure. And it was not possible to put security personnel in or around the work area because their presence would have been so conspicuous as to deter the very activity we wanted to discover taking place.

Any solution strategy must consider the full range of possibilities open to the investigator, and make use of those adaptable to the particular circumstances. In this case the decision was made to enter the stairwell early in the morning, before employees arrived, and to carefully blow a small quantity of baking flour from the cupped hand to form a fine layer of flour on the floor of the stairwell landing. Then, at timed intervals, the patroling security officer was to shine the beam of his flashlight at an oblique angle to the floor to determine if footprints were in evidence in the flour. The inspection intervals were supervised by an investigator in order to insure that the supervisor under investigation was on the job and not near the stairwell, to avoid the risk of having the strategy discovered. Footprints were duly noted, and each day the floor was swept clean and new flour blown onto the floor.

After several days of surveillance it became apparent that the activity took place daily during the morning coffee break for the supervisor's section. Once the time of the event was determined, the couple was soon caught in the act. The supervisor was discharged for misconduct. The young woman resigned. Employees of that section were pleased that management had acted to correct what the employees considered to be an intolerable condition. Morale returned and productivity increased.

The thrust of the "how" aspect of investigation, then, is twofold: It seeks to learn, first, how the crime or activity was carried out, and secondly, to develop an appropriate strategy of solution or apprehension.

HOW WAS IT ACCOMPLISHED? (COMMISSION STRATEGY)

The investigative effort to determine how some act was achieved is either *exploratory* in nature, such as exploration by trial and error, seeking to physically re-create the crime or action, or it is *inspectional* in nature. The latter approach may involve an examination of all steps or processes, looking for loopholes that could logically explain or prove how the deed was accomplished.

In general, the investigative effort at this stage is reconstructive. However, where the activity is ongoing, as in the case of the supervisor's misconduct discussed above, it may be necessary to use covert or constructive means.

Developing the "How" by Exploratory Means

Identifying the "how" by an exploratory approach means just what the word suggests: systematically searching, probing, looking, tracking down every piece of evidence and following up every lead to see where it takes you. It means trying to put yourself in the criminal's shoes — even, as the following case of burglary demonstrates, literally following in his footsteps.

The Case of the Locked House. A fellow employee and executive of the company, though not connected with the security organization, was the victim of a residential burglary. Over the weekend his home had been entered and quantities of his personal property were removed.

There was no evidence of forcible entry. The police came to the house, examined the premises and made their official report. Along with the victim, the police theorized that one of the two doors to the home must hve been inadvertently left unlocked.

Two weeks later the executive, who lived alone, returned to his house after spending the night with a friend, only to find that the place had been burglarized again. This time more property had been stolen. Again, there was no evidence of forcible entry.

Since there was no question about a door being left unlocked after the first experience, the official theory this time was that the burglar must have let himself in with a key. Considerable time and effort was expended in tracking former residents of the house, two single girls, and it was discovered that they had lent the key to the house to one or more boy friends. While this possibility was being investigated, the executive called in a locksmith and had both door locks changed. Shortly thereafter, the house was burglarized once more, this time while the owner was out of town on a business trip.

By now the executive was alarmed. He began to suspect that close friends might be making imprints of his keys in wax, clay or even on paper and, knowing his schedule, were letting themselves into the house with a newly cut key made from the impression. He was becoming that desperate. The central issue, of course, was more concerned with *how* entry was being made into the home than who was doing it.

Although the matter was under police jurisdiction, I wanted to help a company executive if I could. The problem was affecting his work. I wanted to see if I could get in by slipping the locks, by climbing a tree and entering through an attic vent, or in any other way gaining entrance, other than by using force or causing visible damage.

I started at the front door, attempting to slip a pliable plastic card between the edge of the door and the strike plate to push or force back the bolt until it was flush with the edge of the door, thus disengaging the lock. I could not slip the lock. The door's hinge pins were on the inside and not exposed. Had they been accessible, I would have looked for evidence of their removal, which would have allowed the door to be opened from its hinged side.

I worked my way counter-clockwise around the house, checking doors and windows, looking for any way in. At the rear of the house I noted dirt smudges on the stucco siding below the kitchen window. The only logical explanation for dirt to be ground into the stucco was that someone had his shoe against the side of the house. The kitchen window was of the louvered kind, horizontal slats of glass that fit into metal sleeves. The panes or slats can be rotated outward to a horizontal plane to allow ventilation, or closed to a near-vertical plane. Close examination of the glass louvers revealed fingerprint smudges on every one.

I removed the slats from the sleeves of the frames and, by placing my foot on the exterior of the house, at the same height as the dirt smudge I had seen, I was able to hoist myself up and through the window. Satisfied, I left the house the same way I had entered. I replaced each slat and rotated or pressed them down to the original closed or vertical position.

I told my amazed associate, "That is how your burglar friend comes and goes." He said he had wondered why, following one of the burglaries, a house plant next to the kitchen sink and the louvered window had been tipped over.

Now we knew how the crime was being committed. That knowledge offered direction for the next step, which could have been to stake out the home from the inside in order to apprehend the burglar or to correct the weakness in the physical barrier of the home. The executive in this instance chose to have vertical steel bars installed over the window. The pattern of burglaries ceased.

Developing the "How" by Inspectional Means

In attempting to discover how a crime was committed, it is often possible to use inspectional analysis. The investigator must examine internal procedures and practices of the company's operations, examining them for any weakness that the criminal might have taken advantage of. The approach is essentially the same whether one is looking for an accounting loophole exploited by an embezzler or a failure in accountability for goods leaving the company's premises at the shipping dock. The following case shows how a detailed reconstruction of an operating procedure can show where loss is occurring.

The Case of the Missing Checks.   The restaurant operation of a major department store came under suspicion when the general manager noted the net result of the newly acquired Rotary luncheon business amounted to a disappointing $300.00, far below the projected $600.00 or $700.00 planned for. He called the treasurer of the Rotary organization and discovered that the treasurer had cancelled checks for over $600.00 which had been properly endorsed and processed by the company. This meant that one of two possibilities was true: either normal business went down on Tuesdays when the Rotarians had their luncheon meeting at the store's restuarant — or someone was stealing.

The general manager suspected theft and referred the matter to security for investigation. If someone was stealing, the question was how? Not only was it important to learn how, but also how much and for how long.

The restaurant operation followed a very standard procedure. Each waitress was issued a bound guest checkbook and by policy recorded the date and check numbers contained in that book. For example, on Aug. 16, 1980, Book #3455500–3455549 was issued to Marie Waters. Each guest's order, or party of guests' orders, were written on the guest check along with an itemization of the food and drink served. When the guest finished eating, the check was totaled by the waitress and given to the guest as an invoice. The guest presented the invoice, along with cash or a credit card for payment, to the restaurant cashier. The cashier inserted the guest check into a document certification "throat" of the cash register and then certified or recorded the amount of the sale. This certification process imprinted the amount on the guest check. All checks, along with the inner continuous register tape (called a detail tape), charge sales checks and any voided transactions constituted the transaction media for that operation. And, like most business records, they were retained.

Each employee authorized to handle sales transactions used a specifically designated "I-D key" that was part of the imprinted certification. Also, each transaction was supposed to be certified on the register at the time it was negotiated — that is, while the customer was standing there.

Theoretically, then, one could go back in time and determine, on any given date, how many transactions occurred, for what amounts, and by whom recorded — and to verify each transaction on the detail tape with a certified guest check. If there were five hundred transactions on the tape, there should be five hundred certified guest checks. Not only should there be five hundred guest checks, but the checks should be consecutively accounted for by their serialized numbers.

In this investigation we reconstructed the guest checkbooks for Rotarian luncheon days. That meant that we attempted to reassemble the used books by locating and placing in proper order each certified check from a book to see if any were missing. Figure 17-1 provides a sample of the type of check involved. In this case, as suspected, checks were indeed missing.

On Rotary luncheon days, the restaurant manager served as hostess and cashier. It was the manager who was stealing. And now we knew how she was doing it.

Restaurants with a strong luncheon trade experience a hectic peak at that time. Typically, guests who have finished their lunch line up to pay their tabs and return to work. And, typically, cashiers in this situation tend not to certify each transaction at the time it is processed but rather to make change from an open register drawer and, later in the afternoon when things have quieted down, to go back and certify each guest check for its written face value. Missing guest checks told us that the manager-cashier would set aside several larger checks, total them on a scratch pad, and remove the exact amount of the grand total from the register. The money, along with the uncertified guest checks, went into her purse. The register never reflected a loss or shortage because the sales were never recorded.

With the strategy of the crime understood, it was then possible to develop the solution strategy. Because there was no way to place the cashier's area under surveillance, we chose to have integrity shoppers pose as luncheon guests the next time the Rotary Club met at the restaurant. Of the several guest checks gathered by our shoppers, the manager stole the receipts of one. Acting on that evidence, we were able to secure an admission of theft. We then opened the floodgates and overwhelmed the thief with evidence of losses dating back several years.

Of interest then — and even now — was the woman's admission of how she would tear up the guest checks into little pieces and let them flutter out of the wind-wing of her car on the way home at night — the window of a Lincoln Continental she had purchased with our receipts!

HOW CAN THE CRIME BE SOLVED? (SOLUTION STRATEGY)

In many cases the strategy of commission suggests the strategy of solution, as we said at the beginning of this chapter. The basic strategy, at least, is often indicated. Certainly that was the case with the restaurant manager who was stealing by failing to ring up checks. Why not let her steal

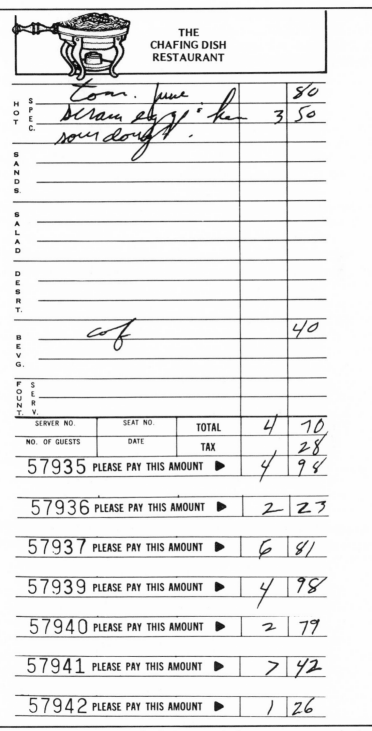

THE
CHAFING DISH
RESTAURANT

HOT SPEC.	*Tom. juce*	80
	scram egg · ham	3 50
	sour dough .	
SANDS.		
SALAD		
DESRT.		
BEVG.	*cof*	40
FOUNT. SERV.		

SERVER NO.	SEAT NO.	TOTAL	4	10
NO. OF GUESTS	DATE	TAX		28
57935	PLEASE PAY THIS AMOUNT ▶		4	98

57936 PLEASE PAY THIS AMOUNT ▶	2	23

57937 PLEASE PAY THIS AMOUNT ▶	6	81

57939 PLEASE PAY THIS AMOUNT ▶	4	98

57940 PLEASE PAY THIS AMOUNT ▶	2	79

57941 PLEASE PAY THIS AMOUNT ▶	7	42

57942 PLEASE PAY THIS AMOUNT ▶	1	26

Figure 17–1.   Reconstructing guest checks in numerical sequence to reveal missing checks.

one of your own sales as the triggering mechanism for the case? Likewise, if an employee is suspected of stealing money from the cash register at closing time each night, it follows that a surveillance should be conducted of that employee at that time and at that location.

This concept of allowing the strategy of the crime's commission to suggest the strategy of solution is exemplified in the following case history.

Case of the Dusty Shelf.   An alert store detective had been inspecting back stock areas when she was puzzled by the odor of what smelled like fresh sawdust. Following her nose, quite literally, she found sawdust on a shelf in a narrow, unlit stockroom. Behind boxed merchandise on that shelf she found the source of the sawdust — a hole drilled through the wall. Leaning on the shelf and looking through the hole, she realized that she was peering into a dressing room used by female customers to try on swimwear.

The first process of elimination in determining the "who" of this case was relatively simple. Customers had no access to that behind-the-scenes part of the store. Without question, the hole had been drilled by an employee — probably a male employee. Because the stockroom housed lingerie items, a male salesperson could never justify his presence in that room. Our "Peeping Tom," then, would have to be in a job classification that would not arouse suspicion if he were seen coming or going or in that room. That narrowed it down to someone in either housekeeping or maintenance.

Carrying this process further, the sawdust chips were relatively large, indicating that the hole was drilled by hand with a brace and bit, the type of tool commonly used by professional carpenters and maintenance people. The most common drill found in the non-professional's toolbox is the ¼-inch electric drill. The conclusion was that the guilty employee would probably be found among the maintenance crew.

I asked three key people in that store — the detective, the store manager and the personal manager — which maintenance man, in their opinion, might be a voyeur. Each picked the same man, basing that opinion on such common observations as the fact that this individual was always talking to female employees; although he was married, he was rumored to be dating some employees; and, according to the personnel manager, she had caught him looking at her one day "with the strangest expression on his face." Hardly evidence, but the unanimity of opinion suggested that the employee named — call him Robert for purposes of this history — was the most likely suspect.

The location and type of construction of the stockroom made it difficult if not impossible for the room to be placed under surveillance. There was thus no way of knowing when Robert would choose to peer through the peephole at unsuspecting customers. Even if he were seen going into that room, there was no guarantee that you could walk in and catch him leaning on the shelf with his eye to the hole. The dressing room might be unoccupied at any given moment, for example, and the suspect might decide not to wait but rather to come back later. How could he be caught in the act, his eye to that hole?

The strategy of solution adopted was to attempt to control both the time and the customer, and to signal that information to our suspect in order to induce him to watch when we wanted him to watch.

Putting myself in the suspect's shoes, in a mental exploratory process, I considered who would be the most satisfying to watch undress. The prettiest girl in the store? The girl he apparently liked most? Neither, I thought. The greatest satisfaction would come from observing someone the voyeur *disliked* most, the secret satisfaction of having seen her exposed and vulnerable. But whom would Robert dislike most in the store? The person who came to mind was the personnel manager. Ironically, personnel people often have a way of irritating other employees.

The personnel manager agreed to assist in the strategy of solution. The manager of the swimwear department was then called to the personnel manager's office and was asked to cooperate in playing out a brief scenario. She agreed, and the two women rehearsed the roles I had sketched out for them.

With the little scenario ready to be enacted, I stood on the desk and loosened one neon light tube in the fixture directly in front of the door to the personnel manager's office. The stage was now set. The secretary called the maintenance department. Robert, our suspect, answered the phone. The secretary asked if he could come to the personnel office to replace a burned out neon tube.

Robert arrived with a stepladder and a box of new neon tubes some fifteen minutes later. While he was standing on the ladder in the process of changing a tube, the swimwear department manager arrived on cue. She paused at the open door of the personnel manager's office and called out, "Marian, that lovely blue swimsuit you ordered last week just came in. Do you have time to come down and slip it on?"

"Oh wonderful!" the personnel manager exclaimed. "I'll be down in about five minutes."

This exchange took place in Robert's hearing — the swimwear manager, in fact, had casually taken hold of the ladder as she spoke to Marian. It was later reported that Robert came down that ladder fast, and in his haste to get out of the office he folded the ladder on one of his legs.

Minutes later the maintenance man was caught in the narrow, unlit stockroom, leaning over the dusty shelf with his eye to the hole that overlooked the dressing room. Subsequently he admitted not only boring that hole but also several other smaller holes designed for the same purpose. He also admitted the need for professional counseling.

The employee was terminated, the holes were patched, and fortunately it never became public knowledge that a "Peeping Tom" had been watching lady customers undress in that store.

The Modus Operandi

More often than not, if an incident is repeated, how a crime or misconduct occurs is predictable. That is to say, the method of operation or *modus operandi* of the criminal is consistent. This in turn can indicate the solution strategy.

If an employee steals funds by fraudulently preparing return or refund documents, you can count on that employee to pursue the same specific avenue of theft because, as he or she perceives it, it is a winning way. If a holdup artist uses a note to announce his intention to rob, that robber will consistently use a note. If a burglar is a residential daylight burglar, you will not find him operating at night against commercial establishments. Commenting on this predictability, Charles O'Hara writes of the repeating criminal that "... he judges the value of his methods solely on the basis of successful accomplishments. Having achieved a few minor successes, he is loath to alter his operational procedure, his reluctance stemming from superstition, lack of imagination and inertia. A summary of the habits, techniques and peculiarities of behavior is often referred to as the Modus Operandi or MO, a term which means no more than method of operation."[26]

Selecting the Solution Strategy

Whereas there is predictability and consistency in how a crime occurs, the MO, there is no such consistency or predictability in how the crime can or will be solved. Earlier in this chapter we said that the strategy of commission *suggests* the strategy of solution. Underscore the word suggests.

There are usually many different ways to solve a crime or apprehend a criminal. Take the case of Robert, the voyeur in the department store. A situation was contrived that, as it unfolded, led to Robert being caught in the act of his offense. But what if the personnel manager had refused to participate in the scenario? What if the swimwear department manager had been unwilling to cooperate — or a poor actress? Or what if company policy, or the interpretation of that policy, had prohibited the strategy used? In any of these circumstances, an entirely different solution would have been required.

Consider the alternatives. One solution might have been to install as 35mm camera loaded with infrared film that would take a series of still photographs once the switch was activated by pressure on the shelf. A variation of that solution would be the installation of either a 16mm motion picture camera with special film or a CCTV camera. Another and very different detection strategy would be to dust the back part of the shelf and the wall behind it through which the hole was bored with one of three powders which fluoresce brightly under an ultraviolet lamp. Then, at least two times each day, the suspect could be exposed to such a lamp without his knowledge that he was being tested for the presence of the powder. (The three powders are Fluorescein, Rhodamine B and Uranyl Nitrate.)

Yet another solution would be the installation of a pressure switch that, when the shelf was depressed by someone's weight, would cause a bulb to light in the corridor down the hall from the door to the stockroom. The light would burn only when the weight was on the shelf; it would go out when the pressure on the shelf was removed. The investigator could monitor the light and open the door to the stockroom only when the lighted bulb told him the voyeur was leaning on the shelf to get a better view.

In assessing these and the various other possible strategies that would apply to a given case, the investigator should consider the following factors:

1. If a given solution strategy failed, would it expose the investigative efforts?
2. Which solution strategy would put the suspect at the greatest disadvantage once caught?
3. Which strategy is the simplest in terms of manpower requirements, technology, the need for sophisticated equipment, etc.?
4. Which strategy would take the least time to implement?
5. Which would be the least expensive?

First consideration would be given to the effectiveness of the strategy if it were successful, and to the potential harm if it failed. But the other questions listed take into account the practical realities of most investigations. The best strategy is one that takes the least time, manpower and expense — and works.

The question of "how" in its twin aspects — the strategies of commission and solution — obviously plays an important role in the investigative process. The way an investigator answers this fundamental question will be a direct reflection of his overall performance and investigative skills.

Chapter 18

Establishing Motive:
The Why of Investigation

In dealing with the question of "why" in the investigative process, we find ourselves in the intriguing as well as controversial area of motive. Motive is that logic or reasoning which constitutes the very root cause of a criminal act or misconduct.

Investigators must have better-than-average insight into human behavior and motivation. However, there is a point beyond which the investigator should not attempt to tread. As an example, one easily understood motive is the narcotic addict's need for money to support his or her habit, resulting in the theft of company funds. That is an apparent or applied motive. Why the person uses narcotics to begin with involves a much deeper examination of motivation, but it is one that belongs more properly in the realm of the psychologist or psychiatrist than the investigator.

Another dimension to the consideration of motive can also be troublesome. That is the ultimate value of motive to the investigation. In *Fundamentals of Law Enforcement,* Brandstatter and Hyman state, "It is almost always necessary to determine the motive for a crime for a successful prosecution. In addition, determining the motive can be an effective first step in discovering the identity of the criminal or the innocence of a suspect."[27]

The assertion that an understanding of the motive behind a crime is "almost always necessary" for successful prosecution may be more true of the public than the private sector. As we saw in an earlier chapter, a successful prosecution is always the ultimate goal in the public sector; it is a secondary consideration in private security.

The emphasis on motive is particularly questionable as it pertains to the crime of theft. We have talked to hundreds of people who have committed theft, including even trusted security personnel, and most of them have been unable to offer a satisfactory explanation of why they did it. Too much weight can be attributed to motive. It is desirable to know why an employee stole property. It can make the whole investigation more comprehensible, perhaps. It could very well be helpful in preventing similar thefts in the future — but it is not essential.

On the other hand, as the authors assert in the same quotation, determining the motive can be an effective first step in discovering the identity of the culprit. Answers to "why" can lead to "who."

The case of Robert the voyeur in the previous chapter offers a good example. How was Robert identified as the prime suspect in this case? Three knowledgeable people in the store were asked, "Who would do such a thing?" That question led to a probable identification of the suspect. But the same three people could just as easily have been asked, "Why would a person bore a peephole in a ladies dressing room?"

The answers might boil down to the conclusion that such a person has a perverted or unsual interest in women or has failed to mature sexually in his relationship with females. Who has exhibited or suggested a possibly perverted or unusual interest or sexual immaturity? Robert. What evidence is there? He spends an inordinate amount of time with and attention toward women; he is apparently unfaithful to his wife, suggesting immaturity; and he has been known to stare at women. The answers to *why* someone would do such a thing can lead to the *who*.

Brandstatter and Hyman also state, "Motives are often uncovered by determining who benefited from the crime."[28] That is to say, reversing our previous point, "who" can lead to "why." Again, however, although there can be both interest and importance to the investigator in knowing the motive, we have some trouble with the *degree of importance* attached to knowing why when we already know who, particularly in the private sector where there is administrative recourse as well as judicial. It is nice, even helpful, to know why; it is *essential* to know who.

MOTIVATION AND DETECTION STRATEGY

There is a clear and important value to the investigator in the private sector in understanding motive as well as knowing who committed a crime when the motive can be used in the detection or apprehension strategy.

The Case of the Early Morning Striker.   A highly unusual case involved an employee who was obviously mentally sick but successfully evaded detection. The case surfaced with the discovery of a paper plate containing human feces along with a hand-printed note saying, "The pooper strikes!" The plate was discovered in an elevator by employees arriving before the building was open to the public.

The shocking and repugnant discovery caused alarm and concern among the staff and had a negative effect on morale. Over a period of days a succession of plates were found in various locations throughout the building, each accompanied by the same kind of note with the added word, "Again!"

Through handwriting comparisons, investigators were confident that they had identified the responsible employee, a janitor. The evidence was not conclusive, however. Surveillances failed to catch the janitor and his activity continued. Morale among employees deteriorated rapidly. It became apparent that random surveillances would in all probability continue to be unproductive. The problem was finally brought to my attention.

Without a doubt, the suspect had a troubled mind and a perverted sense of humor. That was why he was engaging in his "game." Because his motive was perverted, it appeared that the best way to catch him would be to trigger or trip that perversion at a time and place under our control and surveillance.

The next morning investigators entered the building during the early hours prior to the arrival of the janitorial staff. The suspect was known to be assigned to vacuum the third floor. Two undressed mannequins, a male and a female, were set up in a relatively remote location on that floor. The female mannequin was arranged lying face down with the legs spread apart. The male mannequin was placed close to the female, as though looking at her.

Surveillance of that scene commenced. As time passed, the suspect could be heard going about his chores, working his way toward the mannequins. When he came to the prearranged scene and saw the mannequins, he stopped in his tracks and stared. Suddenly he dropped his cleaning equipment and ran off, disappearing from the view of the investigators conducting his surveillance. Some minutes later he reappeared on the scene, carrying a can of spray paint. He began painting the pubic area of the female mannequin. At this point he was promptly taken into custody for defacing company property.

The janitor subsequently admitted defacating on the paper plates, writing the notes and placing his bizarre message at various places around the building. He was a sick man and knew it. His sickness could not handle the mannequin scene. He was terminated and taken into police custody for psychiatric examination. Calm was restored to the building.

The Case of the Frustrated Clerk.   Another example of the value to the detection strategy of knowing the motive for a given act was a case in which a customer was the recipient of an obscene letter.

The customer accused a credit employee in one of the company's stores of being the author of the letter. According to the customer, she had had a confrontation with the employee over her monthly statement. The customer admitted giving the employee a "tongue-lashing" during their confrontation. She received the obscene letter in the mail two days later. The customer's manner was aggressive and abrasive.

The employee, a pleasant woman in her fifties, had been with the company over eighteen years and had a good performance record. Management did not and could not believe that she would author a letter filled with such obscenities. Such an action was simply not like her.

Feeling that the problem might be resolved in the store without the security department's involvement or assistance, the store manager sat down with the employee, told her of the customer's accusation, and asked her if she had sent the letter. The employee emphatically denied having written it.

Because the case was then at an impasse and the customer was putting pressure on the store, the manager referred the matter to the security department. In addition to its obscene comments, the letter referred to the customer as a "slob of a woman" who came into public places with her hair in curlers and her toes sticking out of house slippers. After an analysis of the letter's contents and a comparison of handwritings, I was convinced that our employee did indeed write the letter in question. But why? What was her motive?

At the beginning of this chapter, motive was defined as the logic or reasoning behind a crime or misconduct. In this case the logic seemed apparent. The employee's letter was no more or less than a venting of eighteen years of accumulated frustration over customer abuses, frustration which had never found an outlet. The employee's anger had finally erupted in a single act of resentment.

Understanding that reasoning behind the letter, I talked to her. The fact that she had already lied to her superior about the letter made a second interrogation very difficult. However, because I understood *why* she had acted, I was able to talk to her about the difficulty of her work, the frustrations, the abusive way customers can treat employees whose only response can be a smile and the avoidance of any visible reaction. This is actually a rather unnatural relationship between human beings. Because I understood the motive, the strategy of my interrogation resulted in her admission of guilt.

MOTIVES FOR THEFT

Psychologists cite three factors that commonly motivate individuals to become dishonest: need or desire, rationalization and opportunity.[29]

Need or Desire as Motive

Motivations that come under the category of a perceived need or desire may originate in a problem the individual sees as unsharable or unsolvable.

The problem may be financial, stemming from gambling indebtedness, a drug dependency, living beyond one's means or an extraordinary expense for the family such as cancer treatment. It may be a personal problem such as an extra-marital affair, an unwanted pregnancy or alcoholism. And it may even involve antagonism toward the company, expressing a desire for revenge over the failure to receive a promotion or because of resentment against specific supervisors.

The need may be more purely psychological, prompted by such problems as kleptomania or a menopausal disorientation. Some thieves steal from a need to appear successful, or even out of worthy motives with no desire for personal gain, such as a need to help others.

The desire, finally, may simply be the result of a calculated choice to take rather than to earn.

Rationalized Motives

The thief who rationalizes his actions manages to convince himself that stealing is not really wrong. Common rationalizations include the following:

- It's all right to steal because what he takes was going to be thrown away.
- It's all right because he is only borrowing what he takes.
- It's all right because he is underpaid and deserves what he is stealing.
- It's all right because others are doing it successfully and it would be stupid not to engage in the same thing.
- It's all right because the owner (or company) is so big that what is taken will never be missed.
- It's all right because the boss steals — and if he can do it then so can the little man.

There is, of course, no real limit to the number of excuses that can be found to justify an action, however wrong.

Opportunity as Motive

In this writer's opinion, opportunity does not of and by itself constitute a motive to be dishonest or to steal. Many people have countless opportunities but never steal. Rather, opportunity is a necessary element in theft and must exist *in conjunction with* one or more of the impulses categorized here under need or desire or rationalization.

Hidden Motives

The real motivation for an incident can be hidden by what appears to be the obvious motive. The terrorist's desire for publicity may mean more than the need to cause damage or reap monetary gain. Even an action that appears to be an open-and-shut case of robbery may result from more obscure and complex motives, as the following case illustrates.

The Case of the Man with the Shirt.   A robbery incident took place some years back in a major retail store. An employee walked into the store's public restroom for men and discovered a customer lying unconscious on the floor. The customer had been stabbed in one eye with an ice pick and his wallet had been taken. Witnesses recalled two young men hurriedly leaving the area some minutes before the discovery of the attack.

The customer lost his sight in the wounded eye and subsequently brought suit against the store. The thrust of the civil action was that the company had failed to provide the necessary security or safeguards to protect its customers, and that the customer had the right to assume he could safely use those facilities provided for public use. It was a negligence suit.

The official police report stated that the customer had a need to use the restroom. Upon entering, he observed two male youths of Latin extraction, who approached him. One was holding an ice pick in his hand. They demanded his wallet. He was reluctant to part with it, whereupon the boy with the ice pick jabbed the instrument into his face, penetrating the eye. He fell to the floor unconscious. The wallet was removed from his trouser pocket, and the two youths fled. The wallet was never recovered. The assailants were never identified or apprehended.

Management was concerned that this should happen in our store. Why did it happen to this customer?

An independent investigation conducted by the security department turned up additional information. At about 10:00 a.m., right after the store opened to the public, the customer who was later to be victimized, easily identifiable because he was wearing a neck-brace, approached an employee working on the main floor and asked her for directions to the men's room. This was about five hours prior to the robbery. About an hour later the same customer purchased a name brand white dress shirt and, at the conclusion of the sale, asked the salesgirl the location of the men's restroom. At about 1:00 p.m. another salesperson returning from her lunch period happened to observe the customer with the neck-brace standing outside the store next to a doorway. He was carrying a store bag, the size issued with the purchase of a dress shirt. And sometime between 1:30 and 2:00 p.m. the same customer asked an employee working on the third floor for directions to the men's restroom. She directed him back to the main floor. At 3:00 p.m. the man was found unconscious in that restroom.

A background investigation of the customer disclosed that he was the proprietor of a men's haberdashery not many miles from the department store. The type of shirt he purchased in our store was in the inventory of his own store. As we probed deeper, a criminal check confirmed our growing suspicions. The customer had a criminal history of lewd conduct offenses in public restrooms.

He had made a small purchase to legitimize his presence in the store for several hours. He may have asked numerous clerks about the location of the restroom in the hope that there was more than just one. Although what happened in the restroom could not be proved, it was apparent that the man had solicited the two youths with a sexual proposal. His own action had undoubtedly prompted them to attack him.

Once the details of our investigation were made known to the plaintiff, the civil action was dropped.

MOTIVE AND RESPONSE

Sometimes the "why" of an incident can help the company or individual targeted to react or respond more effectively. Bomb threats, an all too common hazard faced by companies and institutions today, are a good example. The extent of the response to the threat bears a direct correlation to the perception of the motive for it. A series of malicious attacks against a number of stores in Los Angeles offer another illustration.

The Case of the Broken Windows. The case began with a series of incidents in which my company suffered considerable damage to several large plate glass show windows, each costing hundreds of dollars to replace. In the first store victimized, each window had been shattered by a half-inch hexagon nut, apparently hurled against the glass by a slingshot. A few days later another store of ours had an identical experience. Then, on an almost daily basis, similar incidents continued.

Why were our windows being broken?

The attacks then took a new direction. In our downtown store, someone came into the store with a paper sack containing rats, set the sack down on a counter and abandoned it. Soon the rats were out of the sack and running about the store, sending customers and salespeople shrieking with fright into the streets.

Across town, in another store, someone squirted an acid on the sleeves of all the men's suits, causing a total loss of a large quantity of merchandise. Hexagon nuts continued to break windows, and it was discovered that our stores were not the only ones besieged. Other merchants were experiencing similar attacks.

At last, as the pattern of attacks became clearer, the "why" became known. A large newspaper was involved in a labor dispute. Discontented strikers were taking unsanctioned action on their own, attempting to win at the bargaining table by intimidating advertising accounts of the paper. The theory behind the campaign was simple. If those companies which normally advertised in the paper stopped advertising in return for a cessation in harrassment, the cash flow of the newspaper would diminish drastically. The paper would be forced to meet the union's demands.

Now we knew our enemy. The attacks made a bizarre kind of sense. While the company refused to be intimidated and continued its advertising program, knowing that various incidents would continue as long as the advertising continued to appear in the newspaper enabled us to take preventive measures as well as to institute detection efforts.

The response to one type of attack offers an example. Various companies in the city, including ours, were victimized by the use of the chemical *butyl marcaptan,* the odorizing agent for natural gas. The effect of butyl marcaptan is staggering. One small vial, no larger than an iodine bottle, would be opened and set carefully among merchandise. Before long the area around that bottle would take on an odor remarkably similar to vomit. If the bottle was knocked over, which usually occurred, the odor was magnified many times, driving people away. Every fixture and every item of merchandise in the immediate area had to be burned or otherwise destroyed.

Once this threat was known and understood, however, security people were directed to carry or have immediately available a counter-agent to the noxious chemical. The counter-agent came in spray cans. The sooner it could be applied, the less damage occurred.

The security department's protective objective shifted from an emphasis on theft to patrolling for "customers" who were not really shopping but intent on disruptive actions or malicious damage. The motive for the attacks gave us, the victims, purpose and direction in ways we could act upon.

Additionally, establishing a communication network with competitive stores and with a variety of law enforcement agencies helped to stem the frequency of the attacks.

Until we knew the motive behind these acts, we simply reacted to each event. We were not able to respond intelligently and purposefully.

SUMMARY

The process of security investigations essentially involves information collection and, through the application of sound reasoning, analyzing that information to answer questions or solve problems that threaten loss to the company.

Through such basic techniques as undercover investigation, surveillance, background investigation, and the variety of internal strategies that may be used to expose covert crimes, the investigative process develops information. As the investigation focuses on specific acts or individuals, additional procedures are used to build a case, including interviewing suspects and witnesses; the analysis of physical evidence; obtaining statements and confessions; and information gained from clandestine sources such as informants.

All of this effort is directed toward answering the fundamental investigative questions — the *who, where, when, how* and *why* of a crime or incident. The investigator will ferret out and follow up every conceivable piece of information that might be useful in identifying *who* was responsible for an incident. To do that successfully he must know *where* to look — where to find information. He will seek to narrow the scope of his inquiries by limiting and defining the *time factor.* In solving a crime, his investigative strategy is often dependent on finding out *how* the crime was committed. And quite often, learning who was responsible for a given action requires an understanding of human motivation, determining *why* the crime was committed.

In accomplishing this, the investigator must be imaginative and resourceful. He must be tireless and determined. He must understand people, and he must be able to apply logical reasoning. But he is not a magician or, in truth, a Sherlock Holmes who pulls answers out of a hat. His success, when he enjoys it, is more often the result of applying common sense and uncommon persistence. The work is time-consuming and frequently tedious — but it is also a challenging work of deep personal satisfaction to those rare men and women who bring to it the resources of skill, effort and character that make the successful investigator.

Sources

Chapter 3

1. *The American Heritage Dictionary of the English Language.* New York: Houghton Mifflin Company, 1969, p. 978.
2. Donald O. Schultz, *Criminal Investigation Techniques.* Gulf Publishing Co., p. 6.
3. Charles E. O'Hara, *Fundamentals of Criminal Investigation.* Springfield, Ill.: Charles C. Thomas Publishers, p. 222.
4. *Municipal Police Administration.* 4th Edition. International City Managers Assoc., p. 306.
5. *Ibid.,* p. 317.

Chapter 4

6. Charles A. Sennewald, *Effective Security Management.* Los Angeles: Security World Publishing Co., Inc., 1978, p. 58.
7. Schultz, *op. cit.,* p. 9.
8. *Ibid.*
9. Sennewald, *op. cit.,* p. 4.
10. *Ibid.,* p. 179.
11. Charles A. Sennewald, "Give Your People the Opportunity to Fail," *Security Management* (May, 1979), p. 20.

Chapter 7

12. Garzilli v. Howard Johnson's Motor Lodges, Inc., 419 F. Supp. 1210 (U.S. D. Ct. E. D. N. Y., 1976).
13. (Explanatory note.)

Chapter 8

14. Saul D. Astor, *Loss Prevention: Controls and Concepts.* Los Angeles: Security World Publishing Co., Inc., 1978. p. 89.
15. Roger Griffin, *Failure to Record.* Los Angeles: Commercial Service Systems, p. 1.
16. *Ibid.,* p. 2.

Chapter 9

17. James Gilbert, *Criminal Investigation.* Ohio: Merrill Publishing Co., 1980, p. 96.

Chapter 10

18. *Ibid.,* p. 50.

Chapter 11

19. (Explanatory note.)
20. O'Hara, *op. cit.,* p. 137.

Chapter 12

21. Paul Fuqua and Jerry V. Wilson, *Security Investigator's Handbook.* Gulf Publishing Co., p. 16.
22. O'Hara, *op. cit.,* p. 159.
23. J. Kirk Barefoot, *Employee Theft Investigation.* Los Angeles: Security World Publishing Co., Inc., 1979, p. 53.
24. Gene Blackwell, *The Private Investigator.* Los Angeles: Security World Publishing Co., Inc., 1979, p. 23.

Chapter 13

25.   Fuqua and Wilson, *op. cit.,* p. 81.

Chapter 17

26.   O'Hara, *op. cit.,* p. 666.

Chapter 18

27.   A. F. Brandstatter and Allen A. Hyman, *Fundamentals of Law Enforce-ment.* Glencoe Press, 1971, p. 367.
28.   *Ibid.*
29.   Richard J. Healy and Timothy J. Walsh, *Protection of Assets Manual,* Vol. I. The Merritt Company, 1978, pp. 11–15.

INDEX